Not For Tourists Guide™ to **BROOKLYN**

D1527208

Not For Tourists, Inc

2009

published and designed by:
Not For Tourists, Inc
NFT™—Not For Tourists™ Guide to Brooklyn 2009
www.notfortourists.com

Publisher
Jane Pirone

Information Design
Jane Pirone
Rob Tallia
Scot Covey

Managing Editor
Craig Nelson

City Editor
Rob Tallia

Writing and Editing
Reed Fischer
Gina Grintstead
Rebecca Katherine Hirsch
Annie Holt
Aaron Schielke
Jennifer Keeney Sendrow
Sarah Zorn

Research
Melissa Burgos
Ben Bray
Bethany Covey
Michael Dale

Sales and Marketing
Erin Hodson
Annie Holt
Sarah Hocevar
Sho Spaeth
Jennifer Wong

**Graphic Design/
Production**
Aaron Schielke
Carolyn Thomas

Graphic Design Intern
Yumi Endo

Editorial Intern
Allison Dedianko

Contributors
Tom Pryor

Canine Research
Lulu & Beni

Proofing
Sho Spaeth

All rights reserved. No portion of this book may be reproduced without written permission from the publisher.

Printed in China
ISBN# 978-0-9814887-1-4 $14.95
Copyright © 2008 by Not For Tourists, Inc.

Every effort has been made to ensure that the information in this book is as up-to-date as possible at press time. However, many details are liable to change—as we have learned. The publishers cannot accept responsibility for any consequences arising from the use of this book.

Not For Tourists does not solicit individuals, organizations, or businesses for listings inclusion in our guides, nor do we accept payment for inclusion into the editorial portion of our book; the advertising sections, however, are exempt from this policy. We always welcome communications from anyone regarding ANYTHING having to do with our books; please visit us on our website at www.notfortourists.com for appropriate contact information

Dear NFT User:

As you can see, the steroid controversy goes beyond baseball—you're holding a Brooklyn NFT guide that's 25% larger than last year's edition. Clearly we used some sort of performance-enhancers, since the total amount of NFT staff didn't really change. George Mitchell, I think it's time to waste another two years on a completely useless report.

But seriously folks, NFT is back and bigger—and better—than ever. We've now broken down each of the neighborhoods into four separate maps (Essentials, Sundries, Entertainment, and Transportation), increased the point size of our type (so even grandma can read it), threw out a bunch of crappy stuff you didn't even know was there anyway, and just generally overhauled the entire thang.

As usual, now it's up to you, dear reader, to tell us what you want that, for some unknown reason, we completely flaked on for the 2009 edition (possible overdose on beer, steak, or maps). Hit our website at www.notfortourists.com and fire away—we'll be waiting.

Here's hoping you find what you need…

Jane, Rob & Craig

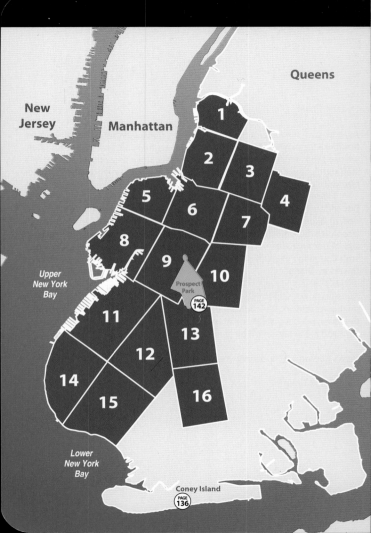

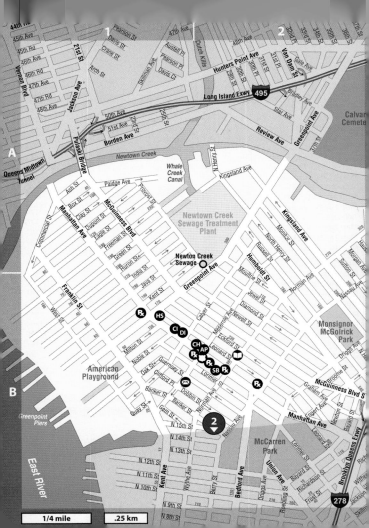

Leafy streets it has, but this predominantly Polish neighborhood is most recognizable for aluminum siding and post-industrial wreckage. Manhattan Avenue is the main thoroughfare, but parts of Franklin swarm with artist-appropriated bars and venues. West Street stretches from abandoned warehouses to the river. Call it the poor man's Promenade.

Banks

AP • Apple • 776 Manhattan Ave [Meserole]
CH • Chase • 798 Manhattan Ave [Calyer]
CI • Citibank • 836 Manhattan Ave [Noble]
DI • Dime • 814 Manhattan Ave [Calyer]
HS • HSBC • 896 Manhattan Ave [Greenpoint]
SB • Sovereign • 717 Manhattan Ave [Norman]

Landmarks

• **Newton Creek Sewage Treatment Plant** •
Greenpoint Ave & Provost St

Libraries

• **Brooklyn Public** • 107 Norman Ave [Leonard]

Pharmacies

• **Chopin Chemists** •
911 Manhattan Ave [Kent St]
• **Murawski Pharmacy** •
94 Nassau Ave [Leonard]
• **Rite Aid** • 723 Manhattan Ave [Norman]
• **Rite Aid** • 783 Manhattan Ave [Meserole]

Police

• **94th Precinct** • 100 Meserole Ave [Manhattan]

Post Offices

• **US Post Office** • 66 Meserole Ave [Guernsey]

Map 1 • Greenpoint

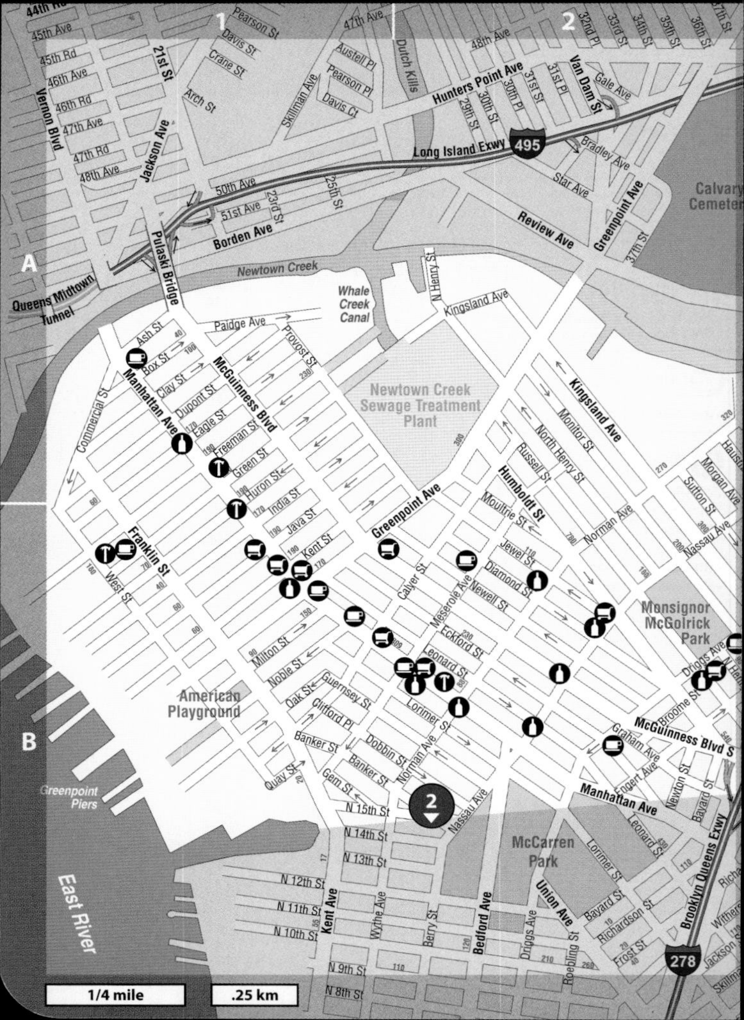

1   2

44th Rd
45th Ave
45th Rd
46th Ave
46th Rd
47th Rd
48th Ave

Pearson St
Davis St
Crane St
Arch St

47th Ave
Austell Pl
Pearson Pl
Davis Ct

48th Ave
32nd Pl
33rd St
34th St
35th St
36th St

Hunters Point Ave
29th St
30th St
30th Pl
31st St
Van Dam St
Gale Ave
Bradley Ave
Star Ave

Vernon Blvd
21st St
Jackson Ave

Dutch Kills
Stillman Ave

Long Island Expwy 495

Greenpoint Ave
Calvary Cemetery

50th Ave
51st Ave
23rd St
25th St

Review Ave
37th St

Borden Ave
Pulaski Bridge

A

Newtown Creek

Queens Midtown Tunnel

Whale Creek Canal
Kingsland Ave

Paidge Ave
Provost St

Ash St
Box St

Newtown Creek Sewage Treatment Plant

Commercial St
Manhattan Ave
McGuinness Blvd
Clay St
Dupont St
Eagle St
Freeman St
Green St
Huron St
India St
Java St
Kent St

Franklin St
West St

Greenpoint Ave

Kingsland Ave
Monitor St
North Henry St
Russell St
Humboldt St
Moultrie St
Norman Ave
Sutton St
Morgan Ave
Nassau Ave

Jewel St
Diamond St
Newell St

Calyer St
Meserole Ave
Eckford St
Leonard St
Lorimer St

Milton St
Noble St
Oak St
Clifford Pl
Banker St
Dobbin St
Gem St

Guernsey St
Norman Ave

Monsignor McGolrick Park

Dobbins St
Broome St
McGuinness Blvd S
Graham Ave
Humbert St

American Playground

B

Greenpoint Piers

Manhattan Ave

N 15th St
N 14th St
N 13th St

McCarren Park

Lorimer St
Leonard St

2

East River

Kent Ave
Wythe Ave
Berry St
Bedford Ave
Union Ave
Bayard St
Richardson St
Frost St

N 12th St
N 11th St
N 10th St
N 9th St
N 8th St

Brooklyn Queens Expwy
278

1/4 mile   .25 km

N

See all the Greenpoint demographics mingle peaceably at Peter Pan Doughnuts—the best nuts in the borough---well worth the 60 cents. Natural Garden does for organic foods what Café Grumpy does for coffee what Goldsholle & Garfinkel does for giant vats of paint.

Coffee

- **Ashbox** • 1154 Manhattan Ave [Ash]
- **Café Grumpy** • 193 Meserole Ave [Diamond]
- **Café Riviera** • 830 Manhattan Ave [Noble]
- **Cafecito Bogota** •
  1015 Manhattan Ave [Green]
- **Champion Coffee** • 1108 Manhattan Ave [Clay]
- **Cup O' Joe's** • 85 Driggs Ave [Monitor]
- **Dunkin' Donuts** •
  892 Manhattan Ave [Greenpoint]
- **Greenpoint Coffee House** •
  195 Franklin St [Green]
- **Maria's** • 769 Manhattan Ave [Meserole]
- **Peter Pan Doughnuts** •
  727 Manhattan Ave [Norman]
- **Starbucks** • 910 Manhattan Ave [Greenpoint]
- **Sole Mio Café** • Manhattan Ave & Green St
- **Utro Café** • 277 Driggs Ave [Leonard]

Liquor Stores

- **Cracovia Liquors** • 150 Nassau Ave [Newel]
- **Dunne Gerald F Wines & Liquors** •
  698 Manhattan Ave [Norman]
- **Eagle Wine & Liquor** •
  1071 Manhattan Ave [Eagle]
- **Greenpoint Wine & Liquor** •
  89 Nassau Ave [Manhattan]
- **Park Place Liquor** • 143 Driggs Ave [Russell]
- **Save-Rite Discount Wine** •
  907 Manhattan Ave [Greenpoint]
- **T&N Wine & Liquor** •
  983 Manhattan Ave [India]
- **Vino Liquor Store** • 182 Norman Ave [Jewel]
- **W&W Wine & Liquor** •
  128 Nassau Ave [McGuinness]
- **Z&J Liquor** • 761 Manhattan Ave [Meserole]

Hardware Stores

- **Fastenal** • 190 West St [Freeman]
- **Goldsholle & Garfinkel** •
  977 Manhattan Ave [India]
- **Simon's Hardware Supplies** •
  1032 Manhattan Ave [Freeman]
- **WR Hardware** • 720 Manhattan Ave [Norman]

Supermarkets

- **Associated Supermarket** •
  802 Manhattan Ave [Calyer]
- **Busy Bee Food Exchange** •
  185 Nassau Ave [Jewel]
- **C-Town** • 953 Manhattan Ave [Java]
- **The Garden** • 921 Manhattan Ave [Kent St]
- **Green Farms** • 918 Manhattan Ave [Kent St]
- **Key Food** • 224 McGuinness Blvd [Greenpoint]
- **Met Food** • 131 Driggs Ave [Russell]
- **Natural Garden** •
  750 Manhattan Ave [Meserole]

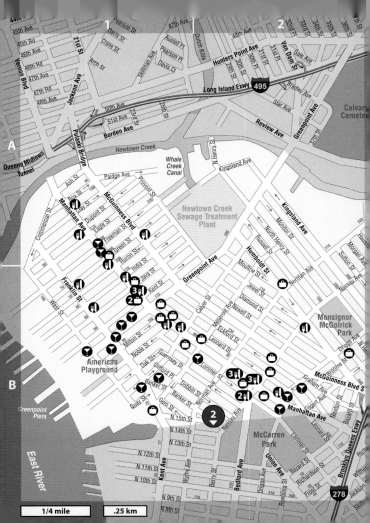

Entertainment

Map 1

The Pencil Factory remains the nightlife favorite of a certain demographic; Polish dance clubs cater to another. Where Wedel's churns out fancy Polish chocolates, legions of Manhattan Avenue meat markets slash out infinite slabs of bloody flesh. The Thing's got everything you never thought would merit a thrift store.

Nightlife

- **Black Rabbit** • 91 Greenpoint Ave [Franklin]
- **Coco 66** • 66 Greenpoint Ave [Franklin]
- **The Diamond** • 43 Franklin St [Calyer]
- **Enid's** • 560 Manhattan Ave [Driggs]
- **Europa** • 98 Meserole Ave [Manhattan]
- **Jack O'Neil's** • 130 Franklin St [Milton]
- **Lost and Found** • 113 Franklin St [Greenpoint]
- **The Mark Bar** • 1025 Manhattan Ave [Green]
- **Matchless** •557 Manhattan Ave [Driggs]
- **Pencil Factory** • 142 Franklin St [Greenpoint]
- **Red Star** • 37 Greenpoint Ave [West]
- **Studio B** • 259 Banker St [Meserole]
- **Tommy's Tavern** •
  1041 Manhattan Ave [Freeman]
- **Warsaw** • 261 Driggs Ave [Eckford]

Restaurants

- **Acapulco Deli & Restaurant** •
  1116 Manhattan Ave [Clay]
- **Amarin Café** • 617 Manhattan Ave [Nassau]
- **Baldo's Pizza** • 175 Nassau Ave [Diamond]
- **Brooklyn Label** • 180 Franklin St [Java]
- **Casanova** • 338 McGuinness Blvd [Green]
- **Christina's** • 853 Manhattan Ave [Noble]
- **Dami's** • 931 Manhattan Ave [Kent St]
- **Divine Follie Café** •
  929 Manhattan Ave [Kent St]
- **Enid's** • 560 Manhattan Ave [Driggs]
- **Erb** • 681 Manhattan Ave [Norman]
- **Fresca Tortilla** • 620 Manhattan Ave [Nassau]
- **God Bless Deli** • 818 Manhattan Ave [Calyer] ⊘
- **Johnny's Café** • 632 Manhattan Ave [Nassau]
- **Lamb & Jaffey** • 1073 Manhattan Ave [Eagle]
- **Lomzynianka** • 646 Manhattan Ave [Nassau]
- **Manhattan 3 Decker** •
  695 Manhattan Ave [Norman]
- **Monsignor's** • 905 Lorimer St [Nassau]
- **Old Poland Restaurant** •
  190 Nassau Ave [Humboldt]
- **OTT** • 970 Manhattan Ave [India]
- **Queen's Hideaway** • 222 Franklin St [Green]
- **Relax** • 68 Newell St [Nassau]
- **San Diego** • 999 Manhattan Ave [Huron]
- **Sapporo Haru** • 622 Manhattan Ave [Nassau]
- **Thai Café** • 925 Manhattan Ave [Kent St]
- **Valdiano** • 659 Manhattan Ave [Bedford]

Shopping

- **Alter** • 109 Franklin St [Greenpoint]
- **Brooklynski** • 145 Driggs Ave [Russell]
- **Chopin Chemists** •
  911 Manhattan Ave [Kent St]
- **Dee & Dee** • 777 Manhattan Ave [Meserole]
- **Film Noir** • 10 Bedford Ave [Manhattan]
- **The Garden** • 921 Manhattan Ave [Kent St]
- **Mini Me** • 123 Nassau Ave [Eckford]
- **Petland Discounts** •
  846 Manhattan Ave [Noble]
- **Photoplay** • 928 Manhattan Ave [Kent St]
- **Polam** • 952 Manhattan Ave [Java]
- **Pop's Popular Clothing** •
  7 Franklin St [Meserole]
- **Sikorski Meat** • 603 Manhattan Ave [Nassau]
- **Steve's Meat Market** •
  104 Nassau Ave [Leonard]
- **Syrena Bakery** • 207 Norman Ave [Humboldt]
- **The Thing** • 1001 Manhattan Ave [Huron]
- **Uncle Louie G's** •
  172 Greenpoint Ave [Leonard]
- **Wedel** • 772 Manhattan Ave [Meserole]
- **Wizard Electroland** •
  863 Manhattan Ave [Milton]

Map 1 · **Greenpoint**

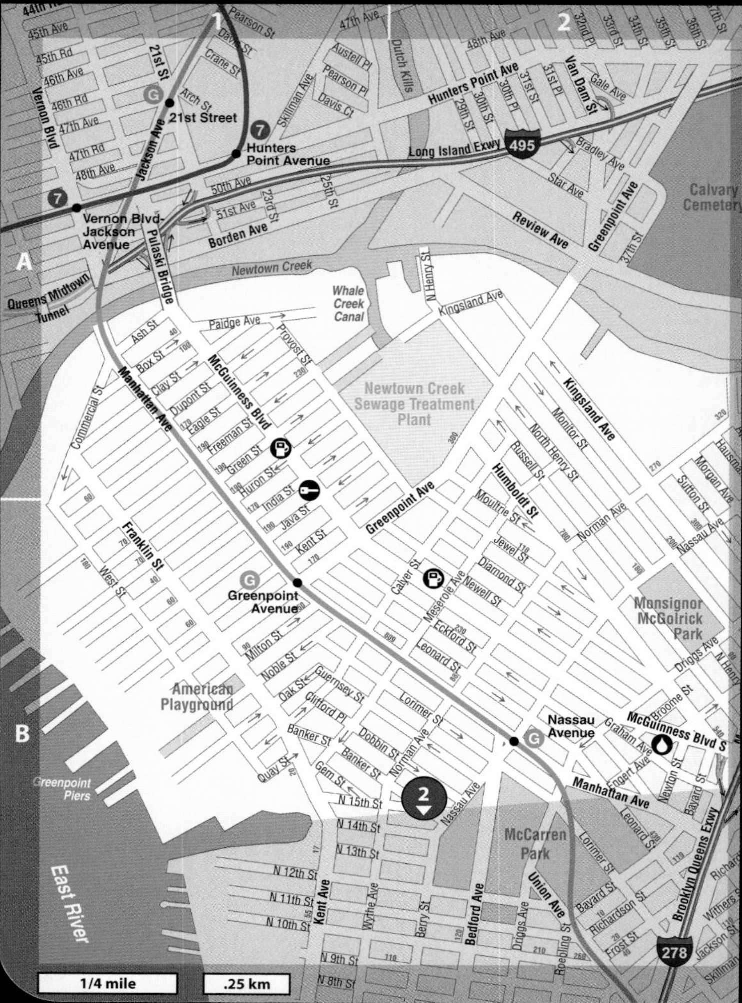

N

44th Rd
45th Ave
47th Ave
48th Ave
2
33rd St
34th St
35th St
36th St

45th Rd
45th Ave
46th Ave
47th Rd
48th Ave
Vernon Blvd
21st Street
Jackson Ave
Arch St
Crane St
Austell Pl
Pearson St
47th Ave
48th Ave
Dutch Kills
Hunters Point Ave
28th St
30th Pl
31st St
Van Dam St
Gale Ave
1st Ave

Hunters
Point Avenue
Stillwell Ave
Pearson Pl
Davis Ct
29th St
30th St
Bradley Ave
Star Ave

Long Island Expwy 495

50th Ave
Borden Ave
51st Ave
23rd St
25th St
Review Ave
5th St
Greenpoint Ave
Calvary
Cemetery

Vernon Blvd-
Jackson
Avenue
Pulaski Bridge
Borden Ave

A
Queens Midtown
Tunnel
Newtown Creek
Kingsland Ave
Whale
Creek
Canal

Manhattan Ave
McGuinness Blvd
Commercial St
Ash St
Box St
Clay St
Dupont St
Eagle St
Freeman St
Green St
Huron St
India St
Java St
Kent St
Paidge Ave
Provost St
Whale
Creek
Canal
Newtown Creek
Sewage Treatment
Plant
Kingsland Ave
Monitor St
North Henry St
Russell St
Humboldt St
Moultrie St
Norman Ave
Morgan Ave
Sutton St
Nassau Ave
278

Franklin St
West St
Greenpoint
Avenue
Greenpoint Ave
Calyer St
Meserole Ave
Newell St
Eckford St
Leonard St
Diamond St
Jewel St
Monsignor
McGolrick
Park
Dobbin St
Driggs Ave
N Henry St

B
Greenpoint
Piers
American
Playground
Milton St
Noble St
Oak St
Clifford Pl
Banker St
Quay St
Gem St
Guernsey St
Lorimer St
Dobbin St
Norman Ave
Banker St
Nassau
Avenue
McGuinness Blvd S
Graham Ave
Manhattan Ave
Russell St
Newton St
Leonard St
Bayard St

East River
N 15th St
N 14th St
N 13th St
N 12th St
N 11th St
N 10th St
N 9th St
N 8th St
Kent Ave
Wythe Ave
Berry St
Bedford Ave
Nassau Ave
Union Ave
McCarren
Park
Lorimer St
Guernsey St
Bayard St
Richardson St
Frost St
Brooklyn Queens Expwy
278

1/4 mile   .25 km

Map 1

Oh, please. The G's so hated it's almost cool. Almost. Give the G a break. The B43, B48, and B61 trek along Manhattan Avenue to that other nearby train, the L. Parking is a breeze (at least if you only work 'til 4 pm.)

Subways

7 .... Hunters Point Avenue
7 .... Vernon Blvd-Jackson Avenue
G .... Greenpoint Avenue
G .... Nassau Avenue

Car Rental

• **Enterprise Rent A Car** •
266 McGuinness Blvd [India]

Car Washes

• **Autoclean Carwash** •
103 Engert Ave [McGuinness]

Gas Stations

• **Exxon** • 321 McGuiness Blvd [Huron]
• **Getty** • 176 McGuiness Blvd [Meserole]

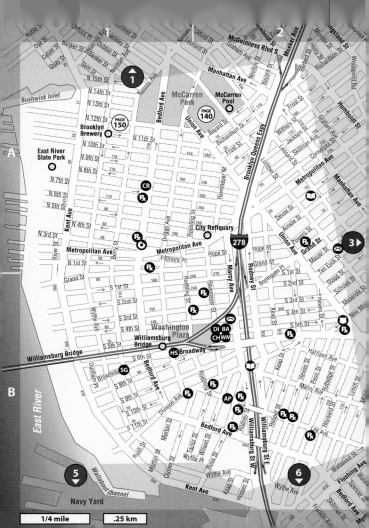

It sure didn't take long for the luxury high-rises to sprout up. This hood is a prime example of how the artist-to-hipster-to-yuppie gentrification cycle continues to churn away. Despite the constant influx of cool, new businesses, don't forget about the offerings from the old guard Hasidic, Puerto Rican, and Italian communities, as well.

 Bagels

• **The Bagel Store** • 247 Bedford Ave [N 3rd]

 Banks

AP • **Apple** • 44 Lee Ave [Wilson St]
BA • **Bank of America** •
266 Broadway [Havemeyer St]
CH • **Chase** • 225 Havemeyer St [Broadway]
CR • **Cross County Federal** •
175 Bedford Ave [N 7th St]
DI • **Dime** • 209 Havemeyer St [S 5th St]
HS • **HSBC** • 175 Broadway [Driggs Ave]
SG • **Signature** • 84 Broadway [Berry St]
WM • **Washington Mutual** •
217 Havemeyer St [S 5th St]

Landmarks

• **Brooklyn Brewery** • 79 N 11th St [Wythe]
• **City Reliquary** •
370 Metropolitan Ave [Havemeyer]
• **East River State Park** • 90 Kent St [N 9th]
• **McCarren Pool** • Lorimer St & Bayard St
• **Williamsburg Bridge** • S 5th St & Driggs St

Libraries

• **Brooklyn Public** • 240 Division Ave [Rodney]
• **Brooklyn Public** • 81 Devoe St [Leonard]

Pharmacies

• **Chopin Chemists** • 189 Grand St [Bedford]
• **Corner Pharmacy** •
166 Division Ave [Roebling]
• **Division Pharmacy** • 134 Division Ave [Driggs]
• **Gardner's Pharmacy** • 371 Broadway [Keap]
• **Kings Pharmacy** • 241 Bedford Ave [N 3rd]
• **Lieb Pharmacy** • 147 Lee Ave [Hewes]
• **Mittman Pharmacy** •
167 Havemeyer St [S 3rd]
• **Northside Pharmacy** •
182 Bedford Ave [N 7th]
• **Rafieh Pharmacy** • 70 Lee Ave [Ross]
• **Rosenblum Pharmacy** •
255 S 2nd St [Havemeyer]
• **S Bros Pharmacy** •
176 Lee Ave [Rutledge]

• **Shimon's Pharmacy** • 115 Lee Ave [Hooper]
• **Slater Stuart Pharmacy** • 63 Lee Ave [Ross]
• **United Pharmacy** • 527 Grand St [Union]
• **Unzer Pharmacy** • 572 Bedford Ave [Rodney]
• **Walgreens** • 210 Union Ave [Montrose]
• **Williamsburg Pharmacy** •
244 Roebling St [S 3rd]

 Police

• **90th Precinct** • 211 Union Ave [Montrose]

Post Offices

• **US Post Office** • 263 S 4th St [Marcy]
• **US Post Office** • 442 Lorimer St [Maujer]

Map 2 • Williamsburg

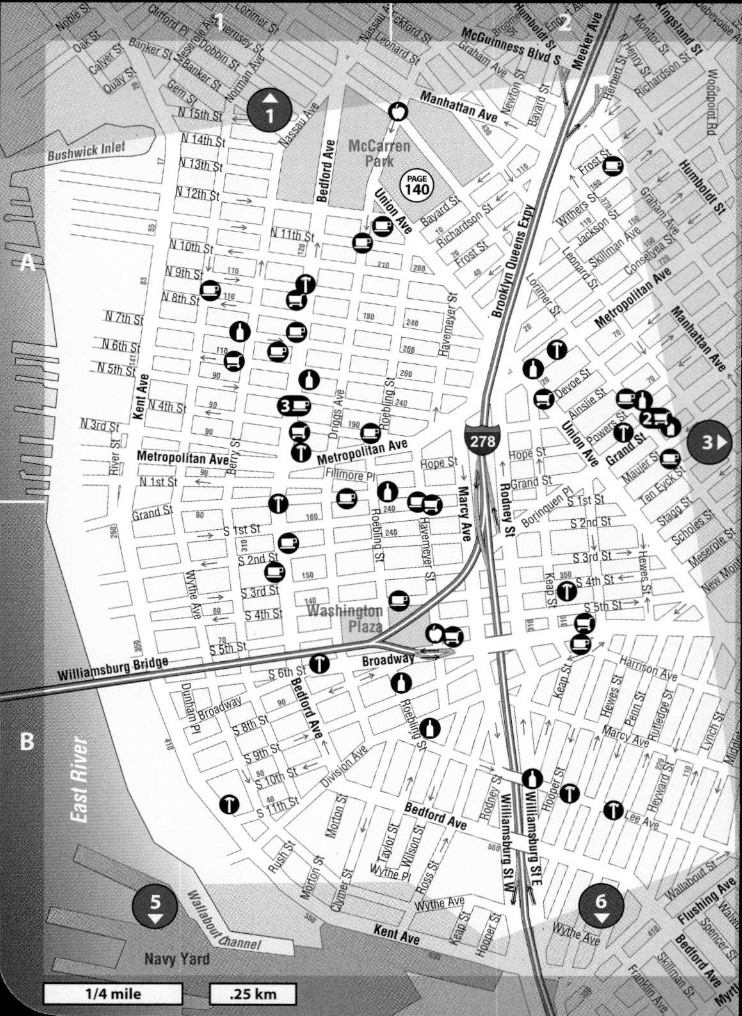

Map 2

Although seeking hardware can result in lengthy treks that ultimately derail your loft-conversion schedule, you can hardly walk without tripping over a coffee shop. Seattle expats will appreciate the offerings at Café 1980, and the baristas at Gimme Coffee boast techniques that result in caffeine-driven art.

Coffee

- **Aldo Coffee Shop** • 241 S 4th St [Havemeyer]
- **Amazon Café** • 236 N 12th St [Driggs Ave]
- **Atlas Café** • 116 Havemeyer St [Grand]
- **Café 1980** • 150 Wythe Ave [N 8th]
- **Caffe Capri** • 427 Graham Ave [Frost]
- **Ella Café** • 177 Bedford Ave [N 7th St]
- **Fabiane's Café** • 142 Bedford Ave [N 9th]
- **Fix Café** • 110 Bedford Ave [N 11th]
- **Gimme Coffee** • 495 Lorimer St [Powers]
- **The Lucky Cat** • 245 Grand St [Roebling]
- **Moto** • 394 Broadway [Hopper]
- **New York Muffins** • 198 Bedford Ave [N 6th]
- **Oslo** • 133 Roebling St [N 4th]
- **Oslo** • 328 Bedford Ave [S 2nd]
- **The Read Café** • 158 Bedford Ave [N 8th]
- **Supercore Café** • 305 Bedford Ave [S 2nd]
- **Verb Café** •
  Mini Mall • 218 Bedford Ave [N 5th]
- **Warma Café** • 442 Lorimer St [Maujer]

Farmers Markets

- **Greenpoint-McCarren Park
  Greenmarket(Sat 8 am–3 pm, July–Nov)** •
  Lorimer St & Driggs Ave
- **Williamsburg Greenmarket
  (Thurs 8 am–5 pm, July–Nov)** •
  Havemeyer St & Broadway

Hardware Stores

- **B&G Hardware** • 292 Bedford Ave [Grand]
- **Bedford Industrial Products** •
  141 Broadway [Bedford]
- **Bedford Lumber & Hardware** •
  176 N 9th St [Bedford]
- **Certified Lumber** • 470 Kent Ave [S 11th]
- **Crest True Value Hardware** •
  558 Metropolitan Ave [Lorimer]
- **Diaz Hardware Store** • 365 S 4th St [Hopper]
- **Discount Hardware** • 179 Lee Ave [Rutledge]
- **Great Century** • 521 Grand St [Union]
- **Lumber City Wide** • 171 N 3rd St [Bedford]
- **Mike's North Star Hardware** •
  136 Bedford Ave [N 10th]
- **Tiv-Tov Store** • 125 Lee Ave [Hopper]

Liquor Stores

- **All Man Wines & Spirits** •
  268 Grand St [Roebling]
- **Donath Wine & Liquor Store** •
  119 Lee Ave [Hooper]
- **Fame Discount Liquors** •
  520 Metropolitan Ave [Union]
- **L'Chaim Kosher Wines & Spirits** •
  348 Roebling St [Division]
- **Lorimer Wines & Spirits** •
  494 Lorimer St [Powers]
- **North Side Liquors** • 110 Berry St [N 7th]
- **Roebling Liquors** • 311 Roebling St [S 9th]
- **Uva Wines** • 199 Bedford Ave [N 5th]
- **Yangs Liquor** • 598 Grand St [Lorimer]

Supermarkets

- **C Town** • 130 Havemeyer St [S 1st]
- **Fine Fare** • 385 Broadway [Hopper]
- **Key Food** • 575 Grand St [Lorimer]
- **Millennium Health** • 241 Bedford Ave [N 3rd]
- **Naturally Healthy Health Food** •
  594 Lorimer St [Lorimer]
- **North Side Health Food** •
  169 Bedford Ave [N 8th]
- **Sunac Natural Food** • 440 Union Ave [Keap] ⊘
- **Tops** • 89 N 6th St [Wythe]
- **Williamsburg Farmers Market** •
  282 Broadway [Havemeyer]

Map 2

You want it, it's here. Carnivores flock to Luger and Fette Sau, beer-lovers throw 'em back at Spuyten Duyvil and Radegast, while Barcade gives joystick junkies their fix. Live music? Pete's Candy Store, Luna Lounge, or Music Hall should do it for ya. And Brooklyn's first new bowling alley in 50 years, The Gutter, was worth the wait.

 Nightlife

• **The Abbey** • 536 Driggs Ave [N 8th]
• **Alligator Lounge** •
600 Metropolitan Ave [Lorimer]
• **Barcade** • 388 Union Ave [Ainslie]
• **Bembe** • 81 S 6th St [Berry]
• **Black Betty** •
366 Metropolitan Ave [Havemeyer]
• **Charleston** • 174 Bedford Ave [N 7th]
• **Clem's** • 264 Grand St [Roebling]
• **Daddy's** • 437 Graham Ave [Frost]
• **East River Bar** • 97 S 6th St [Berry]
• **Greenpoint Tavern** • 188 Bedford Ave [N 7th]
• **The Gutter** • 200 N 14th St [Wythe
• **Iona** • 180 Grand St [Bedford]
• **Larry Lawrence** • 295 Grand St [Havemeyer]
• **The Levee** • 212 Berry St [Metropolitan]
• **Luna Lounge** •
361 Metropolitan Ave [Havemeyer]
• **Mugs Ale House** • 125 Bedford Ave [N 10th]
• **Music Hall of Williamsburg** •
66 N 6th [Kent Ave]
• **Pete's Candy Store** •
709 Lorimer St [Richardson]
• **Radegast Hall & Biergarten** •
113 N 3rd St [Berry]
• **Royal Oak** • 594 Union Ave [Richardson]
• **Savalas** • 285 Bedford Ave [S 1st]
• **Spuyten Duyvil** •
359 Metropolitan Ave [Havemeyer]
• **Trash** • 256 Grand St [Roebling]
• **Turkey's Nest** • 94 Bedford Ave [N 12th]
• **Union Pool** • 484 Union Ave [Rodney]
• **Zebulon** • 258 Wythe Ave [N 3rd]

Restaurants

• **Acqua Santa** • 556 Driggs Ave [N 7th]
• **Anna Maria Pizza** • 179 Bedford Ave [N 7th]
• **Bacci & Abbracci** • 204 Grand St [Driggs]
• **Blackbird Parlour** • 197 Bedford Ave [N 6th St]
• **Bonita** • 338 Bedford Ave [S 3rd]
• **Bozu** • 296 Grand St [Havemeyer]
• **Diner** • 85 Broadway [Berry]
• **Dokebi** • 199 Grand St [Driggs]
• **Dressler** • 149 Broadway [Bedford]
• **DuMont** • 432 Union Ave [Devoe]
• **DuMont Burger** • 314 Bedford Ave [S 1st]
• **Fada** • 530 Driggs Ave [N 8th]
• **Fette Sau** • 354 Metropolitan Ave [Roebling]
• **Juliette** • 135 N 5th St [Berry]
• **Kate's Brooklyn Joint** • 295 Berry St [S 2nd]
• **Lola's** • 454 Graham Ave [Richardson]
• **Marlow & Sons** • 81 Broadway [Berry]

• **Moto** • 394 Broadway [Hopper]
• **Oasis** • 161 N 7th St [Bedford]
• **Peter Luger Steak House** •
178 Broadway [Driggs]
• **Pies N Thighs** • 351 Kent Ave [S 5th]
• **PT** • 331 Bedford Ave [S 3rd]
• **Radegast Hall & Biergarten** •
113 N 3rd St [Berry]
• **Raymund's Place** • 124 Bedford Ave [N 10th]
• **Relish** • 225 Wythe St [N 3rd]
• **Roebling Tea Room** •
143 Roebling St [Metropolitan]
• **Sparky's/Egg** • 135A N 5th St [Bedford]
• **Taco Chulo** • 318 Grand St [Havemeyer]
• **Teddy's Bar and Grill** • 96 Berry St [N 8th]
• **Yola's Café** • 542 Metropolitan Ave [Union]

Shopping

• **Academy Records** • 96 N 6th St [Wythe]
• **Amarcord Vintage Fashion** •
223 Bedford Ave [N 4th]
• **Artist & Craftsman** •
761 Metropolitan Ave [Graham]
• **Beacon's Closet** • 88 N 11th St [Wythe]
• **Bedford Cheese Shop** •
229 Bedford Ave [N 5th]
• **The Brooklyn Kitchen** •
616 Lorimer St [Skillman]
• **Built By Wendy** • 46 N 6th St [Kent Ave]
• **Earwax Records** • 218 Bedford Ave [N 5th]
• **Emily's Pork Store** • 426 Graham Ave [Withers]
• **Future Perfect** • 115 N 6th St [Berry]
• **Houndstooth** • 485 Driggs Ave [N 10th]
• **KCDC Skateshop** • 90 N 11th St [Wythe]
• **The Mini-Market** • 218 Bedford Ave [N 5th]
• **Model T Meats** • 404 Graham Ave [Withers]
• **Moon River Chattel** • 62 Grand St [Wythe]
• **Otte** • 132 N 5th St [Bedford]
• **Passout Record Shop** • 131 Grand St [Berry]
• **Pegasus** • 355 Bedford Ave [S 4th]
• **Roulette** • 188 Havemeyer St [S 3rd]
• **Scandinavian Grace** • 197 N 9th St [Bedford]
• **Sodafine** • 119 Grand St [Myrtle]
• **Soundfix** • 110 Bedford Ave [N 11th]
• **Spoonbill & Sugartown** •
218 Bedford Ave [N 5th]
• **Sprout** • 44 Grand St [Kent Ave]
• **Spuyten Devil Grocery** •
132 N 5th St [Bedford]
• **Treehouse** • 430 Graham Ave [Frost]
• **Two Jakes** • 320 Wythe Ave [Grand]
• **Ugly Luggage** • 214 Bedford Ave [N 5th St]
• **Videology** • 308 Bedford Ave [S 1st St]
• **Yoko Devereaux** • 338 Broadway [Keap]

For many, the Bedford Avenue L stop is either the current epicenter of cool or a hipster fashion show to avoid. Either way, there's no denying that the L, J, and M trains conveniently connect Williamsburg with its brethren across the river, the East Village and the Lower East Side.

Subways

Ⓖ ....Nassau Avenue
ⒼⓁ ...Metropolitan Avenue-Lorimer Street
ⒿⓂ ....Hewes Street
ⒿⓂ Ⓩ ....Marcy Avenue
Ⓛ .... Bedford Avenue
Ⓛ .... Graham Avenue

Car Rental
• **PSPP** • 470 Rodney St [Ainslie]

Car Washes
• **Juan Zapil Car Wash** •
421 Meeker Ave [Manhattan]

Gas Stations
• **Shell** • 351 S 1st St [Keap]

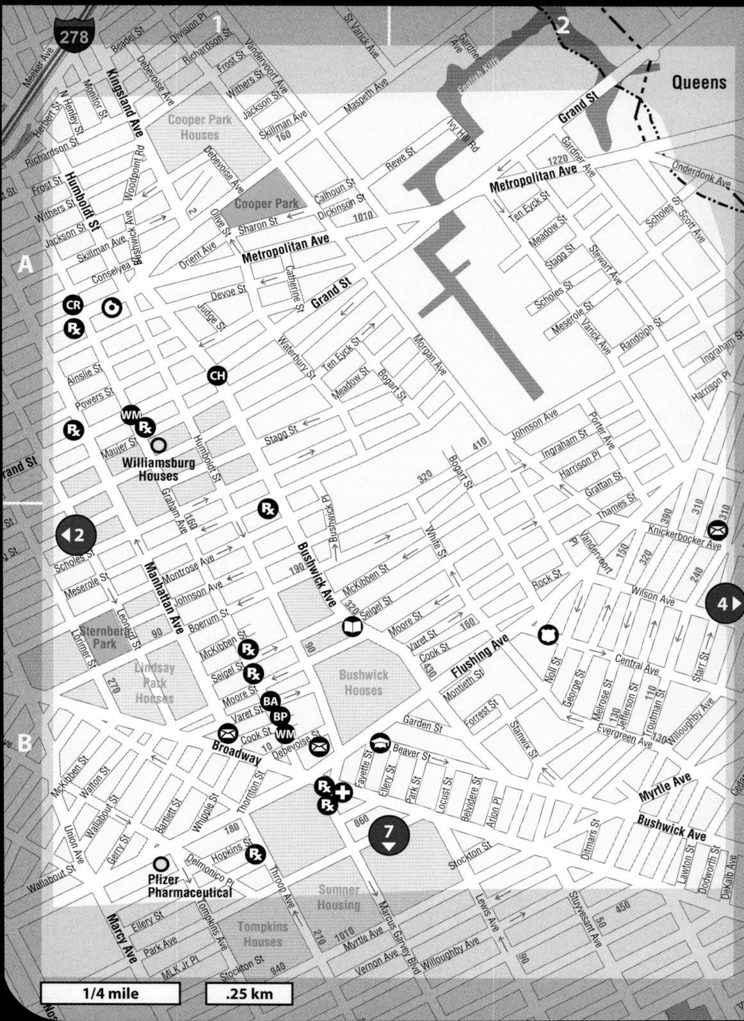

Map 3 · **East Williamsburg**

N

278

Queens

Grand St

Beadel St
Division Pl
St Vincent Ave
Stewart Ave

Vandervort Ave
Bogart St
Frost St
Withers St
Jackson St

Richardson St
Herbert St
Meeker Ave
Monitor St
Kingsland Ave
Woodpoint Rd
Debevoise Ave
Skillman 160
Maspeth Ave

Frost St
Withers St

Jackson St
Humboldt St

Cooper Park
Houses

Calhoun St
Dickinson St
1010

Ten Eyck Ave
Meadow Ave
Stagg Ave
Scholes Ave

Onderdonk Ave

Metropolitan Ave

Grand St

Skillman Ave
Conselyea St

Cooper Park
Orient Ave
Sharon St

Metropolitan Ave

Devoe St
Catherine St

Grand St

Scholes Ave
Meserole Ave
Varick Ave
Randolph Ave
Ingraham St

A

CR
Rx

Ainslie St
Powers St

Frost St
Grand St

Jorelemon St
Wagner St
Ten Eyck St
Meadow St
Bogart St
Morgan Ave

Johnson Ave

Harrison Pl

CH

Rx
WM
Rx

Mauier St
Humboldt St

Stagg St

410

Ingraham St
Harrison St

Grattan St
Thames St

Williamsburg
Houses

Bushwick Ave
320

Vinde St

Knickerbocker Ave
390
310
110
240

2

Rx
Graham Ave
Manhattan Ave
Montrose Ave
190
McKibben St

Vandervoort Ave

Scholes St
Meserole St

Johnson Ave
Boerum St

Wilson Ave

4

Sternberg
Park

Lindsay
Park
Houses
270

McKibben St
Seigel St
Moore St
Varet St

Rx
Rx
BA
BP
WM

Moore St
Seigel St
90

Bushwick
Houses

Flushing Ave
Cook St
160

Garden St
Montieth St
Forrest St

Scott Ave

Cook St
Moore St

Stanwix St
Central Ave

B

Broadway

Rx
Rx

McKibben St
Walton St
Siegel St
Whipple St
Thornton St
Beaver St

Debevoise St
Garden St
Beaver St

Ellery St
Hooper St

Myrtle Ave
Bushwick Ave

Union Ave
Gerry St
Locust St
Stockton St

Rx

7

Hopkins St

Pfizer
Pharmaceutical

Marcy Ave
Ellery St
Park Ave
MLK Jr Pl
Delmonico Pl

Tompkins
Houses

Sumner
Housing

Stockton St
Myrtle Ave
Vernon Ave
Willoughby Ave

1/4 mile | .25 km

Graham Avenue near the L stop is where you'll find old Italian couples strolling the sidewalks beside oh-so-cool youngsters who can't stomach the rents closer to Bedford. Farther south, nail salons, bodegas, and taquerias fill the weathered storefronts of Grand Street and Graham Avenue, while the abandoned factories around Morgan continue to fill with loft-dwellers.

Bagels

- **The Bagel Store** •
  754 Metropolitan Ave [Graham]

$ Banks

BP • Banco Popular •
15 Graham Ave [Debevoise St]
BA • Bank of America •
47 Graham Ave [Varet St]
CH • Chase • 819 Grand St [Bushwick Ave]
CR • Cross County Federal •
731 Metropolitan Ave [Graham Ave]
WM • Washington Mutual •
12 Graham Ave [Debevoise St]
WM • Washington Mutual •
726 Grand St [Graham Ave]

✚ Emergency Rooms

- **Woodhull** • 760 Broadway St [Sumner]

Landmarks

- **Pfizer Pharmaceutical** •
  630 Flushing Ave [Bartlett]
- **Williamsburg Houses** •
  176 Maujer St [Humboldt]

Libraries

- **Brooklyn Public** •
340 Bushwick Ave [Seigel St]

Pharmacies

- **Borinquen Pharmacy** •
  106 Graham Ave [McKibben]
- **DNG Pharmacy** • 249 Graham Ave [Maujer]
- **Duane Reade** • 749 Broadway [Flushing]
- **GST Pharmacy** • 669 Grand St [Manhattan]
- **Marcy Pharmacy** • 170 Throop Ave [Hopkins]
- **MARG Pharmacy** • 76 Graham Ave [Moore]
- **Napolitano** • 335 Graham Ave [Metropolitan]
- **Vista Pharmacy** •
  236 Bushwick Ave [Montrose]
- **Walgreens** • 755 Broadway [Flushing]

Police

- **Police Service Area 3** • 25 Central Ave [Forrest]

✉ Post Offices

- **US Post Office** • 21 Manhattan Ave [Varet]
- **US Post Office** •
  226 Knickerbocker Ave [Troutman]
- **US Post Office** • 47 Debevoise St [Graham]

Sundries

Every stop along the L train has its own java outpost around here (Graham/ Phoebe's, Grand/Stain, Montrose/Potion, Morgan/The Archive). Khim's supplies the natural and organic products, though overpriced, while the Bottle Shoppe remains the top choice for vino.

Coffee

- **American Coffee Shop** •
  108 Moore St [Humboldt]
- **The Archive** • 49 Bogart St [Grattan]
- **Dunkin' Donuts** • 1130 Myrtle Ave [Broadway]
- **Dunkin' Donuts** •
  352 Graham Ave [Metropolitan]
- **Jessie's Coffee Shop** •
  223 Bushwick Ave [Meserole]
- **Phoebe's Café** • 323 Graham Ave [Devoe]
- **Potion Café** • 248 McKibben St [Bushwick Ave]
- **Stain** • 766 Grand St [Humboldt]

Farmers Markets

- **Graham Ave Farmers Market
  (Sat & Sun 8am–6pm, July–Oct)** •
  Cook St & Graham Ave

Hardware Stores

- **Benat Hardware** • 627 Grand St [Leonard]
- **Camporese Hardware** •
  771 Grand St [Humboldt]
- **Florama Hardware** •
  98 Graham Ave [Seigel St]
- **Heavy Construction Lumber** •
  380 Morgan Ave [Skillman]
- **Sampogna Hardware** •
  697 Broadway [Debevoise St]

Liquor Stores

- **Bottle Shoppe** • 353 Graham Ave [Conselyea]
- **Estevez Liquor** •
  202 Knickerbocker Ave [Troutman]
- **Manhattan Liquor Store** •
  64 Manhattan Ave [Seigel St]
- **Pascur Fine Wines & Liquors** •
  303 Graham Ave [Ainslie]
- **Richie's Wine & Liquor** •
  812 Grand St [Bushwick Ave]
- **SMC** • 939 Broadway [Myrtle]

Supermarkets

- **Associated Supermarket** •
  229 Knickerbocker Ave [Troutman]
- **Associated Supermarket** •
  57 Kingsland Ave [Withers]
- **Associated Supermarket** •
  639 Grand St [Leonard]
- **Bravo** • 91 Humboldt St [Seigel St]
- **C-Town** • 330 Graham Ave [Devoe]
- **C-Town** • 830 Flushing Ave [Beaver]
- **Food Bazaar** • 21 Manhattan Ave [Varet]
- **Khim's Millennium Market** •
  260 Bushwick Ave [Johnson]
- **Khim's Millennium Market** •
  324 Graham Ave [Devoe]

Map 3

Map 3 · **East Williamsburg**

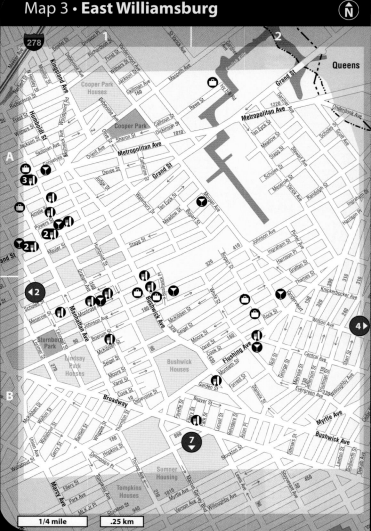

Map 3

The mouth-watering pupusas at Bahia are a must. Head to Carmine's for a slice, Ricos Tacos y Antojitos Mexicanos for the best tacos around, and Grand Morelos for that late night chilaquiles fix. For nighttime fun, hit friendly watering hole duckduck or check out the art parties at Third Ward.

Nightlife

- **Asterisk Art Space** •
  258 Johnson Ave [Bushwick Pl]
- **Bushwick Country Club** •
  618 Grand St [Leonard]
- **Don Pedro** • 90 Manhattan Ave [Boerum]
- **duckduck** • 153 Montrose Ave [Graham]
- **Harefield Road** •
  769 Metropolitan Ave [Graham]
- **Office Ops** • 57 Thames St [Morgan]
- **Sweet Ups** • 277 Graham Ave [Grand]
- **Third Ward** • 195 Morgan Ave [Stagg St]
- **Wreck Room** • 940 Flushing Ave [Evergreen]

Shopping

- **The Archive** • 49 Bogart St [Grattan]
- **Brooklyn Natural** • 49 Bogart St [Grattan]
- **Fortunato Brothers** •
  289 Manhattan Ave [Devoe]
- **GreenDepot** • 20 Rewe St [Vandervoort]
- **Moore Street Market** •
  108 Moore St [Humboldt]
- **The Vortex** • 222 Montrose Ave [Bushwick]
- **Zukkie's** • 279 Bushwick Ave [Johnson]

Restaurants

- **Bahia** • 690 Grand St [Manhattan] ⏱
- **Barzola** • 197 Meserole St [Bushwick Ave]
- **Café Nijasol** • 172 Montrose Ave [Humboldt]
- **Carmine's** • 358 Graham Ave [Conselyea]
- **Cono and Sons O'Pescatore** •
  301 Graham Ave [Ainslie]
- **Danny's Pizzeria** •
  241 Bushwick Ave [Montrose]
- **El Brillante Restaurant** •
  159 Graham Ave [Montrose]
- **El Nuevo Yauca** • 465 Bushwick Ave [Flushing]
- **Garden Grill** • 318 Graham Ave [Devoe]
- **Grand Morelos** • 727 Grand St [Graham] ⏱
- **Latin Cuisine** • 804 Grand St [Bushwick Ave]
- **Life Café NINE83** • 983 Flushing Ave [Bogart]
- **Lily Thai** • 615 Grand St [Leonard]
- **Loco Burrito** • 243 Bushwick Ave [Montrose]
- **Los Primos** • 704 Grand St [Graham]
- **Manna's Restaurant** • 829 Broadway [Park St]
- **Mojito Loco** • 102 Meserole St [Leonard]
- **Najeeb's** • 374 Graham Ave [Skillman]
- **Ricos Tacos y Antojitos Mexicanos** •
  107 Graham Ave [McKibbin St]
- **Tony's Pizzeria** • 355 Graham Ave [Conselyea]
- **Wombat** • 613 Grand St [Leonard]

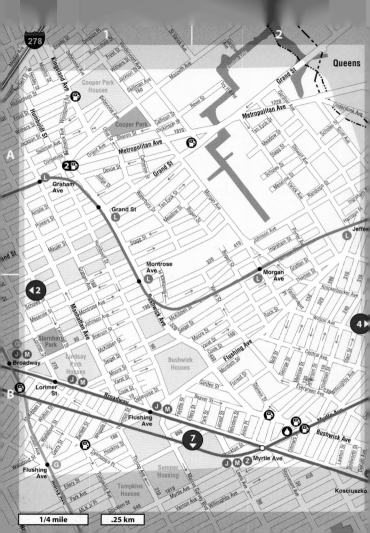

Map 3

While the L is the preferred mode of transit in these parts, the J, M, and G are here as well---not too shabby. Of course, don't forget about the buses, especially the B43 and the B48, both of which can get you all the way to Prospect Park better than any train can.

Subways

G J M	Broadway Avenue
G	Flushing Avenue
J	Kosciusazko Street
J M	Lorimer Street
J M	Flushing Avenue
J M Z	Myrtle Avenue
L	Graham Avenue
L	Grand Street
L	Montrose Avenue
L	Morgan Avenue
L	Jefferson Street

Car Washes

• **GP Car Wash** • 1191 Myrtle Ave [Ditmars]|

Gas Stations

• **BP** • 1049 Grand St [Vandervoort Ave]
• **BP** • 1193 Myrtle Ave [Bushwick Ave]
• **BP** • 152 Union Ave [Lynch]
• **BP** • 655 Flushing Ave [Harrison]
• **Hess** • 810 Metropolitan Ave [Bushwick Ave]
• **Shell** • 2 Bushwick Ave [Metropolitan]
• **Shell** • 613 Bushwick Ave [Jefferson]
• **Sunoco** • 51 Kingsland Ave [Withers]
• **Sunoco** • 644 Bushwick Ave [Troutman]

Bushwick has gotten a lot of hype lately, and sure, it ain't pretty, but squint and you can see the potential. The pioneering artists, cheap(er) loft spaces, and urban grit that made Williamsburg what it is today are all present, and speculators are banking on it to follow in its hipper neighbor's footsteps.

$ Banks

CI • Citibank • 1455 Myrtle Ave [Bleecker St]
CI • Citibank (ATM) •
  Menorah Home & Hospital•
  871 Bushwick Ave [Himrod St]
NF • North Fork • 315 Wyckoff Ave [Gates Ave]

✚ Emergency Rooms

• **Wyckoff Heights Medical Center** •
  374 Stockholm St [St Nicholas]

○ Landmarks

• **St Barbara's Roman Catholic Church** •
  138 Bleecker St [Central]

📖 Libraries

• **Brooklyn Public** • 360 Irving Ave [Woodbine]
• **Brooklyn Public** • 790 Bushwick Ave [DeKalb]
• **Brooklyn Public** •
  8 Thomas S Boyland St [Broadway]

℞ Pharmacies

• **Bellos Pharmacy** •
  179 St Nicholas Ave [Himrod]
• **Burham Pharmacy** •
  715 Knickerbocker Ave [Jefferson]
• **Dekalb Pharmacy** •
  1472 DeKalb Ave [Knickerbocker]
• **Duane Reade** •
  416 Knickerbocker Ave [Himrod]
• **Elkoch Pharmacy** •
  124 Wyckoff Ave [Stanhope]
• **Eve 4 Pharmacy** • 1634 Broadway [Covert]
• **Images Pharmacy** •
  1383 Bushwick Ave [Cooper]
• **Kraupner Pharmacy** •
  457 Knickerbocker Ave [Myrtle]
• **Marino Pharmacy** •
  167 Wyckoff Ave [Stanhope]
• **Mishkin Pharmacy** •
  1153 Broadway [Kosciusko]
• **Noha Pharmacy** •
  291 Knickerbocker Ave [Suydam]
• **Rimco Pharmacy** • 610 Wilson Ave [Decatur]
• **Rite Aid** • 355 Knickerbocker Ave [Stockholm]
• **Rite Aid** • 960 Halsey St [Broadway]
• **St Jude Pharmacy** •
  121 St Nicholas Ave [DeKalb]
• **V G H Pharmacy** • 1454 Myrtle Ave [Menahan]

🚓 Police

• **83rd Precinct** •
  480 Knickerbocker Ave [Bleecker]

✉ Post Offices

• **US Post Office** • 1369 Broadway [Gates]
• **US Post Office** • 86 Wyckoff Ave [Hart]

(31)

Map 4

Not a 'hood for the faint of heart, the aesthetically shallow, or those endeavoring to "be seen," Bushwick does offer what the spartan requires—bodegas aplenty, a place to get a good cup of joe (Wyckoff Starr), and some pleasant green space (Maria Hernandez Park and Irving Square), to boot.

Coffee

- **CM Coffee Shop** • 340 Stanhope St [Wyckoff]
- **Dunkin' Donuts** • 137 Wyckoff Ave [DeKalb]
- **Dunkin' Donuts** •
  1443 Myrtle Ave [Knickerbocker]
- **Dunkin' Donuts** •
  1556 Broadway St [Weirfield]
- **Vinas Torres Coffee Shop** •
  1571 Broadway [Weirfield]
- **Wyckoff Starr** • 30 Wyckoff Ave [Starr]

Farmers Markets

- **CVC Bushwick Farmers Market
  (Wed 9am–4pm, July–Nov)** •
  Linden St & Central Ave

Hardware Stores

- **Broadway Krown True Value** •
  1325 Broadway [Grove]
- **Henry's** • 1674 Broadway [Decatur]
- **Madrid Construction Supply** •
  1363 Myrtle Ave [Stanhope]
- **Nat's Hardware** • 576 Wilson Ave [Covert]
- **Tant Hardware** • 258 Wyckoff Ave [Linden]

Liquor Stores

- **1083 Gates Avenue Wines & Liquors** •
  1083 Gates Ave [Broadway]
- **Central Wine & Liquor** •
  252 Central Ave [Himrod]
- **D&S Wines & Liquors** •
  582 Wilson Ave [Covert]
- **D&W Liquor** • 180 Wilson Ave [DeKalb]
- **J&J Liquors** • 1102 Lafayette Ave [Patchen]
- **Jason Liquor Store** •
  18 Rockaway Ave [Bainbridge]
- **Las Americas Liquors** •
  1096 Jefferson Ave [Bushwick Ave]

Supermarkets

- **Associated Supermarket** •
  1291 Broadway [Lexington]
- **C Town** • 1781 Broadway [Pilling]
- **C Town** • 346 Central Ave [Menahan]
- **C Town** • 72 Wyckoff Ave [Suydam]
- **Key Food** • 1533 Broadway [Hancock]
- **Western Beef** • 1048 Wyckoff Ave [Covert]

While the 'hood has been filling with refugees from rising rents, the bars and restaurants have been slow to follow. The blocks near the Jefferson L station provide the few entertainment options that do exist, where you'll find cozy eatery Northeast Kingdom and thrifters' delight Green Village.

Restaurants

• **Bojangles'** • 1291 Broadway [Lexington]
• **Northeast Kingdom** •
  18 Wyckoff Ave [Troutman]

Shopping

• **Green Village** • 276 Starr St [St Nicholas Ave]
• **Kenco Retail Shops** •
  1451 Myrtle Ave [Bleecker]

Map 4 · **Bushwick**

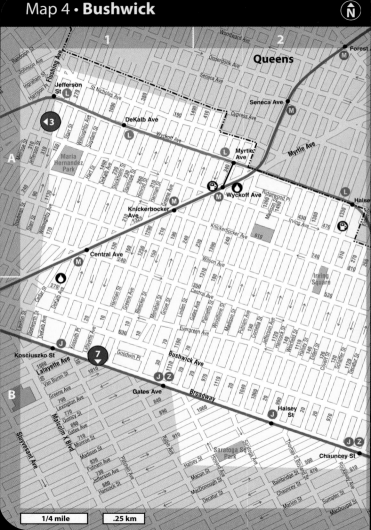

Transportation

Map 4

Bottom line: The L, J, and M trains are the lifelines out here in the 'Wick, shuttling young blood to all of the fun in Williamsburg, the East Village, and the LES. But be warned: The M only runs between Myrtle Avenue and Metropolitan Avenue late night and on the weekend.

Subways

L ....Jefferson Street

L .... Dekalb Avenue

L .... Halsey Street

L **M** ....Myrtle -Wyckoff Avenue

J **Z** ....Chauncey Street

J **Z** .... Gates Avenue

J ....Halsey Street

J ....Kosciuszko Street

M ....Central Avenue

M ....Knickerbocker Avenue

Car Washes

• **Detailing Handwash** •
1257 DeKalb Ave [Evergreen]
• **Sunny Brite Auto Wash** •
1517 Gates Ave [Irving]

Gas Stations

• **Citgo** • 1525 Myrtle Ave [Irving]
• **Exxon** • 1379 Halsey St [Irving]

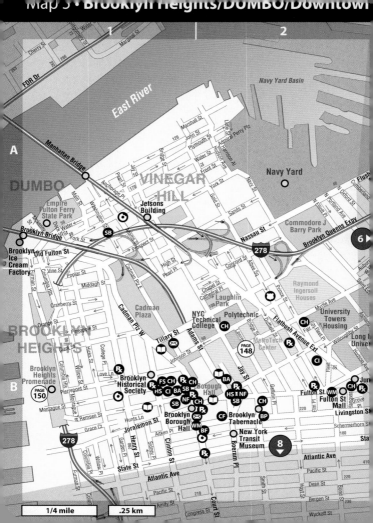

Map 3 • **Brooklyn Heights/DUMBO/Downtown**

1/4 mile   .25 km

Hands down, Brooklyn Heights is the most beautiful nabe in all of NYC. Then add in the views of Manhattan from the Promenade and DUMBO (especially from Empire Fulton Ferry State Park) and quirky Vinegar Hill into the mix, and it's endless fun—except for the horrendous mishmash that is "downtown Brooklyn."

🎯 Bagels

• **La Bagel Delight** • 104 Front St [Adams]
• **La Bagel Delight** • 90 Court St [Schermerhorn]
• **Montague St Bagels** • 108 Montague [Henry]

💲 Banks

BP • **Banco Popular** • 166 Livingston [Smith St]
BA • **Bank of America** • 205 Montague [Clinton]
BA • **Bank of America (ATM)** •
Marriott Hotel • 333 Adams St [Willoughby St]
BF • **Brooklyn Federal** • 81 Court [Livingston St]
CF • **Carver Federal** •
111 Livingston St [Schermerhorn St]
CH • **Chase** • 101 Court St [Schermerhorn St]
CH • **Chase** • 16 Court St [Remsen]
CH • **Chase** • 177 Montague St [Clinton St]
CH • **Chase** • 4 MetroTech Ctr
CH • **Chase (ATM)** • 168 Myrtle Ave [Prince St]
CH • **Chase (ATM)** • 386 Fulton St [Jay St]
CH • **Chase (ATM)** • 44 Court St [Joralemon St]
CH • **Chase (ATM)** • 522 Fulton St [Hanover Pl]
CI • **Citibank** • 181 Montague St [Clinton St]
CI • **Citibank (ATM)** • 1 University Plz [Fleet Pl]
CO • **Commerce** • 211 Montague St [Clinton St]
FS • **Flushing Savings** •
186 Montague St [Clinton St]
HS • **HSBC** • 200 Montague St [Clinton St]
HS • **HSBC** • 342 Fulton St [Red Hook Ln]
NF • **North Fork** • 356 Fulton St [Red Hook Ln]
NF • **North Fork** • 50 Court St [Joralemon St]
SG • **Signature** • 26 Court St [Remsen St]
SB • **Sovereign** • 1 Boerum Pl [Fulton St]
SB • **Sovereign** • 180 Remsen St [Court St]
SB • **Sovereign** • 195 Montague St [Clinton St]
SB • **Sovereign** • 40 Washington St [Water St]
SB • **Sovereign (ATM)** • 156 Henry St [Love Ln]
SB • **Sovereign (ATM)** • 186 Jay St [Nassau St]
SB • **Sovereign (ATM)** •
250 Joralemon St [Court St]
SB • **Sovereign (ATM)** • 300 Jay St [Tillary St]
WM • **Washington Mutual** •
66 Court St [Livingston St]
WM • **Washington Mutual** •
9 DeKalb Ave [Albee Sq]

⊙ Landmarks

• **Brooklyn Borough Hall** •
209 Joralemon St [Cadman Plz W]
• **Brooklyn Bridge** • Adams St & East River
• **Brooklyn Heights Promenade** • n/a
• **Brooklyn Historical Society** •
128 Pierrepont St [Clinton]
• **Brooklyn Ice Cream Factory** •
Fulton Ferry Pier [Everit]
• **Brooklyn Navy Yard** •
Waterfront [Cumberland]
• **Brooklyn Tabernacle** •
17 Smith St [Livingston]
• **Empire Fulton Ferry State Park** • n/a
• **Fulton Street Mall** • Fulton St b/w Flatbush
Ave & Borough Hall Plz
• **Jetsons Building** • 110 York St [Jay St]
• **Junior's** • 386 Flatbush Ave [St Johns]
• **Manhattan Bridge** • n/a
• **New York Transit Museum** •
Boerum Pl & Schermerhorn St

📖 Libraries

• **Brooklyn Bar Association Foundation** •
123 Remsen St [Clinton]
• **Brooklyn Law Library** •
250 Joralemon St [Cadman Plz W]
• **Brooklyn Public** • 280 Cadman Plz W [Tillary]
• **New York State Supreme Court** •
360 Adams St [Joralemon]

℞ Pharmacies

• **CVS** • 156 Henry St [Love]
• **Duane Reade** • 16 Court St [Remsen St]
• **Duane Reade** • 386 Fulton St [Smith] ✆
• **Duane Reade** • 44 Court St [Joralemon]
• **Duane Reade** • 522 Fulton St [Hanover]
• **Gristedes** • 101 Clark St [Monroe Pl]
• **Metro Drug** • 4 MetroTech Ctr
• **Rite Aid** • 120 Court St [State]
• **Rite Aid** • 168 Montague St [Clinton]
• **Rite Aid** • 559 Fulton St [Bond]
• **Siri Pharmacy** • 1 DeKalb Ave [Fleet St]

⭕ Police

• **84th Precinct** • 301 Gold St [Tillary]

✉ Post Offices

• **US Post Office** • 210 Joralemon [Cadman Plz]
• **US Post Office** • 271 Cadman Plz E [Tillary]

Map 5 • Brooklyn Heights/DUMBO/Downtown

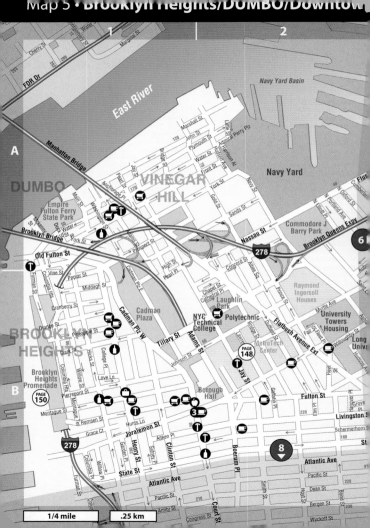

A few more shops in DUMBO and you'd never have to leave; that is, if you could afford it in the first place. Cutely-named Peas & Pickles serves both nabes with essential foodstuff, but it won't be mistaken for Fairway any time soon. Sid's Hardware is a New York classic.

Coffee

- **Amette Jamaican Café** •
  192 Duffield St [Willoughby]
- **The Brooklyn Grind** • LIU, H Bldg •
  1 University Plz [Willoughby]
- **Clarks Corner** • 80 Clark St [Henry]
- **DUMBO General Store** • 111 Front St [Adams]
- **Dunkin' Donuts** • 22 Court St [Montague St]
- **Dunkin' Donuts** • 24 Bond St [Livingston]
- **Dunkin' Donuts** • 451 Fulton St [Jay St]
- **Dunkin' Donuts** • 56 Court St [Joralemon]
- **Equinox** • 194 Joralemon St [Court St]
- **Greeks Coffee Shop** •
  130 Livingston St [Boerum]
- **Starbucks** • 112 Montague St [Henry]
- **Starbucks** • 50 Court St [Joralemon]
- **Starbucks** • 67 Front St [Main]

Farmers Markets

- **Borough Hall**
  (Tue, Thu & Sat 8am–6pm, July–Nov) •
  Court St b/w Remsen St & Montague St

Hardware Stores

- **American Hardware & Home Supply Depot**
  • 85 Court St [Livingston]
- **DUMBO True Value** • 115 Front St [Adams]
- **Sam's Hardware** • 95 Court St [Schermerhorn]
- **Sid's Hardware & Homecenter** •
  345 Jay St [Myrtle Prom]
- **Variety Mart** • 136 Montague St [Clinton]

Liquor Stores

- **Blanc et Rouge Wine & Spirits** •
  81 Washington St [York]
- **Michael Towne Wine & Spirits** •
  73 Clark St [Henry]
- **Montague Wine & Spirits** •
  78 Montague St [Hicks]
- **Zap Liquors** • 105 Court St [Schermerhorn]

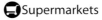Supermarkets

- **Associated Supermarket** •
  91 Tillary St [Jay St]
- **Bridge Fresh Market** • 68 Jay St [Water]
- **Foragers Market** • 56 Adams St [Front St]
- **Key Food** • 102 Montague St [Hicks]
- **Peas & Pickles** • 55 Washington St [Front St] ⊠
- **Peas & Pickles** • 79 Henry St [Orange] ⊠
- **Perelandra Natural Food Center** •
  175 Remsen St [Court St]

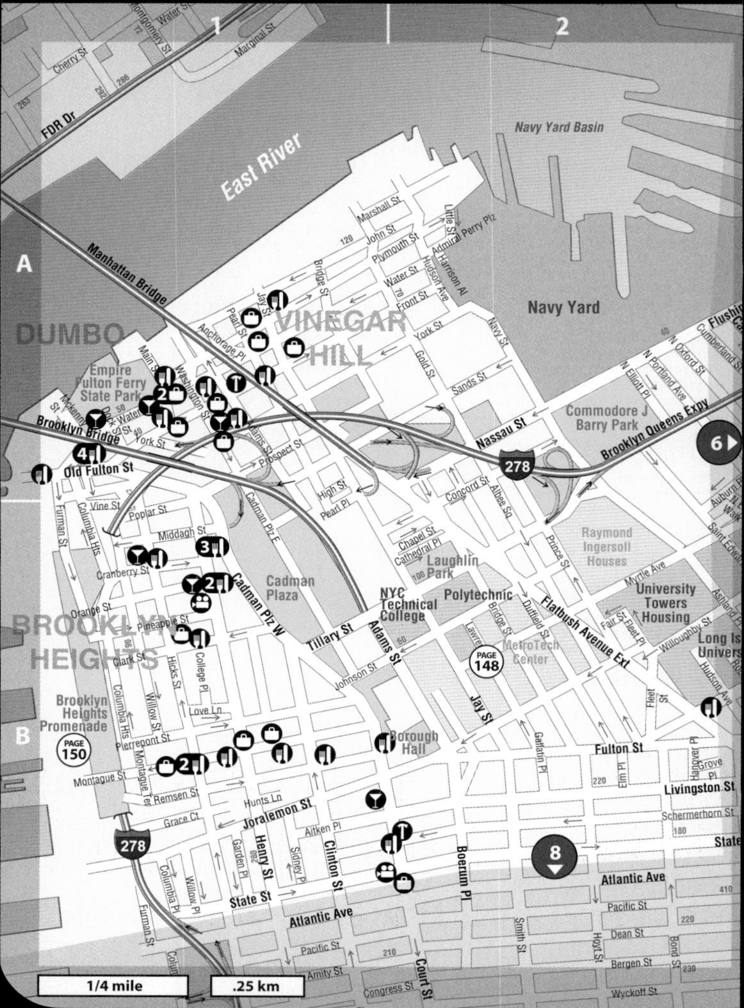

Map 5 • **Brooklyn Heights/DUMBO/Downtown**

East River

Navy Yard Basin

FDR Dr

Cherry St

Manhattan Bridge

Marshall St

John St

Plymouth St

Water St

Front St

York St

Sands St

Nassau St

Navy Yard

Commodore J
Barry Park

Brooklyn Queens Expy

278

6 ▶

DUMBO

Empire
Fulton Ferry
State Park

Brooklyn Bridge

**VINEGAR
HILL**

Old Fulton St

Vine St

Poplar St

Middagh St

Cranberry St

Orange St

Pineapple St

Clark St

Cadman Plz W

Cadman
Plaza

High St

Pearl Pl

Chapel Pl

Cathedral Pl

Laughlin
Park

NYC
Technical
College

Polytechnic

Tillary St

Adams St

Johnson St

Raymond
Ingersoli
Houses

Myrtle Ave

University
Towers
Housing

Long Is
Univers

Flatbush Avenue Ext

MetroTech
Center

PAGE
148

**BROOKLYN
HEIGHTS**

Brooklyn
Heights
Promenade

PAGE
150

Columbia Hts

Willow St

Hicks St

Henry St

Clinton St

Pierrepont St

Montague St

Remsen St

Love Ln

College Pl

Borough
Hall

Jay St

Fulton St

Livingston St

Schermerhorn St

State

Joralemon St

Hunts Ln

Garden Pl

State St

Atlantic Ave

278

Columbia Pl

Furman St

Grace Ct

Willow Pl

Aitken Pl

Sidney Pl

Boerum Pl

8 ▼

Atlantic Ave

Pacific St

Dean St

Bergen St

Amity St

Congress St

Court St

Smith St

Wyckoff St

1/4 mile   .25 km

Map 5

Old-world Henry's End is at the top of our list for food, but also check out ultrahip Superfine, friendly Noodle Pudding, and posh gastropub Jack the Horse. For culture, St. Ann's is the place. For chocolate, two words: Jacques Torres. When Tim and Jason move in together, they accessorize at West Elm.

🎭 Movie Theaters

• **Pavilion Brooklyn Heights** •
70 Henry St [Orange]
• **Regal/UA Court Street** •
108 Court St [State]

🍸 Nightlife

• **68 Jay Street Bar** • 68 Jay St [Front St]
• **Henry St Ale House** • 62 Henry St [Cranberry]
• **Jack the Horse Tavern** •
66 Hicks St [Cranberry]
• **Low Bar** • 81 Washington St [York]
• **Okeefe's** • 62 Court St [Livingston]
• **St Ann's Warehouse** •
38 Water St [Dock St]
• **Water Street Bar** • 66 Water St [Main]

🍴 Restaurants

• **Bubby's** • 1 Main St [Plymouth]
• **Curry Leaf** • 151 Remsen St [Clinton]
• **DUMBO General Store** • 111 Front St [Adams]
• **Fascati Pizzeria** • 80 Henry St [Orange]
• **Five Front** • 5 Front St [Old Fulton]
• **Five Guys** • 138 Montague St [Hicks]
• **Grimaldi's** • 19 Old Fulton St [Doughty]
• **Hale & Hearty Soup** • 32 Court St [Remsen]
• **Heights Café** • 84 Montague St [Hicks]
• **Henry's End** • 44 Henry St [Middagh]
• **Jack the Horse Tavern** •
66 Hicks St [Cranberry]
• **Junior's Restaurant** •
386 Flatbush Ave [St Johns]
• **Miso** • 40 Main St [Front St]
• **Noodle Pudding** • 38 Henry St [Middagh]
• **Pete's Downtown** • 2 Water St [Old Fulton]
• **The Plant** • 25 Jay St [Plymouth]
• **Queen Ristorante** •
84 Court St [Livingston]
• **Rice** • 81 Washington St [York]
• **River Café** • 1 Water St [Old Fulton]
• **Siggy's Good Food** •
76 Henry St [Orange]
• **Superfine** • 126 Front St [Pearl St]
• **Sushi California** • 71 Clark St [Henry]
• **Thai 101** • 101 Montague St [Hicks]
• **Theresa's** • 80 Montague St [Hicks]
• **Toro Restaurant** • 1 Front St [Old Fulton]

🛍️ Shopping

• **Almondine Bakery** • 85 Water St [Main]
• **Design Within Reach** •
76 Montague St [Hicks]
• **Halcyon** • 57 Pearl St [Water]
• **Half Pint** • 55 Washington St [Front St]
• **Heights Prime Meats** • 59 Clark St [Henry]
• **Jacques Torres Chocolate** •
66 Water St [Main]
• **Lassen & Hennigs** • 114 Montague St [Henry]
• **Montague Street VIdeo** •
143 Montague St [Clinton St]
• **New Balance Store** • 125 Court St [State]
• **Pomme** • 81 Washington St [York]
• **Recycle-A-Bicycle** • 35 Pearl St [Plymouth St]
• **Stewart/Stand** • 165 Front St [Jay]
• **West Elm** • 75 Front St [Main]
• **Wonk** • 68 Jay St [Front St]

Map 5 • **Brooklyn Heights/DUMBO/Downtow**

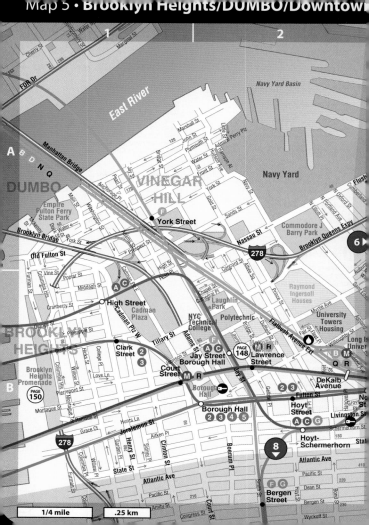

Choose your poison—Brooklyn Bridge or Manhattan Bridge? No trucks on the Brooklyn, and now there's a rush-hour HOV lane on the Manhattan. Tillary's the only good way crosstown here. Both the York Street F and the High Street A/C trains are serviced by elevators—cool. Parking blows.

Subways

② ③	Clark Street
② ③	Hoyt Street
② ③ ④ ⑤	Borough Hall
② ④	Nevins Street
Ⓐ Ⓒ	High Street
Ⓐ Ⓒ Ⓕ	Jay Street-Borough Hall
Ⓐ Ⓒ Ⓖ	Hoyt-Schermerhorn
Ⓑ Ⓜ Ⓠ Ⓡ	DeKalb Avenue
Ⓕ	York Street
Ⓕ Ⓖ	Bergen Street
Ⓜ Ⓡ	Lawrence Street
Ⓜ Ⓡ	Court Street

Car Rental

- **All Car Rent A Car** • Marriott Hotel •
  333 Adams St [Willoughby]
- **Enterprise Rent A Car** •
  291 Livingston St [Bond]

Car Washes

- **Manhattan Bridge Car Wash** •
  285 Flatbush Ave Ext [Willoughby]

45

A tale of two nabes; already-gentrified Fort Greene, with its fabulous park and nice retail strip (DeKalb) + diverse Clinton Hill, with its mix of Pratt students, long-term residents, immigrant Africans, artists, and yuppies on the make. Also check out the great sculpture on Pratt's campus and BAM's many fine offerings. Sweet.

Map C

 Bagels

- **Bagel Boys Express** • 558 Fulton St [Rockwell]
- **Bergen Bagels on Myrtle** •
  486 Myrtle Ave [Hall]
- **La Bagel Delight** •
  73 Lafayette Ave [S Elliott Pl]

$ Banks

AP • Apple • 414 Flushing Ave [Skillman St]
BA • Bank of America •
449 Myrtle Ave [Washington Ave]
CF • Carver Federal •
625 Atlantic Avel [Ft Greene Pll]
CF • Carver Federal (ATM) • Atlantic Center
222 Clinton Ave [Willoughby St]
CH • Chase • 20 Flatbush Ave [Nevins St]
CH • Chase •
210 Flushing Ave [Washington Ave]
CH • Chase • 975 Bedford Ave [DeKalb Ave]
CI • Citibank • 430 Myrtle Ave [Clinton Ave]
HS • HSBC • 118 Flatbush Ave [State St]
SB • Sovereign (ATM) • Pratt •
200 Willoughby Ave [Hall St]
SB • Sovereign (ATM) • BAM •
30 Lafayette Ave [St Felix St]
SB • Sovereign (ATM) • Pratt Bookstore • 550
Myrtle Ave [Emerson Pl]

✚ Emergency Rooms

- **Brooklyn Hospital Center** • 121 DeKalb Ave
  [St Felix]

○ Landmarks

- **Atlantic Terminal Mall** •
  Atlantic Ave & Flatbush Ave
- **Broken Angel** •
  Quincy St b/w Downing St & Classon St
- **Brooklyn Academy of Music** •
  30 Lafayette Ave [Ashland]
- **Brooklyn Masonic Temple** •
  317 Clermont Ave [Lafayette]
- **Fort Greene Park** •
  DeKalb Ave & Washington Park
- **Lafayette Avenue Presbyterian Church** •
  85 S Oxford St [Lafayette]
- **Long Island Rail Road Station** •
  Hanson Pl & Flatbush Ave

- **Pratt Institute Power Plant** •
  200 Willoughby Ave [Hall]
- **Steiner Studios** •
  15 Washington Ave [Flushing]
- **Williamsburg Savings Bank Building** •
  1 Hanson Pl [Ashland]

📖 Libraries

- **Brooklyn Hospital Medical** •
  121 DeKalb Ave [St Felix]
- **Brooklyn Public** • 25 Fourth Ave [Pacific]
- **Brooklyn Public** •
  380 Washington Ave [Lafayette]
- **Brooklyn Public** • 93 St Edwards St [Auburn]

℞ Pharmacies

- **Ashland Pharmacy** • 123 DeKalb Ave [St Felix]
- **Behrens Pharmacy** •
  231 DeKalb Ave [Clermont]
- **Brooklyn Center Pharmacy** •
  104 DeKalb Ave [Ashland]
- **Fine Care Pharmacy** • 981 Fulton St [St James]
- **Flushing Pharmacy** •
  414 Flushing Ave [Skillman]
- **Greene Community Pharmacy** •
  702 Fulton St [S Oxford]
- **Myrtle Avenue Pharmacy** •
  329 Myrtle Ave [Wash Pk]
- **Myrtle Pharmacy** • 446 Myrtle Ave [Waverly]
- **Neighborhood Friendly Pharmacy** •
  712 Myrtle Ave [Spencer St]
- **Pakam Pharmacy** • 597 Marcy Ave [**Vernon**]
- **Target** • Atlantic Terminal •
  139 Flatbush Ave [Atlantic]

⬡ Police

- **88th Precinct** • 298 Classon Ave [DeKalb]

✉ Post Offices

- **US Post Office** • 524 Myrtle Ave [Grand]
- **US Post Office** • 950 Fulton St [Cambridge]

All hail Choice! Good mud and even better baked goods make it the top shop in the nabe, although super-organic Urban Spring, friendly Tillie's, hipster Outpost, and croissant-laden Marquet are all excellent. As for supermarkets, they're all decent, but they ain't Fairway. A co-op is in the planning stages—nice.

Coffee

- **Bittersweet** • 180 Dekalb Ave [Carlton]
- **Choice Market** • 318 Lafayette Ave [Grand]
- **Dunkin' Donuts** • 17 Flatbush Ave [Fulton]
- **Green Apple House** •
  110 DeKalb Ave [Ashland]
- **Marquet** • 680 Fulton St [S Portland]
- **Mike's Coffee Shop** •
  328 DeKalb Ave [St James]
- **Outpost** • 1014 Fulton St [Downing]
- **Tillie's** • 248 DeKalb Ave [Vanderbilt]
- **Urban Spring** • 185 Dekalb Ave [Carlton]

Farmers Markets

- **Fort Greene Park Greenmarket**
  (Sat 8 am–5 pm, July–Nov) •
  Washington Pk & DeKalb Ave

Hardware Stores

- **Bhiuyan Hardware & Paint Supply** •
  249 Nostrand Ave [Kosciusko]
- **Home Depot** • 585 DeKalb Ave [Sandford]
- **Kevin & Richard Hardware** •
  645 Myrtle Ave [Franklin]
- **M&S Hardware & Paint Soundries Supply** •
  203 Clifton Pl [Skillman]
- **New Town Home Center** •
  519 Flushing Ave [Warsoff]
- **Safeway Locksmith** •
  998 Bedford Ave [DeKalb]
- **Sister's Community Hardware** •
  900 Fulton St [Wash Ave]

Liquor Stores

- **Andy's Wines & Liquors** •
  343 Myrtle Ave [Carlton]
- **D&M Pratt Liquor** •
  180 Washington Ave [Myrtle]
- **Franklin DeKalb Liquors** •
  501 DeKalb Ave [Franklin]
- **Greene & Grand Liquors** •
  231 Greene Ave [Grand]
- **The Greene Grape** • 765 Fulton St [S Oxford]
- **Lucky Liquor Store** •
  752 Myrtle Ave [Nostrand]
- **Philip's Liquor Store** •
  403 Myrtle Ave [Vanderbilt]
- **Rand Liquor Store** •
  1029 Bedford Ave [Clifton]

Supermarkets

- **Associated Supermarket** •
  367 Waverly Ave [Greene]
- **Associated Supermarket** •
  492 Myrtle Ave [Hall]
- **Associated Supermarket** •
  535 Marcy Ave [MLK]
- **Greene Farm** • 17 Greene Ave [Cumberland]
- **Met Food** • 991 Fulton St [Cambridge]
- **Pioneer** • 325 Lafayette Ave [Grand]

Map 6 · **Fort Greene / Clinton Hill**

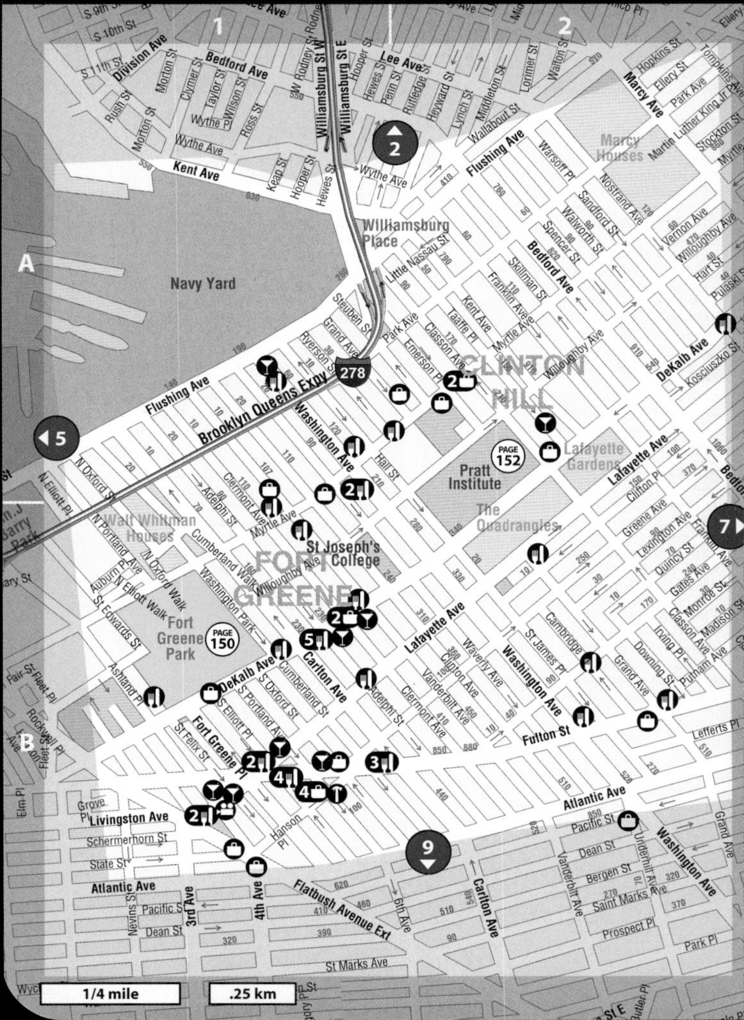

S-10th St
S 9th St
Division Ave
S 11th St
Morton St
Cormeira St
Taylor St
Wilson St
Ross St
Williamsburg St E
Williamsburg St W
Hewes St
Rutledge St
Howard St
Lynch St
Middleton St
Hooper St
Lee Ave

1   2

Bedford Ave
Wythe Ave

Kent Ave

Marcy Ave

Marcy Houses

Flushing Ave

Wilson Pl
Rossrand Ave
Sandford St
Walworth St
Spencer St

Bedford Ave
Franklin Ave
Skillman St
Taaffe Pl
Kent Ave
Classon Ave
Myrtle Ave

Willoughby Ave
DeKalb Ave

Kosciuszko St

A
Navy Yard

Williamsburg Place
Little Nassau St
Steuben St
Emerson Pl
Grand Ave
Ryerson St

CLINTON HILL

5
Flushing Ave
Brooklyn Queens Expwy
278
Washington Ave

Clinton Ave

Clifton Pl
Greene Ave
Lexington Ave
Quincy St
Gates Ave
Monroe St
Putnam Ave

Lafayette Ave

PAGE 152
Lafayette Gardens

Pratt Institute
The Quadrangles

7

Walt Whitman Houses

N Oxford St
N Portland Ave
Adelphi St
Clermont Ave
Myrtle Ave
Willoughby Ave

St Joseph's College

Cambridge Pl
Grand Ave

FORT GREENE

Auburn Pl
N Elliott Walk
Washington Park
Fort Greene Park
PAGE 150

Lafayette Ave
Waverly Ave
Clinton Ave
Vanderbilt Ave
Clermont Ave
St James Pl

Washington Ave
Irving Pl
Classon Ave
Grand Ave

B
Ashland Pl
DeKalb Ave
Carlton Ave

Fulton St

Fort Greene
S Elliott Pl
S Oxford St
S Portland Ave
Adelphi St

Atlantic Ave
Pacific St

Livingston Ave
Schermerhorn St
State St

Grove Pl
Hanson Pl

9

Dean St
Bergen St
Saint Marks Ave

Atlantic Ave
Nevins St
Pacific St
Dean St

Flatbush Avenue Ext
3rd Ave
4th Ave
Carlton Ave
Vanderbilt Ave

Prospect Pl
Park Pl

St Marks Ave

| 1/4 mile | .25 km |

Entertainment

Well, it's missing a cheese shop (supposedly coming soon) and a rock club, but that's about it—check out cool eats and Afro beats at Grand Dakar, friendly French at Chez Oskar, pre-BAM Austrian at Thomas Beisl, killer cheap Mexican at Castro's, posh Italian at Locanda, and short rib heaven at Smoke Joint.

Map 6

 Movie Theaters

- **BAM Rose Cinemas** • BAM •
  30 Lafayette Ave [St Felix]

Nightlife

- **The Alibi**• 242 Dekalb Ave
- **BAMcafé** • 30 Lafayette Ave [Ashland]
- **Frank's Lounge** • 660 Fulton St [S Elliott Pl]
- **Grand Dakar** • 285 Grand Ave [Clifton]
- **Moe's** • 80 Lafayette Ave [S Portland]
- **Reign Bar & Lounge** •
  46 Washington Ave [Flushing]
- **Sputnik** • 262 Taaffe Pl [DeKalb]
- **Stonehome Wine Bar** •
  87 Lafayette Ave [S Portland]
- **Thomas Beisl** • 25 Lafayette Ave [Ashland]

Restaurants

- **1 Greene Sushi and Sashimi** •
  1 Greene Ave [Fulton]
- **67 Burger** • 67 Lafayette Ave [S Elliott Pl]
- **BAMcafé** • 30 Lafayette Ave [Ashland]
- **Black Iris** • 228 DeKalb Ave [Clermont]
- **Café Lafayette** • 99 S Portland Ave [Fulton]
- **Castro's Restaurant** • 511 Myrtle Ave [Grand]
- **Chez Lola** • 387 Myrtle Ave [Clermont]
- **Chez Oskar** • 211 DeKalb Ave [Adelphi]
- **Choice Market** • 318 Lafayette Ave [Grand]
- **Grand Dakar** • 285 Grand Ave [Clifton]
- **Habana Outpost** • 757 Fulton St [S Portland]
- **Ici** • 246 DeKalb Ave [Vanderbilt]
- **Kush** • 17 Putnam Ave [Grand]
- **Locanda Vini & Olii** •
  129 Gates Ave [Cambridge]
- **LouLou** • 222 DeKalb Ave [Clermont]
- **Luz** • 177 Vanderbilt Ave [Myrtle]
- **Madiba** • 195 DeKalb Ave [Carlton]
- **Maggie Brown** • 455 Myrtle Ave [Wash Ave]
- **Mojito Restaurant** • 82 Washington Ave [Park]
- **Night of the Cookers** •
  767 Fulton St [S Oxford]
- **Olea** • 171 Lafayette Ave [Adelphi]
- **Pequena** • 86 S Portland Ave [Lafayette]
- **Red Bamboo** • 271 Adelphi St [Adelphi]
- **Rice** • 166 DeKalb Ave [Cumberland]
- **Ruthie's Restaurant** •
  96 DeKalb Ave [Ashland]
- **Scopello** • 63 Lafayette Ave [S Elliott Pl]

- **The Smoke Joint** • 87 S Elliiot Pl [Lafayette]
- **Soule** • 920 Fulton St [Wash Ave]
- **Thai 101** • 455 Myrtle Ave [Wash Ave]
- **Thomas Beisl** • 25 Lafayette Ave [Ashland]
- **Zaytoons** • 472 Myrtle Ave [Wash Ave]

Shopping

- **Atlantic Terminal Mall** •
  Atlantic Ave & Flatbush Ave
- **Bargains R Us** • 976 Fulton St [Grand]
- **Blue Bass Vintage** • 431 DeKalb Ave [Classon]
- **Cake Man Raven Confectionary** •
  708 Fulton St [Hanson]
- **Carol's Daughter** • 1 S Elliot Pl [DeKalb]
- **Dope Jams** • 580 Myrtle Ave
- **Frosted Moon** • 154 Vanderbilt Ave [Myrtle]
- **The Greene Grape** • 765 Fulton St [S Oxford]
- **Gureje** • 886 Pacific St [Underhill]
- **Kiki's Pet Spa** • 239 DeKalb Ave [Vanderbilt]
- **Malchijah Hats** • 225 DeKalb Ave [Clermont]
- **The Midtown Greenhouse Garden Center** •
  115 Flatbush Ave [Hanson]
- **My Little India** • 96 S Elliot Pl [Fulton]
- **Owa African Market** •
  434 Myrtle Ave [Waverly]
- **Pratt Institute Bookstore** •
  550 Myrtle Ave [Emerson Pl]
- **Target** • Atlantic Terminal •
  139 Flatbush Ave [Atlantic]
- **White Elephant Gallery** •
  572 Myrtle Ave [Classon]
- **Yu Interiors** • 15 Greene Ave [Cumberland]

51

Map 6 · **Fort Greene / Clinton Hill**

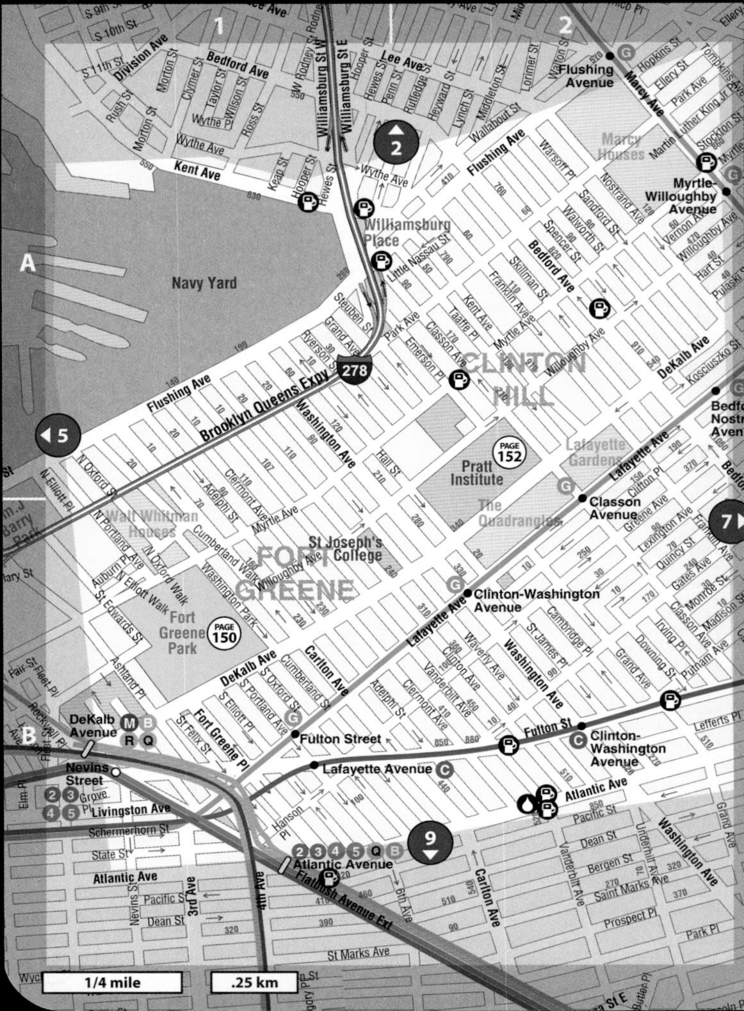

N

1

2

S 16th St

S 16th St

Division Ave

Bedford Ave

Lee Ave

Flushing Avenue

G

Hopkins St

Ellery St

Park Ave

Hewes St

Williamsburg St E

Williamsburg St W

Flushing Avenue

Martin Luther King Jr

Morton St

Clymes St

Taylor St

Wilson St

Wythe Ave

Ross St

Rutledge St

Lynch St

Heyward St

Wallabout St

Wythe Ave

Kent Ave

Flushing Ave

Warsoff Pl

Sandford St

Walworth St

Spencer St

Bedford Ave

Marcy Ave

Marcy Houses

Myrtle-Willoughby Avenue

G

Stockton St

Vernon Ave

Willoughby Ave

Hart St

Pulaski

Kent Ave

Taaffe Pl

Classon Ave

Emerson Pl

Franklin Ave

Skillman Ave

Steuben St

Grand Ave

Ryerson St

278

Navy Yard

A

Williamsburg Place

Little Nassau St

DeKalb Ave

CLINTON HILL

Kosciuszko St

Bedford-Nostrand Avenues

G

5

Flushing Ave

Brooklyn Queens Expwy

Washington Ave

Hall St

PAGE 152

Lafayette Gardens

G

Classon Avenue

Lafayette Ave

Greene Ave

Clinton St

Bedford

7

N Oxford St

N Portland Ave

N Elliott Pl

Clermont Ave

Vanderbilt Ave

Adelphi St

Clifton Pl

Gates Ave

Quincy St

Monroe St

Madison St

Pratt Institute

The Quadrangles

Lexington Ave

Walt Whitman Houses

Carlton Ave

Myrtle Ave

Willoughby Ave

St Joseph's College

FORT GREENE

Cumberland St

Washington Park

Fort Greene Park

PAGE 150

Clinton-Washington Avenue

G

Cambridge Pl

St James Pl

Grand Ave

Downing St

Putnam Ave

DeKalb Ave

Carlton Ave

S Oxford St

S Portland Ave

Fort Greene Pl

S Elliott Pl

Lafayette Ave

Fulton Street

Fulton St

Clinton-Washington Avenue

C

Waverly Ave

Lafferts Pl

Auburn Pl

Cumberland Walk

N Portland Ave

Oxford Walk

S Elliott Pl

St Felix St

Atlantic Ave

Washington Ave

DeKalb Avenue

M B R Q

Nevins Street

2 3 4 5

Grove

Livingston Ave

Schermerhorn St

State St

Atlantic Ave

Pacific St

Dean St

3rd Ave

Flatbush Ave Ext

2 3 4 5 Q B

9

Atlantic Avenue

Hanson Pl

Atlantic Avenue

Carlton Ave

Dean St

Bergen St

Saint Marks Ave

Washington Ave

Prospect Pl

Park Pl

St Marks Ave

| 1/4 mile | | .25 km | |

Parking, not too bad. Subway, not too good (it's the G or a loooong walk to the A/C, folks). The best BQE access is from the Classon-Flushing-Wythe-Kent nexus. Car crap is all on crappy Atlantic. Myrtle needs a subway line, and we await the Flushing Avenue Greenway with the deepest anticipation.

Subways

2 3 4 5 .... Nevins Street
2 3 4 5 B Q .... Atlantic Avenue
B M Q R .... DeKalb Avenue
C .... Lafayette Avenue
C .... Clinton-Washington Avenue
G .... Fulton Street
G .... Clinton-Washington Avenue
G .... Classon Avenue
G .... Bedford-Nostrand Avenue
G .... Flushing Avenue
G .... Myrtle-Willoughby Avenue

🌢 Car Washes

• **Suzie's Car Wash** •
805 Atlantic Ave [Vanderbilt]

🅿 Gas Stations

• **BP** • 577 Marcy Ave [Myrtle]
• **BP** • 677 Kent Ave [Hooper]
• **BP** • 514 Vanderbilt Ave [Atlantic]
• **Citgo** • 569 Myrtle Ave [Classon]
• **Exxon** • 140 Vanderbilt Ave [Myrtle]
• **Getty** • 713 Kent Ave [Penn]
• **Mobil** • 195 Flatbush Ave [5th Ave]
• **Shell** • 74 Classon Ave [Flushing]
• **Shell** • 895 Bedford Ave [Willoughby]
• **Sunoco** • 941 Atlantic Ave [Grand]

"Do-or-die Bed-Stuy" has become softer since the days of *Do the Right Thing*. Historical housing continues to attract the eyes of real-estate savvy yupsters, and now the annual Bedford-Stuyvesant House Tour in October includes a seminar on buying brownstones. Take-out joints haven't dispensed with their bulletproof windows just yet.

Banks

BA • Bank of America •
880 Quincy St [Ralph Ave]
CF • Carver Federal •
1281 Fulton St [Nostrand Ave]
CH • Chase • 1380 Fulton St [Marcy Ave]
CH • Chase (ATM) • Duane Reade •
274 Herkimer St [Brooklyn Ave]
CI • Citibank • 1398 Fulton St [Brooklyn Ave]
RS • Roosevelt Savings •
1024 Gates Ave [Broadway]
WM • Washington Mutual •
1392 Fulton St [Brooklyn Ave]

Landmarks

• Akwaaba Mansion •
347 MacDonough St [Stuyvesant]
• Magnolia Grandiflora •
679 Lafayette Ave [Tompkins]

Libraries

• Brooklyn Public • 617 DeKalb Ave [Nostrand]
• Brooklyn Public • 496 Franklin Ave [Hancock]
• Brooklyn Public Macon Branch •
361 Lewis Ave [Halsey]

Pharmacies

• Bed-Stuy Pharmacy • 1458 Fulton St
[Tompkins]
• County Pharmacy •
580 Nostrand Ave [Herkimer Pl]
• Duane Reade •
247 Herkimer St [Brooklyn]
• Five Star Pharmacy •
1200 Fulton St [Bedford]
• Fulton St Pharmacy •
1413 Fulton St [Brooklyn]
• Gates & Garvey Pharmacy •
276 Marcus Garvey Blvd [Quincy]
• Helfman Pharmacy •
410 Tompkins Ave [Hancock]
• Kingsboro Pharmacy •
868 DeKalb Ave [Marcus Garvey]
• Magnum Pharmacy •
1236 Fulton St [Arlington]
• Qasim Pharmacy •
934 Myrtle Ave [Throop]

• R&R Saks Pharmacy •
1147 Fulton St [Franklin]
• Rite Choice Pharmacy •
1484 Fulton St [Kingston]
• Sumner Ave Pharmacy •
103 Marcus Garvey Blvd [Vernon]
• Thriftway • 524 Nostrand Ave [Macon]

Police

• 79th Precinct • 263 Tompkins Ave [Greene]
• 81st Precinct • 30 Ralph Ave [Gates]

Post Offices

• US Post Office • 1205 Atlantic Ave [Nostrand]
• US Post Office • 1360 Fulton St [Marcy]

Supermarkets

• Associated Supermarket •
301 Marcus Garvey Ave [Gates]
• Bravo Supermarket •
1299 Fulton St [Nostrand]
• C-Town • 631 Gates Ave [Throop]
• Key Food • 1146 Fulton St [Franklin]
• Key Food • 200 Malcolm X Blvd [Putnam]
• Key Food • 367 Nostrand Ave [Monroe]
• Key Food • 952 Myrtle Ave [Throop]
• Met Food • 830 Lafayette Ave [Marcus Garvey]

Lewis Avenue, a few blocks north of Fulton Street, is growing into a cool, little retail district. Grab your morning coffee at Bread Stuy, peruse the local farmers market, and then check out the gorgeous brownstones of Stuyvesant Heights.

Coffee

- **Bread Stuy** • 403 Lewis Ave [MacDonough]
- **Bushbaby** • 1197 Fulton St [Bedford]
- **Common Grounds** •
  376 Tompkins Ave [Putnam]
- **Dunkin' Donuts** • 1309 Fulton St [Nostrand]
- **Dunkin' Donuts** • 1285 Broadway [Lexington]
- **Sista's Place** • 456 Nostrand Ave [Hancock]
- **Tiny Cup** • 279 Nostrand Ave [Clifton]

Farmers Markets

- **Bedford-Stuyvesant
  (Sat 8 am–3 pm, July–Nov)** •
  Lewis Ave & Decatur St

Hardware Stores

- **Big Brother's Hardware** •
  1327 Fulton St [Nostrand]
- **Dave's Hardware & Housewares** •
  849 DeKalb Ave [Throop]
- **Gates Lumber (lumber only)** •
  866 Madison St [Ralph]
- **Macon Hardware Store** •
  418 Marcus Garvey Blvd [Macon]
- **Mad Discount** • 1308 Fulton St [Nostrand]
- **Mike's Hardware** • 80 Ralph Ave [Putnam]

Liquor Stores

- **Cross Liquors** • 369 Nostrand Ave [Monroe]
- **Lovell Liquors** • 126 Putnam Ave [Franklin]
- **Mr Liquor** • 1555 Fulton St [Albany]
- **Nostrand Avenue Wines and Liquors** •
  551 Nostrand Ave [Atlantic]
- **S&S Wines & Liquors** •
  1289 Fulton St [Nostrand]

Supermarkets

- **Foodtown** • 1420 Fulton St [Brooklyn]
- **Western Beef** • 994 Myrtle Ave [Summer]

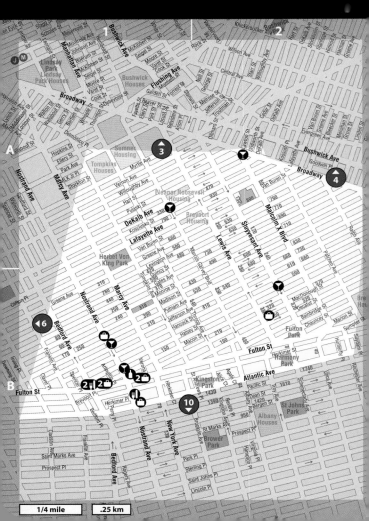

Gentrification has brought with it drinking and dining options such as The Jazz Spot and the hipster-mainstay Goodbye Blue Monday. Alongside these newer venues are fixtures like SugarHill Supper Club, which features dinner and dancing on the weekend and a soul-food Gospel brunch on Sunday. Hallelujah!

Nightlife

- **Goodbye Blue Monday** •
  1087 Broadway [Dodworth]
- **The Jazz Spot** •
  375 Kosciusko St [Marcus Garvey]
- **Sista's Place** • 456 Nostrand Ave [Hancock]
- **Solomon's Porch** •
  307 Stuyvesant Ave [Halsey]

Restaurants

- **A&A Bakes & Doubles** •
  481 Nostrand Ave [Macon]
- **Ali's Roti Shop** • 1267 Fulton St [Macon]
- **Dabakh Malick Resaurant** •
  1191 Fulton St [Bedford]
- **Ricardo Pizza** • 528 Nostrand Ave [Fulton]
- **SugarHill Supper Club** •
  609 DeKalb Ave [Nostrand]

Shopping

- **Andrew Fish Market** •
  1228 B Fulton St [Bedford]
- **Birdell's Records** •
  535 Nostrand Ave [Herkimer St]
- **Foot Locker** • 1258 Fulton St [Nostrand]
- **Happiness Fruit Farm** •
  1307 Fulton St [Nostrand]
- **Original Barber Shop** •
  409 Nostrand Ave [Putnam]
- **Tony's Country Life** •
  1316 Fulton St [Nostrand]

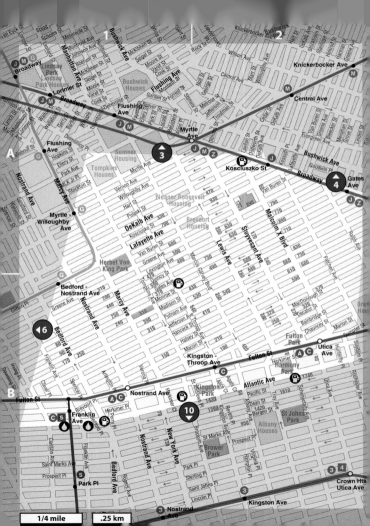

Transportation

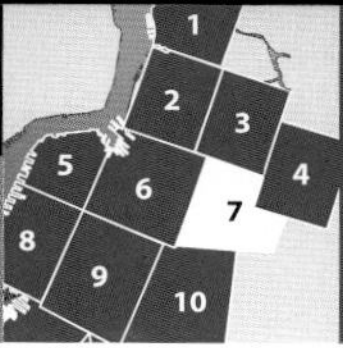

Map 7

While the A/C, J, and G trains run along its edges, much of Bed-Stuy is left without direct access to any trains, requiring you to hop on a bus or seriously hoof it in order to get to the nearest subway station. Hey, at least parking is never a hassle.

Subways

(3) ....Nostrand Avenue
(3) .... Kingston Avenue
(3) (4) .... Crown Heights-Utica Avenue
(A) (C) ....Nostrand Avenue
(A) (C) ....Utica Avenue
(C) .... Kingston-Throop Avenue
(C) (S) ....Franklin Avenue
(G) ....Bedford-Nostrand Avenue
(G) .... Myrtle-Willoughby Avenue
(J) (M) .... Flushing Avenue
(J) (M) (Z) .... Myrtle Avenue
(J) ....Kosciuszko Street
(J) (Z) .... Gates Avenue

Car Washes

- **Atlantic Brushless Car Wash** •
  1090 Atlantic Ave [Classon]
- **Auto Laundry Car Wash** •
  1119 Atlantic Ave [Bedford Pl]

Gas Stations

- **BP** • 1381 Atlantic Ave [Brooklyn]
- **Farmer Hillary Service Station** •
  584 Gates Ave [Throop]
- **Getty** • 1099 DeKalb Ave [Malcolm X]
- **Mobil** • 1143 Atlantic Ave [Bedford]
- **Shell** • 1740 Atlantic Ave [Schenectady]

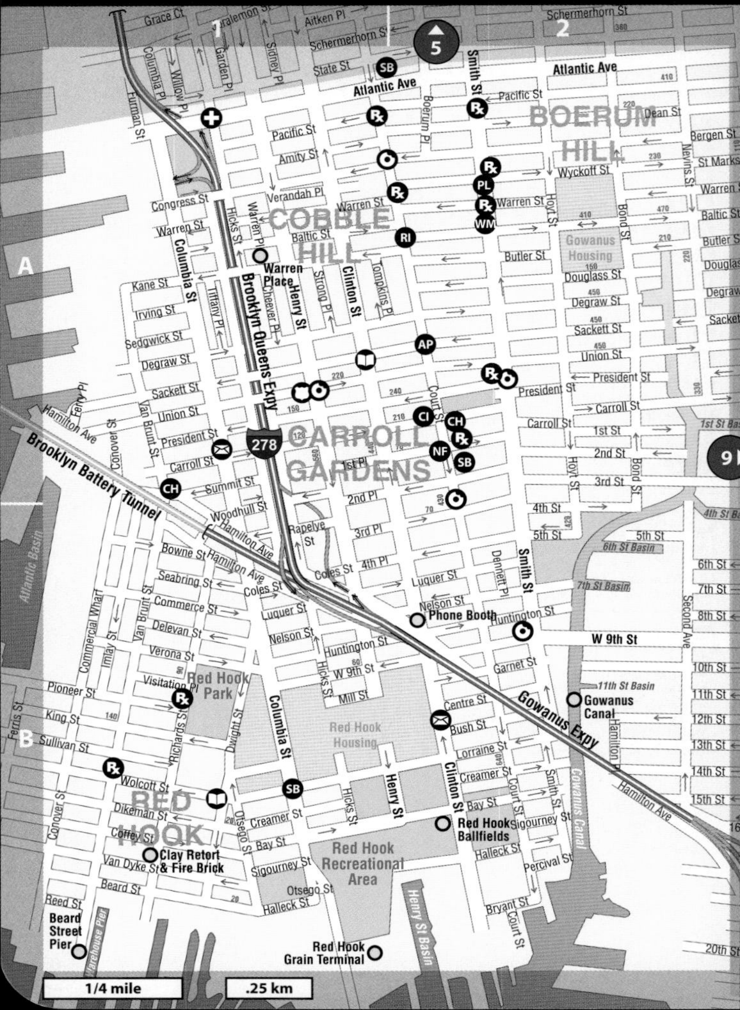

Map 8 · BoCoCa / Red Hook

N

1

2

5

Grace Ct

Falemon St

Aitken St

Schermerhorn St

Grace Ct

Columbia Pl

Willow St

Garden Pl

Sidney Pl

Schermerhorn St

380

Furman St

State St

Atlantic Ave

Boerum Pl

Smith St

Pacific St

Atlantic Ave

410

SB

Pacific St

Rx

Dean St

BOERUM HILL

Congress St

Amity St

Verandah Pl

Warren St

Rx

Wyckoff St

230

St Marks

Rx

PL

Warren St

Hoyt St

Bond St

418

476

210

Warren St

Columbia St

Hicks St

COBBLE HILL

Butler St

WM

RI

Bergen St

Bevins St

Baltic St

Butler St

Douglass St

Gowanus Housing

450

Degraw St

456

Sackett St

Union St

Degraw St

Sackett St

Kane St

Warren Place

Strong Pl

Clinton St

Tompkins Pl

Irving St

Henry St

Sedgwick St

Degraw St

AP

Sackett St

Union St

President St

President St

Carroll St

Carroll St

1st St

President St

CI

CH

2nd St

1st St

Hamilton Ave

Brooklyn Battery Tunnel

278

CARROLL GARDENS

Rx

NF

Court St

SB

Smith St

Hoyt St

Bond St

3rd St

2nd St

3rd St

Summit St

CH

Conover St

Van Brunt St

Woodhull St

2nd Pl

3rd Pl

Rapelye St

4th Pl

5th St

4th St

5th St

6th St Basin

7th St Basin

1st St

9

4th St

5th St

Bowne St

Hamilton Ave

Seabring St

Coles St

Commerce St

Luquer St

Nelson St

Delevan St

Verona St

Huntington St

Luquer St

Nelson St

Coles St

Smith St

Phone Booth

Huntington St

Garnet St

W 9th St

8th St

10th St

Pioneer St

Visitation Pl

Red Hook Park

Rx

Hicks St

Columbia St

W 9th St

Mill St

Centre St

11th St Basin

Gowanus Canal

King St

Sullivan St

140

Red Hook Housing

Bush St

Lorraine St

12th St

Gowanus Expy

Hamilton Ave

14th St

15th St

16

Wolcott St

Rx

RED HOOK

Dikeman St

Coffey St

SB

Creamer St

Henry St

Clinton St

Creamer St

Bay St

Red Hook Ballfields

Sigourney St

Halleck St

Percival St

Clay Retort & Fire Brick

Van Dyke St

Beard St

Red Hook Recreational Area

Sigourney St

Halleck St

Bryant St

Court St

Reed St

Beard Street Pier

Otsego St

Henry St Basin

Red Hook Grain Terminal

20th St

Worthington Pier

Atlantic Basin

Commercial Wharf

Ferris St

Conover St

Imlay St

Van Brunt St

A

B

Brooklyn Queens Expy

1/4 mile

.25 km

Map 3

Boerum Hill, Cobbile Hill, and Carroll Gardens (a.k.a. BoCoCa) is one of the reasons that Manhattanites venture into Brooklyn. Easily accessible by the F train, everything you need or want is located along Court and Smith Streets: Beautiful housing, attractive people, and hundreds of ways to spend lots of money.

Bagels

- **Aroma Bagels** • 520 Henry St [Union]
- **Court Street Bagels** • 181 Court St [Bergen]
- **Bagels by the Park** • 323 Smith St [President]
- **Brooklyn Bread Café** • 436 Court St [2nd Pl]
- **Line Bagels** • 476 Smith St [W 9th]

Banks

AP • **Apple** • 326 Court St [Sackett St]
CH • **Chase** • 390 Court St [Carroll St]
CH • **Chase** • 79 Hamilton Ave [Summit St]
CI • **Citibank** • 375 Court St [Carroll St]
NF • **North Fork** • 420 Court St [1st Pl]
PL • **Ponce de Leon** • 169 Smith St [Wyckoff St]
RI • **Ridgewood** • 244 Court St [Kane St]
SB • **Sovereign** • 498 Columbia St [Lorraine St]
SB • **Sovereign** • 215 Atlantic Ave [Court St]
SB • **Sovereign** • 395 Court St [2nd Pl]
WM • **Washington Mutual** •
192 Smith St [Warren St]

Emergency Rooms

- **Long Island College** • 339 Hicks St [Atlantic]

Landmarks

- **Beard Street Pier** •
Foot of Van Brunt St on the water
- **Brooklyn Clay Retort and Fire Brick Building**
76 Van Dyke St [Richards]
- **Gowanus Canal** • n/a
- **Phone Booth** • Huntington St & Hamilton Ave
- **Red Hook Ballfields** • Clinton St & Bay St
- **Red Hook Grain Terminal** • n/a
- **Warren Place** • Warren Pl [Warren St]

Libraries

- **Brooklyn Public** • 396 Clinton St [Sackett]
- **Brooklyn Public** • 7 Wolcott St [Dwight]

Pharmacies

- **CVS** • 150 Court St [Pacific]
- **CVS** • 395 Court St [1st Pl]
- **Red Hook Pharmacy** •
376 Van Brunt St [Wolcott]
- **Rite Aid** • 182 Smith St [Warren St]
- **Rite Aid** • 320 Smith St [President]
- **S V R H Pharmacy** • 161 Smith St [Wyckoff]
- **Thriftway** • 120 Richards St [Pioneer]
- **Total Care Pharmacy Bk** •
110 Smith St [Pacific]
- **Wyckoff's Corner Pharmacy** •
205 Court St [Wyckoff]

Police

- **76th Precinct** • 191 Union St [Henry]

Post Offices

- **US Post Office** • 257 Columbia St [Carroll]
- **US Post Office** • 615 Clinton St [Centre]

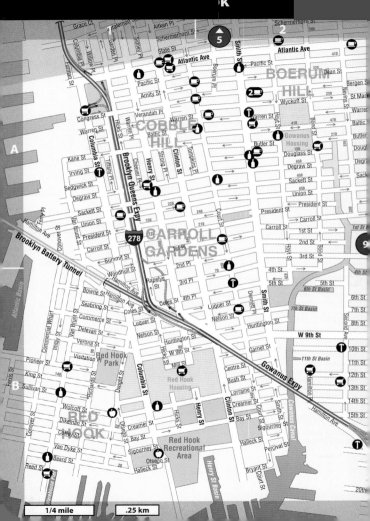

You don't have to walk far to find a quality liquor store or coffee shop in this area. For delicious and affordable wines check out Smith & Vine. D'Amico Foods has been serving up great coffee for over fifty years. For the ultimate supermarket experience with a view, head to the new Fairway.

Map 8

Coffee

- **Amazon Café** • 227 Smith St [Butler]
- **Bococa Café** • 195 Court St [Congress]
- **Coffee Den** • 144 Union St [Hicks]
- **D'Amico Foods** • 309 Court St [Degraw]
- **Dunkin' Donuts** • 148 Smith St [Bergen]
- **Dunkin' Donuts** • 383 Court St [1st Pl]
- **The Fall Café** • 307 Smith St [Union]
- **Flying Saucer** • 494 Atlantic Ave [Nevins]
- **Le Petite Café** • 502 Court St [Nelson]
- **Marquet Patisserie** • 221 Court St [Warren St]
- **Mazzola Bakery** • 192 Union St [Henry]
- **The Nascent** • 143 Nevins St [Bergen]
- **Starbucks** • 164 Smith St [Wyckoff]
- **Starbucks** • 167 Court St [Dean]
- **The Victory Cafe** • 71 Hoyt [State]

Farmers Markets

- **Red Hook Farmers Market (Sat 9 am–3 pm, July–Nov)** • Columbia St & Sigourney St
- **Red Hook Farmers Market (Wed 10 am–2 pm, July–Nov)** • 6 Wolcott St [Dwight]

Hardware Stores

- **Accardi Hardware** • 157 Columbia St [Degraw]
- **Home Depot** • 550 Hamilton Ave [17th]
- **Lowe's** • 118 Second Ave [10th]
- **Mazzone's True Value** • 470 Court St [4th Pl]
- **Tony's Hardware Store** • 181 Smith St [Wyckoff]

Liquor Stores

- **68 Lorraine Liquor** • 68 Lorraine St [Columbia]
- **AFYA Liquors** • 216 Hoyt St [Baltic]
- **Al's Wines & Liquors** • 329 Van Brunt St [Sullivan St]
- **Carroll Gardens Wines & Liquor** • 427 Court St [3rd Pl]
- **Heights Chateau Wines** • 123 Atlantic Ave [Henry]
- **Henry Street Wines & Liquors** • 494 Henry St [Sackett]
- **LeNell's Wine & Spirit Boutique** • 416 Van Brunt St [Coffey]
- **Rubins Liquor Store** • 241 Court St [Baltic]

- **Scotto's Wines Cellar** • 318 Court St [Sackett]
- **Smith & Vine** • 246 Smith St [Douglass]
- **Sterling Wine & Liquor** • 117 Smith St [Pacific]
- **Vintage Cellars** • 311 Smith St [Union]

Supermarkets

- **C Town** • 239 Bond St [Douglass]
- **C Town** • 57 Mill St [Hicks]
- **Fairway** • 480–500 Van Brunt St [Reed]
- **Fine Fare** • 498 Columbia St [Congress]
- **Key Food** • 169 Atlantic Ave [Clinton]
- **Met Food** • 197 Smith St [Warren St]
- **Met Food** • 486 Henry St [Degraw]
- **Park Natural Foods** • 350 Court St [Union]
- **Pathmark** • 1 12th St [Hamilton] ⬤
- **Pioneer Street** • 322 Van Brunt St [Pioneer]
- **Sahadi Importing Company** • 187 Atlantic Ave [Court St]

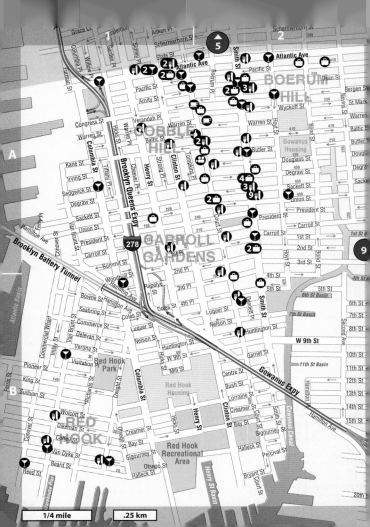

The saturation of shops and restaurants on Court and Smith Streets is complete—seven Thai restaurants between the two, for instance. And CG West (Columbia Street) and Red Hook aren't too far behind, as standouts Alma, Good Fork, and Red Hook Bait & Tackle show. But don't forget Sunny's!

Map 3

🎬 Movie Theaters

- **Cobble Hill Cinemas** • 265 Court St [Butler]

🎤 Nightlife

- **Abilene** • 442 Court St [3rd Pl]
- **Black Mountain Wine House** • 415 Union St [Hoyt]
- **Boat** • 175 Smith St [Wyckoff]
- **Brazen Head** • 228 Atlantic Ave [Court]
- **Brooklyn Inn** • 148 Hoyt St [Bergen]
- **Brooklyn Social** • 335 Smith St [Carroll]
- **Cody's Bar & Grill** • 154 Court St [Dean]
- **Downtown Bar & Grill** • 160 Court St [Amity]
- **Floyd** • 131 Atlantic Ave [Henry]
- **Gowanus Yacht Club** • 323 Smith [President]
- **Issue Project Room** • 232 3rd St [3rd Ave]
- **Kili** • 81 Hoyt St [State]
- **Last Exit** • 136 Atlantic Ave [Henry]
- **Montero Bar and Grill** • 73 Atlantic [Hicks]
- **Moonshine** • 317 Columbia St [Hicks]
- **PJ Hanley's** • 449 Court St [4th Pl]
- **Red Hook Bait & Tackle** • 320 Van Brunt St [Pioneer]
- **Rocky Sullivan's** • 34 Van Dyke St [Dwight]
- **Sugar Lounge** • 147A Columbia St [Kane]
- **Sunny's** • 253 Conover St [Reed]
- **Tini's Wine Bar & Cafe** • 414 Van Brunt St [Coffey]
- **Waterfront Ale House** • 155 Atlantic [Clinton]

🍴 Restaurants

- **Alma** • 187 Columbia St [Degraw]
- **Atlantic Chip Shop** • 129 Atlantic Ave [Henry]
- **Bar Tabac** • 128 Smith St [Dean]
- **Bocca Lupo** • 391 Henry St [Warren St]
- **Caserta Vecchia** • 155 Smith St [Bergen]
- **Chance** • 223 Smith St [Butler]
- **Chestnut** • 271 Smith St [DeGraw]
- **Chicory** • 243 DeGraw St [Clinton]
- **Cubana Café** • 272 Smith St [Degraw]
- **El Nuevo Portal** • 217 Smith St [Butler]
- **Ferdinando's Focacceria Restaurant** • 151 Union St [Hicks]
- **Fragole** • 394 Court St [Carroll]
- **Frankie's 457** • 457 Court St [Luquer]
- **The Good Fork** • 391 Van Brunt St [Coffey]
- **The Grocery** • 288 Smith St [Sackett]
- **Hadramout** • 172 Atlantic Ave [Clinton]
- **Hanco's** • 85 Bergen St [Smith]
- **Hope & Anchor** • 347 Van Brunt St [Wolcott]
- **Joya** • 215 Court St [Warren St]
- **Ki Sushi** • 122 Smith St [Dean]
- **Le Petite Café** • 502 Court St [Nelson]
- **Liberty Heights Tap Room** • 34 Van Dyke St [Dwight]
- **Lucali** • 575 Henry St [Carroll]
- **Panino'teca 275** • 275 Smith St [Sackett]
- **Patois** • 255 Smith St [Degraw]
- **Quercy** • 242 Court St [Baltic]
- **Sam's Restaurant** • 238 Court St [Baltic]
- **Saul** • 140 Smith St [Bergen]
- **Sherwood Café/Robin des Bois** • 195 Smith St [Warren]
- **Soul Spot** • 302 Atlantic Ave [Smith]
- **Yemen Café** • 176 Atlantic Ave [Clinton]
- **Zaytoons** • 283 Smith St [Sackett]

🛍 Shopping

- **A Cook's Companion** • 197 Atlantic Ave [Court]
- **Adam's Fresh Bakery by Design** • 144 Smith St [Bergen]
- **American Beer Distributors** • 256 Court St [Kane]
- **Blue Marble** • 420 Atlantic Ave [Bond]
- **Book Court** • 163 Court St [Dean]
- **Butter** • 389 Atlantic Ave [Bond]
- **Caputo's Fine Foods** • 460 Court St [3rd Pl]
- **D'Amico Foods** • 309 Court St [Degraw]
- **Environment337** • 337 Smith St [Carroll]
- **Exit 9** • 127 Smith St [Dean]
- **Fish Tales** • 296 Smith St [Union]
- **Flight 001** • 132 Smith St [Dean]
- **Marquet Patisserie** • 221 Court St [Warren]
- **Mazzola Bakery** • 192 Union St [Henry]
- **Refinery** • 254 Smith St [Douglass]
- **Rocketship** • 208 Smith St [Baltic]
- **Sahadi Importing Company** • 187 Atlantic Ave [Court]
- **Staubitz Meat Market** • 222 Court St [Baltic]
- **Stinky** • 261 Smith St [Degraw]
- **Swallow** • 361 Smith St [2nd]

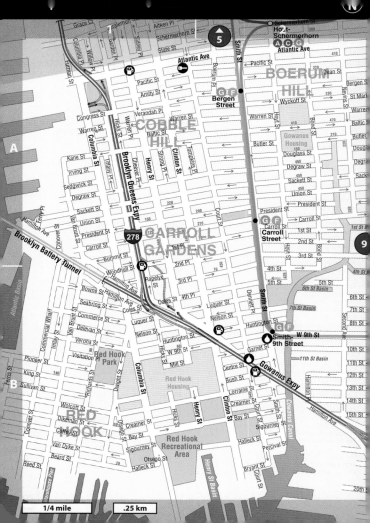

Map 3

The F line is the main form of transport in these parts (for better or worse). The haphazard G will take you into northern Brooklyn and Queens. There are good bus options for hard-to-reach areas: B61 to Red Hook or B71 to northern Park Slope. Take the B75 up Smith and back down Court if you're too lazy to walk.

Subways

F **G** .... Bergen Street
F **G** .... Carroll Street
F **G** .... Smith-9th Street

Car Rental

• **Avis Rent A Car** • 211 Atlantic Ave [Court St]

Car Washes

• **Brooklyn Battery Car Wash** •
  354 Hamilton Ave [Centre]
• **Hamilton Car Care Center** •
  519 Smith St [Garnet]

Gas Stations

• **Gulf** • 640 Hicks St [2nd Pl]
• **Mobil** • 375 Hamilton Ave [Bush]
• **Shell** • 112 Atlantic Ave [Henry]
• **Sunoco** • 289 Hamilton Ave [Clinton]

Bucolic Park Slope features Cosby-esque brownstones, friendly neighbors, and stroller traffic. Seems the renowned public schools and convenient shopping alongside the world-class library, museum, park, and botanic gardens prompt locals to multiply. Residents swear by the Food Co-op and PS 321 Flea Market. Nearby Prospect Heights continues to explode (in a positive way).

Bagels

- **Atlantic Center Bagels** • 625 Atlantic [5th Ave]
- **Bagel Hole** • 400 Seventh Ave [12th St]
- **Bagel World II** • 339 Fifth Ave [4th St]
- **Bagel Factory** • 612 Fifth Ave [17th St]
- **Bergen Bagels** • 473 Bergen St [6th Ave]
- **Fifth Avenue Bageltique Café** • 242 Fifth Ave [Carroll]
- **La Bagel Delight** • 122 Seventh Ave [President]
- **La Bagel Delight** • 252 Seventh Ave [5th]
- **Terrace Bagels** • 224 Prospect Pk W [Windsor]

Banks

- AS • **Astoria Federal** • 110 7th Ave [President]
- AS • **Astoria Federal** • 459 Fifth Ave [10th St]
- BA • **Bank of America** • 534 Fifth Ave [14th St]
- BA • **Bank of America (ATM)** • 139 Flatbush Ave [Atlantic Ave]
- BA • **Bank of America (ATM)** • 92 Seventh Ave [Union St]
- CF • **Carver Federal (ATM)** • Atlantic Terminal • 139 Flatbush Ave [Atlantic Ave]
- CH • **Chase** • 127 Seventh Ave [Carroll St]
- CH • **Chase** • 139 Flatbush Ave [Atlantic]
- CH • **Chase** • 401 Flatbush Ave [Eighth Ave]
- CH • **Chase** • 444 Fifth Ave [9th St]
- CH • **Chase (ATM)** • 300 Flatbush Ave [7th Ave]
- CI • **Citibank** • 114 Seventh Ave [President St]
- CO • **Commerce** • 269 Fifth Ave [Garfield Pl]
- HS • **HSBC** • 325 9th St [Fifth Ave]
- MT • **M&T** • 354 Flatbush Ave [St Johns Pl]
- NY • **New York Commercial** • 478 Fifth Av [11th St]
- NF • **North Fork** • 516 Fifth Ave [13th St]
- RS • **Roosevelt Savings** • 137 12th St [Third Ave]
- RS • **Roosevelt Savings** • Pathmark• 625 Atlantic Ave [Fifth Ave]
- SB • **Sovereign** • 234 Prospect Pk W [Windsor Pl]
- SB • **Sovereign (ATM)** • Brooklyn Public Library 2 Grand Army Plz [Eastern Pkwy]
- SB • **Sovereign (ATM)** • CVS• 341 9th St [5th Ave]
- WM • **Washington Mutual** • 290 Flatbush Ave [Prospect Pl]
- WM • **Washington Mutual** • 533 Fifth Ave [14th St]

Emergency Rooms

- **New York Methodist** • 506 6th St [7th Ave]

Landmarks

- **Brooklyn Botanic Garden** • 900 Washington Ave [Crown]
- **Brooklyn Conservatory of Music** • 58 Seventh Ave [Lincoln]
- **Brooklyn Public Library (Central Branch)** • Grand Army Plz [Grand]
- **Grand Army Plaza** • Flatbush Ave & Plaza St
- **New York Puppet Library** • Grand Army Plz
- **Park Slope Food Co-op** • 782 Union St [7th]

Libraries

- **Brooklyn Public** • 431 Sixth Ave [8th Ave]
- **Brooklyn Public Library (Central Branch)** • Grand Army Plz [Grand]
- **NY Methodist Hospital** • 506 6th St [7th Ave]

Pharmacies

- **Ballard** • 226 Prospect Park W [Windsor]
- **Crest Pharmacy** • 196 Flatbush Ave [Dean]
- **CVS** • 341 9th St [5th Ave]
- **Dante Pharmacy** • 582 Fifth Ave [16th St]
- **Duane Reade** • 300 Flatbush Ave [7th Ave]
- **Emcon Pharmacy** • 49 Fifth Ave [10th St]
- **Hong Kong Pharmacy** • 228 Flatbush [Bergen]
- **Kings Pharmacy** • 357 Flatbush Ave [Park]
- **Neergaard** • 120 Seventh Ave [President]
- **Neergaard** • 454 Fifth Ave [9th St] ☼
- **Oak Park** • 205 Prospect Park W [16th St]
- **Park Slope** • 803 Eighth Ave [8th St]
- **Pathmark Pharmacy** • 625 Atlantic Ave [5th] ☼
- **Prospect Garden** • 89 Seventh Ave [Union]
- **Rite Aid** • 249 Seventh Ave [5th St]
- **Rite Aid** • 462 Fifth Ave [10th St]
- **Rite Aid** • 445 Fifth Ave [9th St]
- **Thriftway** • 759 Washington Ave [Sterling]
- **Walgreens** • 520 Atlantic Ave [3rd Ave]

Police

- **78th Precinct** • 65 Sixth Ave [Bergen]

Post Offices

- **US Post Office** • 198 Seventh Ave [2nd St]
- **US Post Office** • 225 Prospect Park W [Windsor]
- **US Post Office** • 275 9th St [4th Ave]
- **US Post Office** • 542 Atlantic Ave [3rd Ave]

PROSPECT HEIGHTS

PARK SLOPE

WINDSOR TERRACE

Brooklyn Botanic Garden

Prospect Park

Streets and labels:

Flatbush Ave
Hanson Pl
Atlantic Ave
State St
Pacific St
Dean St
Bergen St
St Mark's Pl
Warren St
Baltic St
Third St
Fourth Ave
Fifth Ave
Dean St
Pacific St
Bergen St
Prospect Pl
Park Pl
Sterling Pl
St Johns Pl
Lincoln Pl
Butler St
Douglass St
Degraw St
Sackett St
Nevins St
1st St Basin
4th St Basin
Whitwell Pl
Denton Pl
Berkeley Pl
Union St
President St
Carroll St
Garfield Pl
1st St
2nd St
3rd St
4th St
5th St
6th St
7th St
8th St
9th St
10th St
11th St
12th St
13th St
14th St
15th St
16th St
17th St
18th St
Prospect Expy
Third Ave
Fourth Ave
Fifth Ave
Sixth Ave
Seventh Ave
Eighth Ave
Sterling Pl
St Johns Pl
Lincoln Pl
Vanderbilt Ave
Carlton Ave
Washington Ave
Grand Ave
Park Pl
Plaza St E
Grand Army Plz
Flatbush Ave
West Dr
East Dr
Montgomery Pl
Fiske Pl
Polhemus Pl
Prospect Park W
Prospect Park SW
W Lake Dr
Windsor Pl
Prospect Ave
Jackson Pl
Webster Pl
Calder Pl
Sherman St
Tenth Ave
Eleventh Ave
Fuller Pl
Howard Pl
Hamilton Ave

PAGE 144
PAGE 142

Dutchbury Pl

1/4 mile
.25 km

278
27
6
8
10
11
12
13

Knock out your weekend to-do list efficiently on 7th and 5th Avenues. A fresh cuppa joe from Gorilla, joyce, or Tea Lounge will help you get moving. Peruse the farmer's market, pick up a little something for Fido, select a bottle of fine wine, and you'll still have time for yoga.

Coffee

- **Café Regular** • 318 11th St [5th Ave]
- **Cocoa Bar** • 228 Seventh Ave [4th St]
- **Colson Patisserie** • 374 9th St [6th Ave]
- **Connecticut Muffin** • 206 Prospect Pk W [16th]
- **Delices de Paris** • 321 9th St [5th Ave]
- **Dunkin' Donuts** • 137 12th St [3rd Ave]
- **Dunkin' Donuts** • 244 Flatbush [St Marks Ave]
- **Dunkin' Donuts** • 448 Fifth Ave [9th St]
- **Dunkin' Donuts** • 552 Third Ave [14th St]
- **Dunkin' Donuts** • 578 Atlantic Ave [4th Ave St]
- **El Cafetin** • 227 Fourth Ave [President]
- **Fifth Avenue Café** • 432 Fifth Ave [8th St]
- **Gorilla Coffee** • 97 Fifth Ave [Park]
- **Heights Coffee Lounge** • 335 Flatbush [7th]
- **joyce** • 646 Vanderbilt Ave [Park Pl]
- **Ladybird Bakery** • 1112 8th Ave [11th St]
- **Little Miss Muffin** • 174 Park Pl [Flatbush]
- **Mule Café** • 67 Fourth Ave [Bergen]
- **Naidre's** • 384 Seventh Ave [12th St]
- **Ozzie's Coffee** • 249 Fifth Ave [Carroll]
- **Ozzie's Coffee** • 57 Seventh Ave [Lincoln]
- **Parco** • 427 Seventh Ave [14th St]
- **Paris Bakery** • 321 9th St [Fifth Ave]
- **Perch** • 365 Fifth Ave [5th St]
- **Postmark Café** • 326 6th St [Fifth Ave]
- **Prospect Perk** • 183 Sterling Pl [Flatbush]
- **Red Horse** • 497 Sixth Ave [12th St]
- **7th Avenue Donuts** • 324 Seventh Ave [9th St]
- **Starbucks** • 139 Flatbush Ave [Atlantic]
- **Starbucks** • 164 Seventh Ave [Garfield]
- **Tea Lounge** • 350 Seventh Ave [10th St]
- **Tea Lounge** • 837 Union St [7th Ave]
- **Two Little Red Hens** • 1112 Eighth Ave [11th]
- **Zilli Bar Lounge** • 289 Fifth Ave [2nd St]

Farmers Markets

- **Grand Army Plaza (Sat 8 am–4 pm, July–Nov)** • Prospect Park entrance & Flatbush Ave
- **Park Slope–5th Ave Farmers Market (Sun 11 am–5 pm, July–Nov)** • Fifth Ave & 4th St
- **Windsor Terrace (Wed 8 am–3 pm, July–Oct)** Prospect Park • Prospect Park W & 15th St

Hardware Stores

- **5th Ave Hardware** • 593 Fifth Ave [Prospect]
- **Allstar Hardware** • 284 Flatbush [Prospect Pl]
- **Brooklyn Hardware** • 550 Prospect Ave [10th]
- **Brooklyn Hardware** • 58 Fifth Ave [Bergen]

- **Flatbush Hardware** • 265 Flatbush [St Marks]
- **Joe Leopoldi Hardware** • 415 Fifth Ave [8th St]
- **LTW** • 299 Third Ave [Carroll]
- **Mayday Hardware** • 755 Washington [Sterling]
- **Pintchik** • 478 Bergen St [Flatbush]
- **Prospect Hardware** • 517 Seventh Ave [17th]
- **R&A Houseware** • 109 Fifth Ave [Park]
- **Tarzian Hardware** • 193 Seventh Ave [2nd St]

Liquor Stores

- **Bay River Wine & Liquor** • 539 Fifth Ave [14th]
- **Big Nose Full Body** • 382 Seventh Ave [11th]
- **Fields Fine Wines** • 469 16th St [Prospect Park]
- **Gary's Wines & Liquor** • 234 Flatbush [6th]
- **Grand Plaza Liquor** • 764 Washington [Park]
- **Hamilton Plaza Liquors** • 137 12th St [3rd]
- **Liquor Warehouse** • 749 Bergen St [Wash Ave]
- **Love Liquors** • 797 Washington [Lincoln]
- **Martinez Liquor Store** • 468 Fourth Ave [10th]
- **Mei Chi Liquors** • 391 Flatbush Ave [Sterling]
- **Park Slope Liquor** • 158 Park Pl [Flatbush]
- **Prospect Wine Shop** • 322 Fifth Ave [8th]
- **Red, White and Bubbly** • 211 Fifth Ave [Union]
- **Schwartz Wine & Liquors** • 427 Fifth Ave [8th]
- **Shawn's Wine** • 141 Seventh Ave [Garfield]
- **Slope Cellars** • 436 Seventh Ave [15th]
- **Sterling Grapes** • 115 Fifth Ave [Sterling]
- **Wine Exchange** • 595 Vanderbilt Ave [Bergen]

Supermarkets

- **Ace Supermarket** • 75 Seventh Ave [Berkeley]
- **Associated** • 216 Fifth Ave [Union]
- **Associated** • 617 Fifth Ave [17th]
- **Back to the Land** • 142 Seventh Ave [Carroll]
- **Blue Apron Foods** • 814 Union St [7th Ave]
- **C Town** • 329 Ninth St [5th Ave]
- **C Town** • 720 Washington Ave [Prospect Pl]
- **Key Food** • 120 Fifth Ave [Park]
- **Key Food** • 130 Seventh Ave [Carroll]
- **Key Food** • 369 Flatbush Ave [Sterling] ⊕
- **Key Food** • 589 Prospect Ave [11th Ave]
- **Key Food** • 801 Washington Ave [Lincoln]
- **Met Food** • 185 Seventh Ave [2nd]
- **Met Food** • 595 Fifth Ave [Prospect Ave]
- **Met Food** • 632 Vanderbilt Ave [Prospect Pl]
- **Pathmark** • 625 Atlantic Ave [5th Ave] ⊕
- **Pumpkin's** • 1302 Eighth Ave [13th]
- **Shop Smart** • 238 Prospect Park W [Windsor]
- **Traditions** • 465 Fifth Ave [10th St]
- **United Meat Market** • 219 Prospect Pk W

73

Park Slope/Prospect Heights/Windsor Terrace

Flatbush Ave
Hanson Pl
State St
Atlantic Ave
Pacific St
Dean St
Bergen St
Carlton Ave
Vanderbilt Ave
Washington Ave
Grand Ave
Pacific St
Dean St
Bergen St
St Mark's Ave

PROSPECT HEIGHTS

Park Pl
Sterling Pl
St Johns Pl
Lincoln Pl

St Mark's Pl
Warren St
Baltic St
Butler St
Douglass St
Degraw St
Sackett St

Fourth Ave
Fifth Ave
Sixth Ave
Seventh Ave

Prospect Pl
Park Pl
Sterling Pl
St Johns Pl
Lincoln Pl
Berkeley Pl
Union St
President St
Carroll St
Garfield Pl
1st St
2nd St
3rd St
4th St
5th St
6th St
7th St
8th St
9th St
10th St
11th St
12th St
13th St
14th St
15th St
16th St

Plaza St E

Brooklyn Botanic Garden
PAGE 144

Grand Army Plz

Eighth Ave
Polhemus Pl
Fiske Pl
Montgomery Pl

Flatbush Ave
West Dr
East Dr

PARK SLOPE

PAGE 142
Prospect Park

Prospect Park W

Third Ave
Fourth Ave
Fifth Ave
Sixth Ave
Seventh Ave

Eighth Ave

Whitwell Pl
Denton Pl

Nevins St
1st St Basin
4th St Basin

Jackson Pl
Webster Pl
Calder Pl
Windsor Pl

W Lake Dr
Prospect Park SW

WINDSOR TERRACE

Tenth Ave
Howard Pl
Fuller Pl
Sherman St

Prospect Expy
Prospect Ave

17th St
18th St

Harman Ave

278
11
27
12
13

1/4 mile   .25 km

State St
530
410
320
650
640
350
690
378
310
375
618
420
490
450
380
290
210
200
270
620
515
390
110
110
120
780
670
3100
550
630
590
620
670
610
590
450

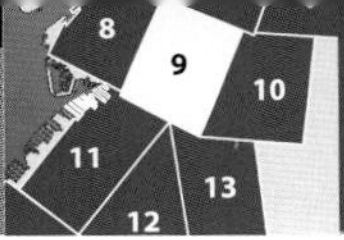

Map 9

As if 7th and 5th Avenues didn't have enough already, now 4th (Sheep Station, Cherry Tree, etc.) gets into the act. Top food abounds—Applewood, Franny's, Blue Ribbon, Stone Park—as does great nabe hangouts Beast, The Gate, and Flatbush Farm. For live acts, head to Barbes, Southpaw, and Union Hall.

Movie Theaters

• **Pavilion Movie Theatres** • 188 Prospect Park W [Greenwood]

Nightlife

• **Bar Toto** • 411 11th St [6th Ave]
• **Barbes** • 376 9th St [6th Ave]
• **Buttermilk** • 577 Fifth Ave [16th]
• **Canal Bar** • 270 Third Ave [President St]
• **Cherry Tree** • 65 4th Ave [Bergen St]
• **Commonwealth** • 497 5th Ave [12th St]
• **Flatbush Farm** •
  76 St Marks Ave [Flatbush Ave]
• **Freddy's Bar and Backroom** •
  485 Dean St [6th Ave]
• **Fourth Avenue Pub** • 76 4th Ave [Bergen St]
• **The Gate** • 321 Fifth Ave [3rd St]
• **Ginger's** • 363 Fifth Ave [5th]
• **Great Lakes** • 284 Fifth Ave [1st St]
• **Good Coffeehouse Music Parlor** •
  53 Prospect Park West [2nd St]
• **Hank's Saloon** • 46 Third Ave [Atlantic]
• **Lighthouse Tavern** • 243 Fifth Ave [Carroll]
• **Loki Lounge** • 304 Fifth Ave [2nd]
• **O'Connor's** • 39 Fifth Ave [Bergen]
• **Pacific Standard** • 82 Fourth Ave [St Marks Pl]
• **Park Slope Ale House** • 356 Sixth Ave [5th]
• **Patio Lounge** • 179 Fifth Ave [Berkeley]
• **Puppet's Jazz Bar** • 294 Fifth Ave [1st]
• **Soda** • 629 Vanderbilt Ave [Prospect Pl]
• **Southpaw** • 125 Fifth Ave [Sterling]
• **Timboo's** • 477 5th Ave [11th St]
• **Union Hall** • 202 Union St [5th Ave]

Restaurants

• **12th Street Bar and Grill** •
  1123 Eighth Ave [11th]
• **2nd Street Café** • 189 Seventh Ave [2nd]
• **Al Di La Trattoria** • 248 Fifth Ave [Carroll]
• **Amorina** • 624 Vanderbilt Ave [Propect Pl]
• **Anthony's** • 426 Seventh Ave [14th]
• **Applewood** • 501 11th St [7th Ave]
• **Beast** • 638 Bergen St [Vanderbilt]
• **Belleville** • 332 Fifth Ave [3rd St]
• **Blue Ribbon Brooklyn** • 280 Fifth Ave [1st St]
• **Bogota Latin Bistro** • 141 Fifth Ave [St Johns]
• **Bonnie's Grill** • 278 Fifth Ave [1st St]
• **Brooklyn Fish Camp** •
  162 Fifth Ave [Douglass]
• **ChipShop** • 383 Fifth Ave [6th]

• **Cousin John's Café and Bakery** •
  70 Seventh Ave [Lincoln]
• **Dizzy's** • 511 Eighth Ave [5th St]
• **Elora's** • 272 Prospect Park W [17th]
• **Flatbush Farm** •
  76 St Marks Ave [Flatbush Ave]
• **Franny's** • 295 Flatbush Ave [Prospect Pl]
• **Garden Café** •
  620 Vanderbilt Ave [Prospect Pl]
• **Gen Restaurant** •
  659 Washington Ave [St Marks Ave]
• **Jpan Sushi** • 287 5th Ave [1st St]
• **Kinara** • 473 Fifth Ave [11th]
• **La Taqueria** • 72 Seventh Ave [Berkeley]
• **The Minnow** • 442 9th St [7th Ave]
• **Mitchell's Soul Food** •
  617 Vanderbilt Ave [St Marks Ave]
• **Moim** • 206 Garfield Pl [7th Ave]
• **Nana** • 155 Fifth Ave [Lincoln]
• **Noo Na** • 565 Vanderbilt Ave [Pacific St]
• **Olive Vine Café** • 54 Seventh Ave [St Johns]
• **Red Hot** • 349 Seventh Ave [10th]
• **Rose Water** • 787 Union St [6th Ave]
• **Sheep Station** • 149 4th Ave [Douglass]
• **Stone Park Café** • 324 Fifth Ave [3rd St]
• **Sushi Tatsu** • 347 Flatbush Ave [Sterling]
• **Tom's** • 782 Washington Ave [Sterling]
• **Watana** • 420 7th Ave [14th]

Shopping

• **3R Living** • 276 Fifth Ave [Garfield]
• **Artesana Home** • 170 Seventh Ave [1st St]
• **Beacon's Closet** • 220 Fifth Ave [President]
• **Bierkraft** • 191 5th Ave [Berkeley Pl]
• **Bird** • 430 Seventh Ave [14th]
• **Brooklyn Superhero Supply** •
  372 Fifth Ave [5th]
• **Buttercup's PAW-tisserie** • 63 5th Ave [10th]
• **Clay Pot** • 162 Seventh Ave [Garfield]
• **Fabrica** • 619 Vanderbilt Ave [Prospect Pl]
• **JackRabbit Sports** •
  151 Seventh Ave [Garfield]
• **Leaf and Bean** • 83 Seventh Ave [Berkeley]
• **Loom** • 115 Seventh Ave [President]
• **Mostly Modern** • 383 Seventh Ave [12th]
• **Movable Feast** • 284 Prospect Park W [18th]
• **Nancy Nancy** • 244 Fifth Ave [Carroll]
• **Rare Device** • 453 Seventh Ave [16th]
• **Root Stock & Quade** •
  297 Seventh Ave [7th St]
• **Somethin' Else** • 294 Fifth Ave [1st St]
• **Stitch Therapy** • 176 Lincoln Pl [7th Ave]
• **Trailer Park** • 77 Sterling Pl [6th Ave]

Atlantic Avenue

Atlantic Ave
State St
Pacific St
Dean St
Bergen St
St Mark's Ave
Carlton Ave
Washington Ave

PROSPECT HEIGHTS

Pacific Street
M N R D
Pacific St
Dean St
Bergen St

Bergen Street
Prospect Pl
7th Avenue
Park Pl
Fifth Ave
Dusenbury Pl
Sixth Ave
Seventh Ave

St Mark's Pl
Warren St
Baltic St
Butler St
Douglass St
Degraw St
Sackett St

Prospect Pl
Park Pl
Sterling Pl
St Johns Pl
Lincoln Pl
Berkeley Pl
Union St
President St
Carroll St
Garfield Pl

Sterling Pl
St Johns Pl
Lincoln Pl
Plaza St E

Grand Army Plaza

Grand Army Plz

Brooklyn Botanic Garden (PAGE 144)

Third Ave
Flatbush Ave

Union Street
M R

Eighth Ave
Fiske Pl
Polhemus Pl
Montgomery Pl
West Dr
East Dr

Whitwell Pl
Denton Pl

1st St
2nd St
3rd St
4th St
5th St
6th St
7th St
8th St

PARK SLOPE

Prospect Park W

(PAGE 142)

Prospect Park

4th Avenue-9th Street
M F
R

9th St
7th Avenue
F

10th St
11th St
12th St
13th St
14th St
15th St
16th St

Third Ave
Fifth Ave
Sixth Ave
Seventh Ave
Eighth Ave

15th Street-Prospect Park F
Prospect Park SW
W Lake Dr

WINDSOR TERRACE

Tenth Ave
Prospect Park W

Prospect Avenue
M R

Prospect Expy

17th St
18th St
Windsor Pl
Prospect Ave

Jackson Pl
Webster Pl
Cutler Pl

Howard Pl
Fuller Pl
Sherman St

17th St
18th St

278

1/4 mile   .25 km

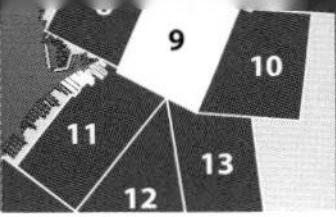

Parking: It's a nightmare. Why? Because residents who own 2-million-dollar brownstones can also afford a Volvo, stupid! All your car needs—gas, car wash, auto parts, etc.—can be found on 4th Avenue. Subway service is good unless you live on 3rd Street. Can anyone say "Union Street Light Rail?"

Map 9

Subways

2 3 .... Bergen Street
2 3 .... Grand Army Plaza
4 5 2 3 B Q .... Atlantic Avenue
B Q .... 7th Avenue
D M N R .... Pacific Street
F .... 7th Avenue
F ....15th Street-Prospect Park
F M R ....4th Avenue-9th Street
M R .... Prospect Avenue
M R .... Union Street

Car Rental

- **All Car Rent A Car** • 610 Warren St [4th Ave]
- **Enterprise** • 453 Third Ave [9th St]
- **Express Car Rental** •
  496 Seventh Ave [Prospect Ave]
- **Forever Ten Rentals** • 569 Grand Ave [Bergen]
- **Speedy Rent A Car** • 800 Union St [7th Ave]

Car Washes

- **Golden Touch Car Wash** •
  296 Fourth Ave [1st St]

Gas Stations

- **BP** • 164 Fourth Ave [Douglass]
- **Citgo** • 169 Third Ave [Butler]
- **Getty** • 538 Third Ave [13th St]
- **Mobil** • 185 Flatbush Ave Ext [Gold]

Fulton St

1

2

Fulton St

Lefferts Pl

Brevoort Pl

Herkimer St

Kingston Park
St Andrews Pl

Aria Ct
OcCt
Aria Ct

Atlantic Ave

Dean St

820

Herkimer St
Perry Pl

820
420
670

Dean St
Bergen St

Pacific St

New York Ave
1530

CROWN
HEIGHTS

950

Prospect Pl

490

Prospect Pl

St Marks Ave
670

Brooklyn
Children's
Museum

SB

Brower
Park

Albany
Housing

510

Bedford Ave

670

740
226

Park Pl
1060
Sterling Pl
1070

Virginia Pl

A

Lincoln Pl

Brooklyn
Museum

Saint Francis Pl
Saint Charles Pl

St Johns Pl

St Johns Pl

Lincoln Pl

Eastern Pkwy

BA

1430
1440

AP

Brooklyn
Botanic
Garden

PAGE
144

1189

Rogers Ave

1040

989

117

835

Franklin Ave

WM

CF

CI CF

BP

CF

Union St

President St

Carroll St

Crown St

1330

Brooklyn Ave

525

Kingston Ave
378
669

493

Albany Ave

440

The
Carousel

McKeever Pl

376

Dean Ct

Sullivan Pl

315

Ludlum St
Shepherd Ave

Montgomery St

Malbone St

411

Empire Blvd

Lamont Ct
Balfour Pl

556

Lefferts
E New Yo
Maple S
Midwoo

Prospect
Park Zoo

PAGE
142

110

Empire Blvd

CH CF

New York Ave

420

Rutla
Fenim
Haw

Sterling St

Lefferts Ave

Flatbush Ave

Lincoln Rd
110

Ocean Ave
200

Maple St
60

Beekman Pl

PROSPECT -
LEFFERTS
GARDENS

Midwood St

420

Palm Ct
Miami Ct

Prospect
Park

B

60

Chester Ct

Westbury Ct
280

Rutland Rd

Fenimore St

Hawthorne St

Winthrop St

340

340

Kings County
Hospital
460

590

Prospect
Lake

Parkside Ave

300
60

Bedford Ave

2
CH

Clarkson Ave

Lenox Rd
2110

Rogers Ave
1320

290
CH

CH

SUNY
Health Science
Center

350

2 Rx
1120

South Lake Dr

Parkside Ave
Woodruff Ave

SB

13

Linden Blvd

820

E 35th St
E 34th St

E 37th St
E 38th St
E 39th St

Parade
Grounds

Parkside Ave

Crooke Ave

Caton Ave

St Pauls Ct

Johnson Ave

Church Ave

Lloyd St
Erasmus St

Martense St

Snyder Av

1/4 mile

.25 km

Got a need to breed? Affordable rents, big apartments, and proximity to Prospect-Lefferts Gardens have long made Prospect-Lefferts Gardens attractive for families. The Brooklyn Museum, Children's Museum, Botanic Garden, Zoo, and Carousel are all here for your infotainment.

Bagels

• **Bagels & High Tea** • 854 Nostrand Ave [Union]

Banks

AP • Apple • 318 Albany Ave [Eastern Pkwy]
BP • Banco Popular •
539 Eastern Pkwy [Nostrand Ave]
BA • Bank of America •
781 Eastern Pkwy [Kingston Ave]
CF • Carver Federal •
1009 Nostrand Ave [Empire Blvd]
CF • Carver Federal (ATM) • Medgar Evers
College • 1150 Carroll St [Rogers Ave]
CF • Carver Federal (ATM) • Medgar Evers
College • 1650 Bedford Ave [Crown St]
CH • Chase • 1000 Nostrand Ave [Sullivan Pl]
CH • Chase (ATM) • SUNY-HSCB Health Science
Center • 450 Clarkson Ave [E 36th St]
CH • Chase (ATM) • Duane Reade •
724 Flatbush Ave [Parkside Ave]
CH • Chase (ATM) • Duane Reade •
750 New York Ave [Clarkson Ave]
CI • Citibank (ATM) • Medgar Evers College •
1650 Bedford Ave [Crown St]
SB • Sovereign Bank • Brooklyn Children's
Museum • 145 Brooklyn Ave [St Marks Ave]
WM • Washington Mutual •
391 Eastern Pkwy [Bedford Ave]

Emergency Rooms

• **Downstate Medical Center** •
450 Clarkson Ave [E 37th St]
• **Interfaith Medical Center** •
1545 Atlantic Ave [Albany]
• **Kings County** • 451 Clarkson Ave [New York]

Landmarks

• **Brooklyn Children's Museum** •
145 Brooklyn Ave [St Marks Ave]
• **Brooklyn Museum** •
200 Eastern Pkwy [Wash Ave]
• **The Carousel** •
Ocean Ave & Flatbush Ave & Empire Blvd
• **Prospect Park Zoo** •
450 Flatbush Ave [Empire]

Libraries

• **Brooklyn Public** • 560 New York Ave [Maple]
• **Brooklyn Public** • 725 St Marks Ave [Nostrand]

Pharmacies

• **Albany Pharmacy** • 178 Albany Ave [St Marks]
• **Clarkson Pharmacy** •
524 Clarkson Ave [E 38th St]
• **CVS** • 1251 Nostrand Ave [Winthrop]
• **Duane Reade** • 724 Flatbush Ave [Parkside]
• **Duane Reade** • 750 New York Ave [Clarkson]
• **Empire Pharmacy** •
353 Empire Blvd [Nostrand]
• **Health Wise** • 1233 Nostrand Ave [Winthrop]
• **Kings Pharmacy** • 492 Clarkson Ave [E 38th St]
• **Krimko Pharmacies** •
954 Nostrand Ave [Montgomery]
• **M & F** • 712 Nostrand Ave [Prospect Pl]
• **Maiman's Pharmacy** •
821 Franklin Ave [Eastern]
• **Maxi Care Pharmacy** •
1645 Bedford Ave [Crown]
• **Noor Pharmacy** •
2036 Bedford Ave [Clarkson Ave]
• **Pharmacy Express** •
701 Flatbush Ave [Parkside]
• **Prime Care Pharmacy** •
1126 Nostrand Ave [Midwood]
• **Raees Pharmacy** • 750 Flatbush Ave [Clarkson]
• **Rite Aid** • 1040 St Johns Pl [Brooklyn]
• **Rite Aid** • 1679 Bedford Ave [Montgomery]
• **Rubin Chemists** • 828 Nostrand Ave [Eastern]
• **S&T Pharmacy** • 391 Eastern Pkwy [Bedford]
• **St John's Place Pharmacy** •
1106 St Johns Pl [Rogers]
• **Sunshine Pharmacy** •
411 Kingston Ave [Montgomery]
• **Swan Pharmacy** •
650 Franklin Ave [St Marks Ave]
• **Thriftway** • 542 Flatbush Ave [Lincoln Rd]
• **Thriftway** • 720 Classon Ave [Prospect Pl]

Police

• **71st Precinct** • 421 Empire Blvd [New York]

Post Offices

• **US Post Office** •
315 Empire Blvd [Nostrand]

Fulton St

Lefferts Pl

Brevoort Pl

Herkimer St

Fulton St

Atlantic Ave

Dean St

820

820

420

Prospect Pl

490

510

Lincoln Pl

Brooklyn Botanic Garden

PAGE 144

Flatbush Ave

East Dr

Center Dr

East Lake Dr

PAGE 142

Prospect Park

Prospect Lake

South Lake Dr

Parkside Ave

Woodruff Ave

Crooke Ave

Caton Ave

Franklin Ave

Classon Ave

Saint Francis Pl

Saint Charles Pl

Bedford Ave

Rogers Ave

Nostrand Ave

Pacific St

Dean St

Bergen St

St Marks Ave

670

740

St Johns Pl

220

Union St

President St

Carroll St

Crown St

Montgomery St

Sullivan Pl

Malbone St

Empire Blvd

Sterling Pl

Lefferts Ave

Lincoln Rd

Maple St

Midwood St

Rutland Rd

Fenimore St

Hawthorne St

Winthrop St

Parkside Ave

Clarkson Ave

Lenox Rd

New York Ave

CROWN HEIGHTS

Brower Park

Park Pl

Prospect Pl

Sterling Pl

Lincoln Pl

Eastern Pkwy

1430

1440

1330

Brooklyn Ave

Kingston Ave

Albany Ave

493

669

525

556

New York Ave

PROSPECT LEFFERTS GARDENS

420

420

340

340

290

Bedford Ave

Rogers Ave

Nostrand Ave

350

820

Kings County Hospital

SUNY Health Science Center

Linden Blvd

460

Albany Ave

Empire Blvd

Lefferts Ave

E New York Ave

13

Martense St

St Pauls Pl

Snyder Ave

| 1/4 mile | .25 km |

The large Caribbean-American population in Crown Heights makes it a great place to scarf delectable jerk chicken, get your hair braided, or stock up on cheap international phone cards. Too much Red Stripe last night? Morning coffee from Kdog and Dunebuggy will revive you.

Coffee

- **Boulevard Café** • 510 Empire Blvd [New York]
- **Café Royal** • 453 Albany Ave [Montgomery]
- **Dunkin' Donuts** • Exxon •
  1550 Bedford Ave [Eastern]
- **Dunkin' Donuts** •
  40 Empire Blvd [Washington Ave]
- **Dunkin' Donuts** • 506 Clarkson Ave [E 38th St]
- **Kdog & Dunebuggy** •
  43 Lincoln Rd [Flatbush]

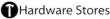 Hardware Stores

- **Carroll Hardware** • 873 Nostrand Ave [Carroll]
- **Franklin Hardware** •
  646 Franklin Ave [St Marks Ave]
- **Garvey's Hardware** •
  583 Nostrand Ave [Pacific]
- **Glen Hardware** • 723 Flatbush Ave [Parkside]
- **Goldsmith Hardware Houseware** •
  225 Rogers Ave [Union]
- **Hawthorne Hardware** •
  660 Flatbush Ave [Hawthorne]
- **Nazar Hardware** • 959 Nostrand Ave [Sullivan]
- **Nostrand Midwood Hardware** •
  1134 Nostrand Ave [Midwood]
- **Winthrop Hardware** •
  1221 Nostrand Ave [Hawthorne]

Liquor Stores

- **Cheng's Liquor Store** •
  253 Kingston Ave [St Johns]
- **Crosstown** • 1042 Nostrand Ave [Sterling St]
- **Dragon Liquors** • 274 Albany Ave [St Johns]
- **Eagle Liquors** • 77 Kingston Ave [Pacific]
- **Eastern Franklin Liquors** •
  808 Franklin Ave [Eastern]
- **Eber's Liquor & Wine** •
  314 Kingston Ave [Union]
- **First Class Liquor** •
  699 Flatbush Ave [Winthrop]
- **JCJ Liquors** • 830 St Johns Pl [Nostrand]
- **Liquor Town** • 559 Flatbush Ave [Maple]
- **Pop's Liquor Store** •
  884 Nostrand Ave [President]
- **Tin Choi Liquor** • 808 Prospect Pl [Nostrand]
- **XING Da Liquor Store** •
  1318 Nostrand Ave [Lenox]

Supermarkets

- **Associated Supermarket** •
  529 Empire Blvd [Balfour]
- **Associated Supermarket** •
  650 Flatbush Ave [Fenimore]
- **Associated Supermarket** •
  905 Franklin Ave [Carroll]
- **Associated Supermarket** •
  975 Nostrand Ave [Sullivan]
- **C-Town** • 210 Clarkson Ave [Rogers]
- **Fine Fare** • 261 Kingston Ave [St Johns]
- **Key Food** • 1232 Nostrand Ave [Winthrop]
- **Key Food** • 653 Nostrand Ave [St Marks Ave]
- **Key Food** • 786 Flatbush Ave [Lenox]
- **Met Food** • 739 Nostrand Ave [Sterling]
- **Met Food** • 2035 Bedford Ave [Clarkson Ave]
- **Pioneer** • 199 Parkside Ave [Ocean Ave]
- **Pioneer** • 822 Franklin Ave [Union]
- **Western Beef** • 44 Empire Blvd [Franklin]

Prospect-Lefferts Gardens / Crown Heights

Caribbean cooking is ubiquitous. around here. Taste the best of Barbados at Culpeppers, and try Jamaican at The Islands or Lily's. Imhotep's tasty, all-organic vegan and vegetarian meals will let you save your calories for the grapenut ice cream at Scoops—if it's ever open!

Nightlife

- **Empire Roller Skating Center** •
  200 Empire Blvd [Bedford Ave]
- **Maximillian Bells** •
  1146 Nostrand Ave [Rutland Ave]
- **Wingate Field** • Brooklyn Ave & Winthrop Ave

Restaurants

- **Ali Roti Shop** • 589 Flatbush Ave [Midwood]
- **Bombay Masala** •
  687 Franklin Ave [Prospect Pl]
- **Brooklyn Exposure** •
  1401 Bedford Ave [St Marks Ave]
- **Culpepper's** • 1082 Nostrand Ave [Lincoln Rd]
- **Enduro** • 51 Lincoln Rd [Flatbush]
- **Golden Krust** •
  1014A Nostrand Ave [Flatbush]
- **Golden Krust** • 568 Flatbush Ave [Maple]
- **Imhotep Health and Vegan Restaurant** •
  734 Nostrand Ave [Park Pl]
- **Irie Vegetarian** • 804 Nostrand Ave [Lincoln]
- **The Islands** • 803 Washington Ave [Lincoln]
- **Lily's** • 707 Nostrand Ave [Park]
- **Mike's International Restaurant** •
  552 Flatbush Ave [Lincoln Rd]
- **Paradise Foods** • 843 Franklin Ave [Union]
- **Peppa's Jerk Chicken** •
  738 Flatbush Ave [Woodruff Ave]
- **Sabah Falafel** •
  1166 Nostrand Ave [Rutland Rd]
- **Saje** • 710 Franklin Ave [Park Pl]
- **Sushi Tatsu II** • 609 Franklin Ave [Dean St]
- **Tavern on Nostrand** •
  813 Nostrand Ave [Union St]

Shopping

- **Allan's Quality Bakery** •
  1109 Nostrand Ave [Maple St]
- **Barbara's Flower Shop** •
  615 Nostrand Ave [Bergen]
- **Phat Albert's** • 495 Flatbush Ave [Lefferts]
- **Scoops** • 624 Flatbush Ave [Fenimore]

It's not as glam as Park Slope, but PLG/Crown Heights offers a much quicker commute with seven express lines—B, Q, 2, 3, 4, 5, and A—to pick up the working stiffs. Catch the B48/B43 to Greenpoint, the B71 to Cobble Hill, the B41/B45 to Downtown, and the B44 to Manhattan Beach.

Subways

② ③	. . . . Eastern Parkway-Brooklyn Museum
② ⑤	. . . . Church Avenue
② ⑤	. . . . President Street
② ⑤	. . . . Sterling Street
② ⑤	. . . . Winthrop Street
② ③ ④ ⑤ S	. . . . Franklin Avenue
③	. . . . Kingston Avenue
③	. . . . Nostrand Avenue
Ⓐ Ⓒ	. . . . Nostrand Avenue
Ⓒ	. . . . Kingston-Throop Avenue
Ⓒ S	. . . . Franklin Avenue
B Q S	. . . . Prospect Park
Q	. . . . Parkside Avenue
S	. . . . Franklin Avenue
S	. . . . Park Place

Car Rental

• **Image Rent-a-Car** • 391 Empire Blvd [Clove]

Car Washes

• **Brooklyn Hand Car Wash & Spa** •
1236 Atlantic Ave [Perry]
• **Utica Enterprises** • 63 Midwood St [Bedford]

Gas Stations

• **BP** • 250 Empire Blvd [Rogers]
• **BP** • 513 Flatbush Ave [Lefferts]
• **BP** • 720 New York Ave [Parkside]
• **BP** • 1525 Bedford Ave [Lincoln]
• **Exxon** • 155 Empire Blvd [Bedford]
• **Exxon** • 1550 Bedford Ave [Eastern]
• **Gasteria** • 43 Empire Blvd [Wash Ave]
• **Mobil** • 415 Empire Blvd [New York]
• **Shell** • 136 Empire Blvd [Bedford]

Map 11 • Sunset Park / Green-Wood Heights

GREEN-WOOD HEIGHTS

GREEN-WOOD

Green-Wood Cemetery

PAGE 138

Gowanus Bay

BMT Yard

39th St

Sunset Park

SUNSET PARK

Bush Terminal Warehouses

Whale Sq

LIRR Yard

278

Gowanus Expy

Prospect Ave

Prospect-Expy

1

8

2

9

27

12

14

1/4 mile   .25 km

17th St
18th St
19th St
20th St
21st St
22nd St
23rd St
24th St
25th St
26th St
27th St
28th St
29th St
30th St
31st St
32nd St
33rd St
34th St
35th St
36th St
37th St
38th St
39th St
40th St
41st St
42nd St
43rd St
44th St
46th St
47th St
48th St
49th St
50th St
51st St
52nd St
53rd St
54th St
55th St
56th St
57th St
58th St
59th St
60th St
61st St
62nd St
63rd St
64th St
65th St
66th St

Fifth Ave
Sixth Ave
Seventh Ave
Tenth Ave
 Fort Hamilton Pkwy
First Ave
Second Ave
Third Ave
Fourth Ave
Fifth Ave
Sixth Ave
Seventh Ave
Eighth Ave
Ninth Ave

Bay St
Sigourney St
Halleck St
Percival St
Bryant St
Clinton Court St

Woodrow Ct
Roosevelt Ct

Marginal St E

Shore Road Dr

Here's the plan: Stroll through the elegantly creepy, eminently historic Green-Wood Cemetery, taking in the skyline views from atop the hill. Eat seriously good grub. Stock up on paper towels at you favorite 99 cents store. Go bowling at Melody Lanes. What's not to love about Sunset Park?

 Bagels

- **Sunset Bagel** • 5309 Fourth Ave [53rd St]
- **Sunset Bagels** • 4903 Fifth Ave [49th St]

$ Banks

BP • Banco Popular • 5216 Fifth Ave [52nd St]
CY • Cathay • 5402 Eighth Ave [54th St]
CY • Cathay • 5501 Eighth Ave [55th St]
CH • Chase • 5101 Fourth Ave [51st St]
CH • Chase • 5423 Eighth Ave [54th St]
CH• Chase (ATM) • Duane Reade •
  4721 Sixth Ave [47th St]
CI • Citibank • 5324 Fifth Ave [53rd St]
CI • Citibank (ATM) • 7-Eleven •
  6415 Third Ave [64th St]
CO • Commerce • 987 Fourth Ave [38th St]
FA • First American International •
  5503 Eighth Ave [55th St]
HS • HSBC • 5515 Eighth Ave [55th St]
  • United Commerical •
  5801 Eighth Ave [58th St]
WM • Washington Mutual •
  5323 Fifth Ave [53rd St]

➕ Emergency Rooms

- **Lutheran Medical Center** •
  150 55th St [2nd Ave]

○ Landmarks

- **Green-Wood Cemetery** • 500 25th St [5th Ave]

📖 Libraries

- **Brooklyn Public** • 5108 Fourth Ave [51st]

Rx Pharmacies

- **5th Avenue Pharmacy** •
  4818 Fifth Ave [48th St]
- **A M Pharmacy** • 5702 Eighth Ave [57th St]
- **Aaushadh Pharmacy** • 4615 Fifth Ave [46th St]
- **Abc Pharmacy** • 5015 Fourth Ave [50th St]
- **American Pharmacy** •
  5524 Eighth Ave [55th St]
- **Compashion Pharmacy** •
  5002 Fourth Ave [50th St]
- **Costco** • 976 Third Ave [37th St]
- **Duane Reade** • 5423 Second Ave [54th St]
- **Family Pharmacy** • 6109 Fifth Ave [61st St]
- **First Choice Pharmacy** •
  5912 Eighth Ave [59th St]
- **Get Well Pharmacy** •
  5218 Eighth Ave [52nd St]
- **Global Care Pharmacy** •
  5905 Eighth Ave [59th St]
- **Good Health Pharmacy** •
  5820 Seventh Ave [58th St]
- **Grand Buy Pharmacy** •
  4717 Eighth Ave [47th St]
- **Health Max Pharmacy** •
  5313 Fifth Ave [53rd St]
- **Ideal Pharmacy** • 5409 Fifth Ave [54th St]
- **JNJ Pharmacy** • 761 61st St [8th Ave]
- **Kelly's Pharmacy** • 5825 Fifth Ave [58th St]
- **Kenby Pharmacy** • 6024 Fifth Ave [60th St]
- **Kinetic Pharmacy** • 6009 Eighth Ave [60th St]
- **Medina Pharmacy** • 5721 Fifth Ave [57th St]
- **Parker & Megna Pharmacy** •
  5124 Fifth Ave [51st St]
- **Phillips Pharmacy** • 3921 Ninth Ave [39th St]
- **Rite Aid** • 5224 Fifth Ave [52nd St]
- **Rite Aid** • 6201 Fourth Ave [62nd St]
- **Rite-Care Pharmacy** • 677 Fourth Ave [21st St]
- **TW Pharmacy** • 804 54th St [8th Ave]
- **V L S Pharmacy** • 4402 Fifth Ave [44th St]

🚓 Police

- **72nd Precinct** • 830 Fourth Ave [29th St]

✉ Post Offices

- **US Post Office** • 5501 Seventh Ave [55th St]
- **US Post Office** • 6102 Fifth Ave [61st St]
- **US Post Office** • 900 Third Ave [33rd St]

Map 1

Slope-ification has been quietly advancing for years now, but this remains a diverse, thriving immigrant community. For proof, just walk down Fifth Avenue, filled with Latino businesses, then walk back up Eighth Avenue, where most everything is Asian-influenced.

Coffee

- **39th St Donuts** • 889 Fifth Ave [38th St]
- **Dunkin' Donuts** • 5425 Fifth Ave [54th St]
- **Dunkin' Donuts** • 5702 Second Ave [57th St]
- **Dunkin' Donuts** • 737 Fourth Ave [24th St]
- **Dunkin' Donuts** • 928 Third Ave [35th St]

Farmers Markets

- **Sunset Park
  (Saturday 8 am–3 pm, July–Nov)** •
  Fourth Ave b/w 59th St & 60th St

Hardware Stores

- **4510 Hardware** • 4510 Fifth Ave [45th St]
- **Anbro Supply** • 4102 Eighth Ave [41st St]
- **Apple Locksmith** • 760 Third Ave [25th St]
- **C&W Hardware** • 5701 Sixth Ave [57th St]
- **Estrella Hardware** • 4723 Fourth Ave [47th St]
- **Fastenal** • 951 Third Ave [36th St]
- **Greschlers' Hardware & Paint** •
  660 Fifth Ave [19th St]
- **J&C Hardware** • 5406 Eighth Ave [54th St]
- **Kamco True Value** • 80 21st St [3rd Ave]
- **King Hardware** • 4104 Fifth Ave [41st St]
- **Kings Material** • 833 39th St [8th Ave]
- **Luck Eight Hardware** •
  4819 Eighth Ave [48th St]
- **Mangual Hardware & Paint Supplies** •
  5419 Fourth Ave [54th St]
- **Newman Hardware** •
  5819 Eighth Ave [58th St]
- **OK Hardware Store** • 4619 Fifth Ave [46th St]
- **Peter Hardware** • 5610 Eighth Ave [56th St]

Liquor Stores

- **5 Avenue Liquor Store** •
  5611 Fifth Ave [56th St]
- **60th Street Wine & Spirits** •
  712 60th St [7th Ave]
- **Brooklyn Liquors** • 976 Third Ave [37th St]
- **Claremont Wine & Liquor** •
  3826 Third Ave [30th St]
- **Double K Liquor** • 4723 Fifth Ave [47th St]
- **L&M Liquors** • 4223 Eighth Ave [42nd St]
- **Mari's Liquor Store** • 4423 Fifth Ave [44th St]
- **Sunset Liquor & Wine** •
  5812 Fourth Ave [58th St]

Supermarkets

- **Associated Supermarket** •
  5009 Sixth Ave [50th St]
- **C-Town** • 4511 Eighth Ave [45th St]
- **C-Town** • 4705 Fifth Ave [47th St]
- **Key Food** • 4320 Fifth Ave [43rd St]
- **National Supermarket** •
  4808 Fouth Ave [48th St]
- **Met Food** • 5817 Fifth Ave [58th St]
- **Pioneer** • 5612 Fifth Ave [56th St]

Map 11 • Sunset Park / Green-Wood Heights

GREEN-WOOD
HEIGHTS

Prospect Ave
27
Prospect Expy

Gowanus Bay

PAGE
138

Green-Wood
Cemetery

BMT Yard

39th St

Sunset
Park

44th St

SUNSET
PARK

Bush
Terminal
Warehouses

Whale Sq

LIRR
Yard

278

14

Fort Hamilton Pkwy

1/4 mile   .25 km

Wakeman Pl

Shore Road Dr

Entertainment

Map 11

The feed is fine, especially at Castlillo Ecuatoriano, Super Pollo, Elite Turkish, Mas Que Pan, Nyonya, and Shi Wei Xian. Everybody hangs at Melody Lanes, but bars are few. East Coast Beer has kegs, though, so you can always just take the party home.

Nightlife

- **Kitchenbar** • 687 Sixth Ave [20th St]
- **Melody Lanes** • 461 37th St [5th Ave]

Restaurants

- **Bar BQ** • 689 Sixth Ave [20th St]
- **Brothers Pizza and Restaurant** • 647 Fourth Ave [20th St]
- **Castillo Ecuatoriano** • 4020 Fifth Ave [40th St]
- **Double Dragon** • 4318 Fourth Ave [43rd St]
- **Eclipse** • 4314 Fourth Ave [43rd St]
- **El Tesoro Ecuatoriano Restaurant** • 40-15 Fifth Ave [40th St]
- **Elite Turkish Restaurant** • 805 60th St [8th Ave]
- **Gina's** • 3905 Fifth Ave [39th St]
- **Full Doe** • 5905 Fourth Ave [59th St]
- **International Restaurant** • 4408 Fifth Ave [44th St]
- **Jade Plaza** • 6022 Eighth Ave [60th St]
- **Kakala Café** • 5302 Eighth Ave [53rd St]
- **Mas Que Pan** • 5401 Fifth Ave [54th St]
- **Nick's Restaurant** • 876 Fourth Ave [32nd St]
- **Nyonya** • 5323 Eighth Ave [53rd St] ♿
- **Pacificana** • 813 55th St [8th Ave]
- **Piaxtla es Mexico Deli** • 505 51st St [5th Ave] ♿
- **Rosticeria Mexicana Los Pollitos** • 5911 Fourth Ave [59th St]
- **Shi Wei Xian** • 5701 Seventh Ave [57th St]
- **Sunset Park Empanada Cart** • 5th Ave & 48th St
- **Super Pollo Latino** • 4102 Fifth Ave [41st St]
- **Tacos Matamoros** • 4503 Fifth Ave [45th St]
- **Ti An** • 5604 Eighth Ave [56th St]

Shopping

- **Costco** • 976 Third Ave [37th St]
- **East Coast Beer Co** • 969 Third Ave [37th St]
- **Hong Kong Supermarket** • 6023 Eighth Ave [60th St]
- **Petland Discounts** • 5015 Fifth Ave [50th St]
- **Ten Ren Tea & Ginseng** • 5817 Eighth Ave [58th St]

Map 11 · **Sunset Park / Green-Wood Heights**

The subways here are local, so express buses—X27, X28, X37, and X38—are a commuter's fastest way to Manhattan. The B63 gets to Downtown Brooklyn, while the B70 just heads for the heart of Bay Ridge retail. Parking shouldn't be a problem.

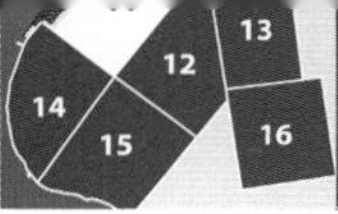

Subways

D M N R .... 25th Street

D M N R .... 36th Street

D M .... Ninth Avenue

D M .... Fort Hamilton Parkway

M R .... Prospect Avenue

N .... Eighth Avenue

N .... Fort Hamilton Parkway

N R .... 59th Street

R .... 45th Street

R .... 53rd Street

Car Rental

• **Speedy Rent-A-Car** • 822 Fourth Ave [29th St]

Car Washes

• **Mali Car Wash** •
  5701 Second Ave [57th St]
• **Marina Wash & Wax** • 462 36th St [5th Ave]
• **Sam's Car Wash** • 4013 Fourth Ave [40th St]

Gas Stations

• **Citgo** • 4001 Fourth Ave [40th St]
• **Citgo** • 745 Fifth Ave [25th St]
• **Getty** • 889 Seventh Ave [64th St]
• **Getty** • 4302 Fort Hamilton Pkwy [43rd St]
• **Getty** • 6423 Third Ave [33rd St]
• **Sunoco** • 668 Third Ave [21st St]
• **Mobil** • 875 Fourth Ave [33rd St]
• **Shell** • 842 Fifth Ave [36th St]

Map 1

12 13

14 15 16

Boro Park: Where the men wear beards, the women wear wigs, the children wear matching outfits, and the ATMs speak Yiddish—welcome to the largest concentration of Orthodox Jews in America. The best time to visit is during spring's Purim festival, when religious duty demands dressing in costume, eating plenty of sweets, and getting drunk!

⊙ Bagels

- **Bagel Express Shop** •
  4912 Ft Hamilton Pkwy [49th St]
- **Bagels & More** • 4305 14th Ave [43rd St]
- **Dale Bagels** • 6201 18th Ave [62nd St]
- **New 13th Avenue Bagel Bakery** •
  4807 13th Ave [48th St]
- **Nosh-A-Bagel Plus** • 5721 16th Ave [57th St]

$ Banks

AP • **Apple** • 1575 50th St [16th Ave]
AP • **Apple** • 4519 13th Ave [45th St]
AS • **Astoria Federal** • 5220 13th Ave [52nd St]
BK • **Berkshire** • 4917 16th Ave [49th St]
BK • **Berkshire** • 5010 13th Ave [50th St]
CH • **Chase** • 4901 13th Ave [49th St]
CH• **Chase (ATM)** • Duane Reade •
  4318 13th Ave [43rd St]
CI • **Citibank** • 5420 13th Ave [55th St]
CO • **Commerce** • 4526 13th Ave [45th St]
HS • **HSBC** • 4410 13th Ave [44th St]
NF • **North Fork** • 4612 13th Ave [46th St]
PA • **Park Avenue** • 4419 13th Ave [44th St]
RS • **Roosevelt Savings** • Pathmark •
  1245 61st St [12th Ave]
SB • **Sovereign** • 4514 16th Ave [45th St]
SB • **Sovereign** • 4823 13th Ave [48th St]
WM • **Washington Mutual** •
  4724 13th Ave [47th St]

✚ Emergency Rooms

- **Maimonides Medical Center** •
  4802 Tenth Ave [48th St]

○ Landmarks

- **Shmura Matzoh Factory** • 36th St & 13th Ave

📖 Libraries

- **Brooklyn Public** • 1265 43rd St [12th Ave]
- **Brooklyn Public** • 1702 60th St [17th Ave]

℞ Pharmacies

- **16th Avenue Pharmacy** •
  4408 16th Ave [44th St]
- **18 Avenue Pharmacy** •
  5411 18th Ave [54th St]
- **Ad Pharmacy** • 1310 48th St [13th Ave]
- **Drug Mart Pharmacy** •
  4914 New Utrecht Ave [49th St]
- **Duane Reade** • 4402 13th Ave [44th St]
- **Duane Reade** • 4721 16th Ave [47th St]
- **Fine Care Pharmacy** • 4723 13th Ave [47th St]
- **Klein's Pharmacy** • 4818 13th Ave [48th St]
- **Leonaum Pharmacy** •
  4910 Ft Hamilton Pkwy [49th St]
- **Lieb Pharmacy** • 4924 16th Ave [49th St]
- **Life Pharmacy** • 4301 14th Ave [43rd St]
- **Miele Pharmacy** • 4224 15th Ave [42nd St]
- **Mmc Pharmacy** • 948 48th St [9th Ave]
- **New Utrecht Pharmacy** •
  4624 New Utrecht Ave [46th St]
- **Pathmark** • 1245 61st St [12th Ave] ⊙
- **Quick Aid Pharmacy** • 3814 13th Ave [38th St]
- **Rite Aid** • 5102 13th Ave [51st St]
- **Rite Aid** • 6101 18th Ave [61st St]
- **Scarpa Pharmacy** • 6216 11th Ave [62nd St]
- **Walgreens** • 114 Beverley Rd [E 2nd St]

⬤ Police

- **66th Precinct** • 5822 16th Ave [58th St]

✉ Post Offices

- **US Post Office** • 1200 51st St [12th Ave]
- **US Post Office** • 5504 13th Ave [55th St]

95

The Orthodox and Hasidic community here supports a vast array of shops and kosher restaurants, all closed from sundown Friday to sundown Saturday. This is the place to shop for Judaica, from scholarly tomes to talking matzo balls, as well as kosher groceries and prepared foods, modest clothing, and well-priced housewares.

Coffee

- **Best Coffee Shop** •
  4906 New Utrecht Ave [49th St]
- **Café Shalva** • 1305 53rd St [13th Ave]
- **Dunkin' Donuts** • 6309 18th Ave [63rd St]

Farmers Markets

- **Borough Park (Thurs 8 am–3 pm, July–Nov)** •
  • 14th Ave b/w 49th St & 50th St

Hardware Stores

- **13th Avenue Home Center** •
  4405 13th Ave [44th St]
- **Boro Park Lumber & Home Center** •
  4601 New Utrecht Ave [46th St]
- **Cohen's Discount Hardware Houseware & Gift** • 5212 13th Ave [52nd St]
- **Express Lumber and Plumbing** •
  1301 60th St [13th Ave]
- **Fourteen Avenue Hardware** •
  4312 14th Ave [43rd St]
- **N&G Hardware** • 5917 18th Ave [59th St]
- **Pacific Supplies** •
  6007 Ft Hamilton Pkwy [60th St]
- **Park Lumber** • 1071 38th St [Ft Hamilton]
- **Pasternack's True Value** •
  5504 18th Ave [55th St]
- **Pine Sash Door & Lumber** •
  6202 14th Ave [62nd St]
- **Yossel's 18th Avenue House-Ware & Hardware** • 4908 18th Ave [49th St]

Liquor Stores

- **A Touch of Spirit Liquors** •
  4720 16th Ave [47th St]
- **A&B Liquor Store** • 5006 12th Ave [50th St]
- **Boro Park Wine & Liquor** •
  5502 13th Ave [55th St]
- **H&H Wine & Liquor** • 4109 13th Ave [41st St]
- **Joe's Liquor Store** • 6405 20th Ave [64th St]
- **Lurio's Liquors Kuddish KUP** •
  5105 16th Ave [51st St]
- **Orlander H Wines & Liquors** •
  4812 13th Ave [48th St]
- **STD Wines & Liquors** •
  89 Church Ave [McDonald]
- **Trovato Liquors** • 6415 18th Ave [64th St]
- **The Winery** • 4616 18th Ave [46th St]

Supermarkets

- **Boro Park Natural Health Food** •
  5203 13th Ave [52nd St]
- **Borough Park Supermarket** •
  382 McDonald Ave [Albemarle Rd]
- **Foodtown** • 1891 50th St [19th Ave]
- **Pathmark** • 1245 61st St [12th Ave]

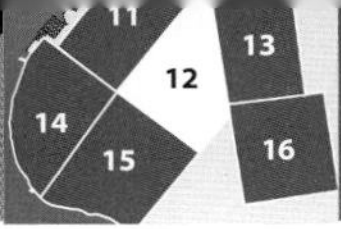

Underworld Plaza is not a crime-ridden mall, but a source of modest—and modestly priced—underwear. If you do mix your milk and your meat, Coluccio & Sons, Agnati Meze, and World Tong are well worth a visit. Israeli-owned falafel shops are the only nighttime hangouts around here, unless you count shul.

Map 14

Restaurants

- **AJ's Restaurant & Pizzeria** •
  4412 Ft Hamilton Pkwy [New Utrecht]
- **Agnanti Maeze** • 4720 16th Ave [47th St]
- **Cheskel's Shwarma King** •
  3715 13th Ave [37th St]
- **China Glatt** • 4413 13th Ave [44th St]
- **Cracovia Deli** • 5503 13th Ave [55th St]
- **Crown Deli** • 4909 13th Ave [49th St]
- **Donut Man** • 4708 13th Ave [47th St]
- **El Morro** • 4018 14th Ave [40th St]
- **Glatt a la Carte** • 5123 18th Ave [51st St]
- **Kosher Delight Family Restaurant** •
  4600 13th Ave [46th St]
- **La Asuncion** •
  3914 Ft Hamilton Pkwy [39th St]
- **Mendel's Pizza** • 4923 18th Ave [49th St]
- **Vesuvio** • 4720 16th Ave [47th St]
- **World Tong Seafood** •
  6202 18th Ave [62nd St]

Shopping

- **Antiques & Decorations** •
  4319 14th Ave [43rd St]
- **Benetton** • 4610 13th Ave [46th St]
- **Bulletproof Games II** •
  4507 Ft Hamilton Pkwy [45th St]
- **Circus Fruits** •
  5915 Ft Hamilton Pkwy [59th St]
- **Coluccio & Sons** • 1214 60th St [12th Ave]
- **Jacadi** • 5005 16th Ave [50th St]
- **Kaff's Bakery** •
  4518 Ft Hamilton Pkwy [45th St]
- **Kosher Candy Man** • 4702 13th Ave [47th St]
- **Scribbles** • 3720 14th Ave [38th St]
- **Strauss Bakery** • 5115 13th Ave [51st St]
- **Trainworld** • 751 McDonald Ave [Ditmas]
- **Underworld Plaza** •
  1421 62nd St [New Utrecht]
- **Weiss Bakery** • 5011 13th Ave [50th St]

Parking is extremely scarce in this densely populated neighborhood, especially along the bustling commercial strip on 13th Avenue. Consider yourself warned.

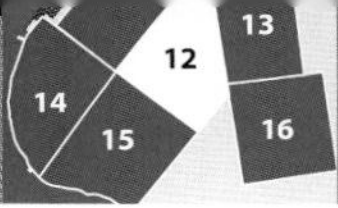

Map 1

Subways

D **M** ....50th Street
D **M** ....55th Street
D **M** .... Fort Hamilton Parkway
D **M** .... Ninth Avenue
D **M** **N** .. New Utrecht Avenue-62nd Street
F .... 18th Avenue
F .... Avenue I
F ....Church Avenue
F ....Ditmas Avenue
F .... Fort Hamilton Parkway
N .... 18th Avenue
N .... 20th Avenue
N .... Fort Hamilton Parkway

Car Rental

• **All Car Rent A Car** •
3475 Ft Hamilton Pkwy [Chester]
• **Econo Car Rental** • 5010 12th Ave [50th St]
• **Express Car Rental** • 475 Dahill Rd [39th St]
• **Perfect Car Rental** • 6302 17th Ave [63rd St]
• **Speedy** • 4515 18th Ave [45th St]

Gas Stations

• **Getty** • 5818 18th Ave [58th St]
• **Shell** • 1 Cortelyou Rd [Dahill]
• **Sunny Triangle** •
4302 Ft Hamilton Pkwy [43rd St]

Kensington / Ditmas Rd / Windsor Terrace

Yuppies have made this once-gritty area cleaner and safer, but, alas, it's still pretty uninteresting. Think Park Slope in attitude but with less charm and fewer amenities. Still, Victorian mansion fetishists adore Ditmas Park: Turrets, stone street markers, and quaint yards galore.

Bagels

- **Giant Bagel** • 1416 Cortelyou Rd [Rugby]
- **Hot Bagels** • 127 Church Ave [E 2nd St]
- **Twin Towers** • 975 McDonald Ave [Webster]

Banks

- **AS • Astoria Federal** • 101 Church [McDonald]
- **AS • Astoria Federal** • 1045 Flatbush [Duryea]
- **AS • Astoria Federal** • 1550 Flatbush [Nostrand]
- **AS • Astoria Federal** • 4302 18th Ave [E 2nd St]
- **BA • Bank of America** • 515 Ocean Ave [Church]
- **CH • Chase** • 1509 Foster Ave [Marlborough Rd]
- **CH • Chase** • 1599 Flatbush Ave [Ave H]
- **CH • Chase** • 4323 18th Ave [E 2nd St]
- **CI • Citibank** • 1871 Nostrand Ave [Newkirk Ave]
- **CI • Citibank** • 885 Flatbush Ave [Church Ave]
- **CO • Commerce** •
  210 Prospect Park SW [Greenwood]
- **HS • HSBC** • 1545 Flatbush Ave [Nostrand Ave]
- **HS • HSBC** • 815 Flatbush Ave [Caton Ave]
- **NF • North Fork** • 927 Flatbush Ave [Snyder Ave]
- **SB • Sovereign** • 23 Newkirk Plz [Newkirk Ave]
- **SB • Sovereign (ATM)** • 1070 Flatbush [Beverly]
- **UC • United Commerical** • 1801 Church [E 18th]
- **WM • Washington Mutual** •
  1462 Nostrand Ave [Church Ave]
- **WM • Washington Mutual** •
  2125 Nostrand Ave [Glenwood Rd]
- **WM • Washington Mutual** •
  833 Flatbush Ave [Linden Blvd]

Landmarks

- **Erasmus Hall Academy** • 911 Flatbush [Church]
- **Flatbush Dutch Reform Church** •
  890 Flatbush Ave [Church]
- **Kensington Stables** • 51 Caton Ave [McDonald]

Libraries

- **Brooklyn Public** • 1305 Cortelyou Rd [Argyle]
- **Brooklyn Public** • 160 E 5th St [Ft Hamilton]
- **Brooklyn Public** • 2035 Nostrand Ave [Farragut]
- **Brooklyn Public** • 22 Linden Blvd [Flatbush]
- **Brooklyn Public** • 410 Ditmas Ave [E 4th St]

Pharmacies

- **1101** • 1101 Flatbush Ave [Cortelyou]
- **Al Medina** • 1321 Flatbush Ave [Ditmas]

- **Aldav Pharmacy** • 749 Ocean Pkwy [Foster]
- **Cityline Pharmacy** • 511 Cortelyou Rd [E 5th]
- **CVS** • 1070 Flatbush Ave [Beverley]
- **CVS** • 411 Ditmas Ave [E 4th St]
- **Dan's Pharmacy** • 99 Church Ave [McDonald]
- **Ditmas Pharmacy** • 509 Ditmas Ave [E 5th]
- **Duane Reade** • 1517 Cortelyou [Marlborough]
- **Duane Reade** • 1833 Nostrand Ave [Newkirk]
- **Duane Reade** • 2141 Nostrand Ave [Flatbush]
- **Flatbush Express** • 860 Flatbush Ave [Martense]
- **Flatbush** • 2134 Beverley Rd [Flatbush]
- **Foster** • 1056 Coney Island Ave [Glenwood]
- **Geo Pharmacy** • 685 Coney Island Ave [Ave C]
- **Greenfield** • 1526 Cortelyou [Marlborough]
- **GS Pharmacy** • 1932 Nostrand Ave [Foster]
- **Harrico Church** • 3016 Church Ave [Nostrand]
- **Junction** • 2109 Nostrand Ave [Glenwood]
- **Mbg Pharmacy** • 119 Church Ave [Beverly]
- **Michael's Pharmacy** • 163 Linden Blvd [Rogers]
- **Parkway Pharmacy** • 531 Church Ave [E 5th St]
- **Personal Care Pharmacy** •
  836 Coney Island Ave [Dorchester]
- **Punjab** • 1018 Coney Island Ave [Parkville]
- **Rite Aid** • 1419 Newkirk Ave [Rugby]
- **Rite Aid** • 1559 Flatbush Ave [Nostrand]
- **Rite Aid** • 2819 Church Ave [Lloyd]
- **Rite Aid** • 302 Church Ave [E 3rd St]
- **Rite Aid** • 892 Flatbush Ave [Church]
- **Rockaway** • 1214 Flatbush Ave [Ditmas]
- **Royal Pharmacy** • 2239 Church Ave [Flatbush]
- **Sky** • 1100 Coney Island Ave [Glenwood]
- **Spectrum** • 952 McDonald Ave [18th Ave]
- **Stop & Shop** • 1009 Flatbush Ave [Tilden]
- **Sun Care Pharmacy** • 533 E 7th St [Cortelyou]
- **Thriftway** • 1621 Church Ave [E 16th St]
- **Thriftway** • 1717 Foster Ave [E 17th St]
- **Thriftway** • 1875 Nostrand Ave [Newkirk Ave]
- **Walgreens** • 2101 Church Ave [E 3rd St]
- **Welcome Pharmacy** • 1403 Foster Ave [Rugby]

Police

- **67th Precinct** • 2820 Snyder Ave [Rogers]
- **70th Precinct** • 154 Lawrence Ave [Seton]

Post Offices

- **US Post Office** • 1451 Nostrand Ave [Church]
- **US Post Office** • 1525 Newkirk [Marlborough]
- **US Post Office** • 2273 Church Ave [Flatbush]
- **US Post Office** • 419 McDonald Ave [Church]

Sundries

Get organic groceries at the charming Flatbush Food Co-op, caffeinate at sadly-named Lonelyville, or mix coffee with readings and book browsing at Vox Pop. While 99 cent stores abound on Flatbush, trust Cortelyou Road for decidedly less blighted retail options.

Map 13

Coffee

- **Armando & Pablo's** •
  43 Newkirk Plz [Newkirk Ave]
- **Connecticut Muffin** •
  1106 Cortelyou Rd [Statford Rd]
- **Crossroads Café** • 1241 Prospect Ave [Reeve]
- **Dunkin' Donuts** • 10 Newkirk Plaza [E 16th St]
- **Dunkin' Donuts** • Exxon •
  418 Coney Island Ave [Friel]
- **Dunkin' Donuts** •
  872 Flatbush Ave [Martense St]
- **Dunkin' Donuts** •
  906 Coney Island Ave [Ditmas]
- **Dunkin' Donuts** • 1700 Church Ave [E 17th St]
- **John's Bakery and Café** •
  1322 Cortelyou Rd [Argyle]
- **Lonelyville** • 154 Prospect Park SW [Vanderbilt]
- **Starbucks** • 33 Hillel Pl [Flatbush]
- **Vox Pop** • 1022 Cortelyou Rd [Coney Island]

Farmers Markets

- **Midwood-Cortelyou Greenmarket
  (Sat 8:30 am–3 pm Jul–Nov)** •
  330 Rugby Rd [Cortelyou]

Hardware Stores

- **18th Avenue Hardware & Houseware** •
  4322 18th Ave [E 2nd St]
- **Able Hardware** •
  1437 Newkirk Ave [Martense St]
- **Almac Hardware** • 2 Newkirk Plz [Newkirk Ave]
- **Bobman's Hardware & Houseware** •
  311 Ditmas Ave [E 3rd St]
- **Brooklyn Paint & Hardware** •
  1010 Coney Island Ave [Parkville]
- **Coney Island Hardware** •
  814 Coney Island Ave [Dorchester]
- **Cortelyou Hardware** •
  1004 Cortelyou Rd [Coney Island]
- **Empire State Supply** •
  639 McDonald Ave [Cortelyou]
- **Glenwood Hardware** •
  1453 Flatbush Ave [E 28th St]
- **Hoque Building Supply** •
  493 McDonald Ave [Church]
- **Kramers Supply Corporation** •
  511 Coney Island Ave [Turner]
- **Marks Tools & Hardware** •
  557 McDonald Ave [Ave C]

- **Mega Hardware & Houseware** •
  1406 Cortelyou Rd [Rugby]
- **National Hardware & Building Material
  Corporation** •
  694 Coney Island Ave [Cortelyou]
- **Nostrand True Value Hardware** •
  1785 87 Nostrand Ave [Clarendon]
- **S&E Building Materials** •
  744 McDonald Ave [Ditmas]
- **Singer & Singer Hardware** •
  1266 Flatbush Ave [Stephens]

Liquor Stores

- **Affordable Liquors** •
  1135 Coney Island Ave [Ave H]
- **B&C Spirits** • 2841 Church Ave [Lloyd]
- **Behia Liquor** • 1842 Nostrand Ave [Ditmas]
- **Cortelyou Wine & Liquor** •
  1524 Cortelyou Rd [Marlborough Rd]
- **Derby Liquors** • 2123 Nostrand Ave [Glenwood]
- **Discount Liquor Store** •
  501 Cortelyou Rd [E 5th St]
- **Discount Wine & Liquors** •
  4330 18th Ave [43rd St]
- **GWA Liquor Store** •
  2345 Newkirk Ave [Flatbush]
- **Jobby Wine & Liquor Corporation** •
  334 E 3rd St [Church]
- **John's Brother Liquor Store** •
  55 E 18th St [Church]
- **Newkirk Liquors & Wines** •
  11 Newkirk Plz [Newkirk Ave]
- **Ortiz Liquor Store** • 797 Flatbush Ave [Lenox]

Supermarkets

- **Associated Supermarket** •
  2720 Church Ave [Rogers]
- **C Town** • 1188 Flatbush Ave [Vanderveer]
- **C Town** • 1301 Church Ave [Argyle]
- **C Town** • 597 E 16th St [Newkirk Ave]
- **C Town** • 710 Coney Island Ave [Ave C]
- **Flatbush Food Co-op** •
  1318 Cortelyou Rd [Argyle]
- **Key Food** • 1407 Foster Ave [Rugby]
- **Key Food** • 1905 Nostrand Ave [Foster]
- **Met Food** • 1498 Flatbush Ave [E 29th St]
- **Met Food** • 1610 Cortelyou Rd [E 16th St]
- **Met Food** • 4030 18th Ave [E 5th St]

Kensington / Ditmas Park / Windsor Terrace

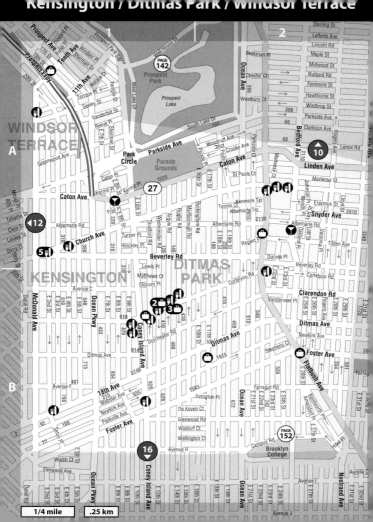

If phrases like "upscale comfort food" and "local ingredients" get you hot, try Picket Fence or The Farm on Adderley. Recovering suburbanites find Fribbles and Funions at Friendly's. Fancy kids get dressed at Belle & Maxie, while the hoi polloi shop the Old Navy Outlet.

 Nightlife

- **Michelle's Cocktail Lounge •**
  2294 Bedford Ave [Albemarle]
- **Shenanigans Pub •** 802 Caton Ave [E 8th St]

Restaurants

- **Bahar •** 984 Coney Island Ave [Ditmas]
- **Cinco De Mayo Restaurant •**
  1202 Cortelyou Rd [E 12th St]
- **Douglas BBQ & Grill •**
  4310 18th Ave [E 2nd St]
- **Farm on Adderley •**
  1108 Cortelyou Rd [Stratford]
- **Friendly's •** 125 Church Ave [E 2nd St]
- **George's •**
  753 Coney Island Ave [Cortelyou] ☺
- **Jhinuk •** 478 McDonald Ave [Church]
- **Joe & Joe Pizzeria & Restaurant •**
  121 Church Ave [E 2nd St]
- **Korner Pizzeria •** 226 Church Ave [E 2nd St]
- **Little Bangladesh •**
  483 McDonald Ave [Church]
- **Los Mariachis •**
  805 Coney Island Ave [Dorchester]
- **Mirage Restaurant •**
  2143 Cortelyou Rd [Flatbush]
- **Picket Fence •** 1310 Cortelyou Rd [Argyle]
- **San Remo Pizza •** 1408 Cortelyou Rd [Rugby]
- **Strictly Vegetarian Restaurant •**
  2268 Church Ave [Flatbush]
- **Sybil's •** 2210 Church Ave [Flatbush]
- **Yen Yen •** 404 Church Ave [E 4th St]
- **Yummy Taco •** 129 Church Ave [Beverley Rd]

Shopping

- **Belle & Maxie •**
  1209 Cortelyou Rd [Westminster]
- **Cortelyou Vintage •**
  1118 Cortelyou Rd [Stratford]
- **Flatbush Food Co-op •**
  1318 Cortelyou Rd [Argyle]
- **Natural Frontier Market •**
  1104 Cortelyou Rd [Stratford Rd]
- **Newkirk Plaza •**
  Above Newkirk Ave Subway [Foster]
- **Old Navy Outlet •**
  1009 Flatbush Ave [Tilden]
- **Trailer Park •** 1211 Cortelyou Rd [Stratford Rd]
- **Uncle Louie G's •** 1306 Flatbush Ave [Foster]
- **Uncle Louie G's •**
  157 Prospect Park Sw [Reeve]

1

2

Sterling St

Sterling St

Lefferts Ave

Prospect Ave

Howard Pl

Prospect Park SW

Prospect Park W

Windsor Pl

Sherman St

Lincoln Rd

Maple St

Midwood St

Rutland Rd

Fenimore St

Hawthorne St

Winthrop St

Lincoln Rd

10th Ave

11th Ave

17th St

16th St

PAGE 142

Prospect Park

Well House Dr

Beekman Pl

Chester Ct

Ocean Ave

Westbury Ct

Parkside Ave

11th Ave

Seeley St

Terrace Pl

Temple Ct

Vanderbilt St

West Lake Dr

Prospect Lake

South Lake Dr

Winthrop St

Parkside Ave

Clarkson Ave

Bedford Ave

Rogers Ave

Lenox Rd

Nostrand Ave

A

WINDSOR TERRACE

Greenwood Ave

Reeve Pl

Sherman St

Park Circle

Parkside Ave

Woodruff Ave

Crooke Ave

Parkside Ave

Linden Ave

Fort Hamilton Pkwy

Parade Grounds

Caton Ave

St Pauls Ct

Martense St

Martense St

Church Ave

Caton Ave

Kermit Pl

27

Caton Ave

Church Ave

Kenmore Ter

Albemarle Ter

Johnson Pl

Woods Pl

Snyder Ave

Erasmus St

12

Albemarle Rd

Fenton Pl

E 2nd St

Stratford Rd

Argyle Rd

Rugby Rd

Marlborough Rd

Buckingham Rd

Tennis Ct

Albemarle Rd

E 18th St

E 19th St

Regent Pl

Tilden Ave

Snyder Ave

Veronica Pl

Beverley Rd

Church Ave

Turner Pl

Hinckley Pl

Church Ave

KENSINGTON

Beverley Rd

Lewis Pl

Matthews Ct

Slocum Pl

DITMAS PARK

Beverley Rd

Duryea Pl

Beverley Rd

Cortelyou Rd

Clarendon Rd

Cortelyou Rd

Vanderveer Pl

Avenue C

Ocean Pkwy

McDonald Ave

E 2nd St

E 7th St

E 8th St

E 9th St

Coney Island Ave

Dorchester Rd

Cortelyou Rd

Ditmas Ave

Ditmas Ave

Newkirk Ave

Foster Ave

Flatbush Ave

Ditmas Ave

E 16th St

Stephens Ct

Newkirk Ave

B

Ditmas Ave

Newkirk Ave

Newkirk Ave

18th Ave

Webster Ave

Irvington Pl

Farragut Rd

Avenue C

Avenue D

Newkirk Ave

Parkville Ave

De Koven Ct

Foster Ave

Glenwood Rd

Ocean Ave

18 Ave

Waldorf Ct

Wellington Ct

PAGE 152

Brooklyn College

16

Avenue H

Avenue H

Campus Rd

Brooklyn College Flatbush Ave

Foster Ave

Walsh Ct

Elmwood Ave

Coney Island Ave

Ocean Pkwy

Avenue I

Dahill Rd

Avenue J

Avenue J

1/4 mile

.25 km

Aurelia Ct

Transportation

Map 13

East side commuters have express B, Q, 2, and 5 trains, while west siders ride the glacially slow F or the X29 express bus. The B68 reaches Brighton Beach, the B16 heads to Bay Ridge, and the B41 goes down Flatbush Ave. Forget Kensington Stables—the locals drive rather than ride horseback.

Subways

② ⑤	.....................Beverley Road
② ⑤	.....................Church Avenue
② ⑤	.....................Newkirk Avenue
② ⑤	.....................Sterling Street
② ⑤	.....................Winthrop Street
② ⑤	....Brooklyn College-Flatbush Avenue
Ⓑ Ⓠ	.....................Church Avenue
Ⓑ Ⓠ	.....................Newkirk Avenue
Ⓠ	.....................Avenue H
Ⓠ	.....................Avenue J
Ⓠ	.....................Beverley Road
Ⓠ	.....................Cortelyou Road
Ⓠ	.....................Parkside Avenue
Ⓕ	.....................18th Avenue
Ⓕ	.....................Avenue I
Ⓕ	.....................Church Avenue
Ⓕ	.....................Ditmas Avenue
Ⓕ	.....................Fort Hamilton Parkway

Car Rental

- **Auto Mall Rentals** •
705 McDonald Ave [Ditmas]

Car Washes

- **Hollywood Car Wash** •
488 Coney Island Ave [Albemarle]
- **Magic Car Wash** •
1092 Rogers Ave [Clarendon]

Gas Stations

- **BP** • 852 Coney Island Ave [Ditmas]
- **BP** • 4210 Farragut Rd [E 42nd St]
- **Exxon** • 418 Coney Island Ave [Friel]
- **Mobil** • 3132 Ft Hamilton Pkwy [E 2nd St]
- **Mobil** • 378 Coney Island Ave [Kermit]
- **Mobil** • 619 Coney Island Ave [Slocum]
- **Shell** • 546 Coney Island Ave [Beverley]
- **Shell** • 865 Rogers Ave [Erasmus]
- **Shell** • 2193 Bedford Ave [Church Ave]

Map 14 · **Bay Ridge**

N

1 · 11

Conrail Railroad

64th St

Wakeman Pl · Shore Road Dr

65th St

66th St

Shore Road Dr

Leif Ericsson

67th St

Leif Ericsson Runestone

Senator St

Leif Ericsson Square

Owls Head Park

Sedgwick Pl

Berger Ct

68th St

Bay Cliff Ter

Madeline Ct

390

Senator St

Bay Ridge Ave

Ovington Ave

Seventh Ave

Eighth Ave

68th St

69th Street Pier/ 9/11 Memorial

Bay Ridge Ave

Bliss Ter

Louise St

70th St

Ridge Crest Ter

440

Bennett Ct

71st St

FS
MA

72nd St

Sixth Ave

73rd St

AP
WM
CH

Gowanus Expwy

Mackay Pl

The Barkaloo Cemetery

71st St

72nd Ct

Colonial Rd

72nd St

73rd St

Fourth Ave

Fifth Ave

74th St

CI DI
SB

74th St

Bay Ridge Pkwy

130

75th St

350

278

McKinley Park

76th St

77th St

Bell Pkwy

Shore Rd

160

78th St

360

MA
MT

79th St

BA

80th St

15

81st St

AT
RS
CO

80th St

Colonial Rd

Narrows Ave

Harbor Ln

82nd St

83rd St

Dyker Pl

The Gingerbread House

84th St

330

Ft Hamilton Athletic Field

85th St

RI

LI
WM

HS NF
PA

CI

Seventh

Shore Road Ln

86th St

Ridge Blvd

Colonial Rd

87th St

Third Ave

MA

88th St

Fort Hamilton Pkwy

Gatling Pl

88th St

Gelston Ave

Dahlgren Pl

Battery Ave

88th St

SB
CI

Forest Pl

Shore Ct

88th St

89th St

320

90th St

90th St

Gowanus Expwy

Monastery Square

90th St

Colonial Gdns

91st St

HS
CH

92nd St

92nd St

Hamilton Walk

93rd St

Wo...

95th St

Bell Pkwy

92nd St

93rd St

Oliver St

94th St

Marine Ave

94th St

95th St

NF

Ridge Blvd

95th St

Fort Hamilton Pkwy

Fort Hill Pl

96th St

Barwell Ter

The Narrows

James F Farrell House

97th St

Ridge Blvd

97th St

St. John's Episcopal Church

Fontbonne Hall

98th St

99th St

480

Fort Hamilton

100th St

101st St

Jackson...

John P Jones Park

US Government Reservation

Verrazano Bridge

A

B

1/4 mile · .25 km

Lately, Bay Ridge has made news for acquiring a sewer stench courtesy of a pipeline project gone wrong. That puts a crimp in plans to enjoy the harbor views from the 69th Street Pier, but at least the shopping corridors along 86th Street and Fifth Avenue and Third Avenue's "Restaurant Row" are out of nose-shot.

🎯 Bagels

- **5 Star Bagels** • 8614 Fourth Ave [86th St]
- **Bagel Boy** • 8002 Third Ave [80th St]
- **Bake Ridge Bagels** • 9417 Third Ave [94th St]
- **Dale Bagels on Fifth** • 7715 Fifth Ave [77th St]
- **DVA Bagels** • 7017 Third Ave [Ovington]
- **Fourth Avenue Bagel Boy** •
  6907 Fourth Ave [Bay Ridge Ave]
- **H&L Bagels** • 8818 Third Ave [88th St]
- **Shore Road Bagel & Deli** •
  9401 Fifth Ave [94th St]

💲 Banks

- **AP • Apple** • 7415 Fifth Ave [74th St]
- **AT • Atlantic** • 8010 Fifth Ave [80th St]
- **BA • Bank of America** •
  6901 Fifth Ave [Bay Ridge Ave]
- **BA • Bank of America** • 7923 Third Ave [79th St]
- **CH • Chase** • 7510 Fifth Ave [Bay Ridge Pkwy]
- **CH • Chase** • 9313 Third Ave [93rd St]
- **CI • Citibank** • 502 86th St [Fifth Ave]
- **CI • Citibank** • 7501 Third Ave [Bay Ridge Pkwy]
- **CI • Citibank (ATM)** • 7-Eleven•
  8813 Fourth Ave [89th St]
- **CO • Commerce** • 8206 Fifth Ave [82nd St]
- **DI • Dime** • 7524 Third Ave [Bay Ridge Pkwy]
- **FS • Flushing Savings** •
  7102 Third Ave [71st St]
- **HS • HSBC** • 447 86th St [Fourth Ave]
- **HS • HSBC** • 9201 Third Ave [92nd St]
- **LI • Long Island Commerical** •
  375 86th St [Fourth Ave]
- **MT • M&T** • 7807 Fifth Ave [78th St]
- **MA • Marathon** • 7123 Third Ave [71st St]
- **MA • Marathon** • 7826 Fifth Ave [78th St]
- **MA • Marathon** • 8724 Fourth Ave [87th St]
- **NF • North Fork** • 413 86th St [Fourth Ave]
- **NF • North Fork** •
  7110 Fourth Ave [Ovington Ave]
- **NF • North Fork** • 9502 Third Ave [95th St]
- **PA • Park Avenue** • 464 86th St [5th Ave]
- **RI • Ridgewood** • 8522 Third Ave [85th St]
- **RS • Roosevelt Savings** • 8110 Fifth Ave [81st St]
- **SB • Sovereign** •
  7500 Bay Ridge Pkwy [Third Ave]
- **SB • Sovereign** • 8808 Fifth Ave [88th St]
- **WM • Washington Mutual** •
  426 86th St [Fourth Ave]
- **WM • Washington Mutual** •
  7427 Fifth Ave [74th St]

ⓞ Landmarks

- **69th Street Pier/9/11 Memorial** •
  Shore Rd & Bay Ridge Ave
- **Barkaloo Cemetery** • Narrows Ave & Mackay Pl
- **Fontbonne Hall** • 9901 Shore Rd [99th St]
- **Fort Hamilton** • 101st St [4th Ave]
- **The Gingerbread House** •
  Narrows Ave & 83rd St
- **James F Farrell House** • 95th St & Shore Rd
- **Leif Ericsson Runestone** •
  Fourth Ave & 67th St
- **St John's Episcopal Church** •
  9818 Ft Hamilton Pkwy [Marine]
- **Verrazano-Narrows Bridge** •
  Easternmost point of I-278 at Ft Wadsworth

📖 Libraries

- **Brooklyn Public** • 7223 Ridge Blvd [72nd St]
- **Brooklyn Public** • 9424 Fourth Ave [94th St]

℞ Pharmacies

- **Alleon Pharmacy** • 7133 Fifth Ave [Ovington]
- **Best Care Pharmacy** • 8510 Third Ave [85th St]
- **Bridge Pharmacy** • 8912 Third Ave [89th St]
- **CVS** • 6702 Ft Hamilton Pkwy [67th St]
- **Duane Reade** • 436 86th St [4th Ave St] ⊕
- **Farmacon Pharmacy** • 8007 Fifth Ave [80th St]
- **Miel Pharmacy** • 8410 Fifth Ave [84th St]
- **Narrows Pharmacy** • 9920 Fourth Ave [99th St]
- **New Victory** • 9202 Fourth Ave [92nd St]
- **Nu-Edge Pharmacy** • 7707 Fifth Ave [77th St]
- **Pharmacy On Fifth** • 6914 Fifth Ave [69th St]
- **Powell** • 7517 Third Ave [Bay Ridge Pkwy]
- **Qualicare Pharmacy** • 8312 Third Ave [83rd St]
- **Rite Aid** • 6717 4th Ave [67th St]
- **Rite Aid** • 6900 Fourth Ave [Bay Ridge Ave]
- **Rite Aid** • 7501 5th Ave [Bay Ridge Pkwy]
- **St Mary's Pharmacy** • 9720 Fourth Ave [97th]
- **Waldinger's** • 8318 Fifth Ave [83rd St]

👮 Police

- **68th Precinct** • 333 65th St [3rd Ave]

✉ Post Offices

- **US Post Office** • 7323 3rd Ave [72nd St]
- **US Post Office** • 6803 Fourth Ave [68th St]
- **US Post Office** • 8801 Fifth Ave [88th]

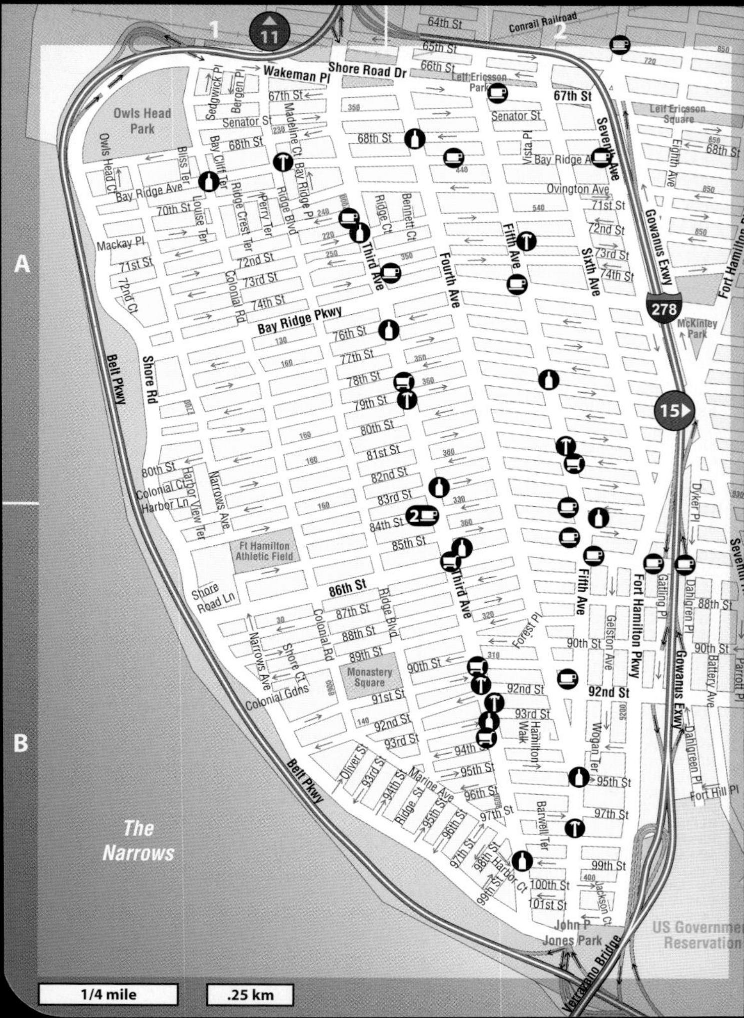

Map 14 • **Bay Ridge**

N

1

11

Conrail Railroad

2

64th St

65th St

66th St
Leif Ericsson
Park

67th St

Wakeman Pl

Shore Road Dr

Shore Road Dr

720

Owls Head
Park

Senator Pl

68th St

Senator Pl

Vista Pl

Bay Ridge Ave

Leif Ericsson
Square

850

68th St

Seventh Ave

Owls Head Park

Bliss Ter

Sedgwick Pl

Harbor Pl

Madeline Ct

Bay Cliff Ter

350

Bay Ridge Ave

68th St

Ovington Ave

71st St

850

Bay Ridge Ave

Ridge Blvd

Bay Ridge Pl

Perry Ter

Ridge Crest Ter

Bennett Ct

240

220

540

72nd St

Fifth Ave

Sixth Ave

Gowanus Expwy

850

70th St

Louise Ter

73rd St

74th St

Fort Hamilton

A

Mackay Pl

71st St

72nd St

Colonial Rd

72nd Ct

74th St

Third Ave

350

350

Fourth Ave

278

McKinley
Park

Bay Ridge Pkwy

130

76th St

160

77th St

78th St

79th St

360

15

Shore Rd

Bell Pkwy

814

160

80th St

81st St

160

82nd St

83rd St

84th St

85th St

300

330

360

Fifth Ave

Dyker Pl

Gatling Pl

Dahlgren Pl

Seventh

80th St

Colonial Rd

Harbor Ln

Narrows View Ter

Ft Hamilton
Athletic Field

86th St

87th St

88th St

89th St

Third Ave

Ridge Blvd

320

Forest Pl

Fort Hamilton Pkwy

88th St

90th St

Battery Ave

Parrot Pl

Shore
Road Ln

30

Colonial Rd

Narrows Ave

Shore Ct

Monastery
Square

90th St

310

91st St

Gelston Ave

90th St

91st St

Dahlgren Pl

Gowanus Expwy

B

Colonial Gdns

Bell Pkwy

Oliver St

83rd St

84th St

85th St

Marine Ave

92nd St

93rd St

Hamilton Walk

Fifth Ave

92nd St

Wogan Pl

Fort Hill Pl

94th St

95th St

96th St

97th St

Ridge Blvd

95th St

96th St

97th St

98th St

99th Harbor Ct

99th St

100th St

101st St

400

Jackson Ct

Barwell Ter

95th St

97th St

The
Narrows

John P.
Jones Park

US Government
Reservation

Verrazano Bridge

Bay Ridge has all the amenities one would expect from a solidly middle class neighborhood: Plenty of restaurants from fast food to fancy schmancy, diverse retail strips stocked with chain stores, mom-and-pop shops alike, and nightlife to suit everyone from crotchety old boozehounds to shiny young club kids....from Staten Island.

Coffee

- **Best Coffee Shop** • 8612 Fifth Ave [86th St]
- **Brooklyn's Finest Café** •
  611 86th St [Ft Hamilton]
- **Caffe Café** • 8401 Third Ave [84th St]
- **Dunkin' Donuts** • 6402 Seventh Ave [64th St]
- **Dunkin' Donuts** • 6755 Fifth Ave [Senator]
- **Dunkin' Donuts** • 7111 Third Ave [72nd St]
- **Dunkin' Donuts** •
  7519 Fifth Ave [Bay Ridge Pkwy]
- **Dunkin' Donuts** • 8425 Fifth Ave [84th St]
- **Dunkin' Donuts** • 9243 Fourth Ave [93rd St]
- **Meena House Café** •
  690 Bay Ridge Ave [7th Ave]
- **Starbucks** • 514 86th St [5th Ave]
- **Starbucks** • 7419 Third Ave [74th St]
- **Starbucks** • 9202 Third Ave [92nd St]

Hardware Stores

- **Fergus Hardware** • 9733 Fourth Ave [97th St]
- **Jose Hardware** • 9301 Third Ave [93rd St]
- **M&M Hardware** •
  6915 Ft Hamilton Pkwy [Bay Ridge Ave]
- **Ovington Hardware** •
  6926 Third Ave [Bay Ridge Ave]
- **Pearson's Home Center** •
  7305 Fifth Ave [73rd St]
- **Ridge Paint Hardware** •
  9108 Third Ave [91st St]
- **Sunset Hardware** • 8111 Fifth Ave [81st St]
- **United Hardware** • 7905 Third Ave [79th St]

Liquor Stores

- **Chun Liquor** • 6813 Fourth Ave [68th St]
- **Five Star Wine & Liquors** •
  8412 Fifth Ave [84th St]
- **Harde Henry** • 9314 Third Ave [93rd St]
- **Harmon Wines & Liquors** •
  9425 Fifth Ave [94th St]
- **Hendricks Wines & Liquors** •
  7624 Third Ave [76th St]
- **Kings Cellars** • 8304 Third Ave [83rd St]
- **Long's Discount Wines** •
  7917 Fifth Ave [79th St]
- **McGovern's Wine & Liquor** •
  7207 Third Ave [72nd St]
- **McKey Liquors** • 308 86th St [3rd Ave]
- **Petzinger's Wines & Liquors** •
  123 Bay Ridge Ave [Colonial Rd]
- **Valens Liquor** • 9901 Third Ave [99th St]

Supermarkets

- **Foodtown** • 9105 3rd Ave [91st St]
- **Frank & Eddie's** • 302 86th St [3rd Ave]
- **Key Food** • 9408 Third Ave [94th St]
- **Met Food** • 8222 Fifth Ave [82nd St]

(113)

Map 14

The local branch of Century 21 is better stocked than its Manhattan counterpart, or maybe it's just the lack of tourists we adore. The Middle Eastern feasts at Tanoreen still reign foodie supreme, best followed with Lebanese sweets from Aryassi. Nordic Delicacies evokes the neighborhood's Norwegian past, which is still celebrated with a parade of blondes each May.

🍸Nightlife

- **Bean Post** • 7525 Fifth Ave [Bay Ridge Pkwy]
- **Delia's Lounge** • 9224 Third Ave [93rd St]
- **Hall of Fame Billiards** •
  505 Ovington Ave [5th Ave]
- **JJ Bubbles** • 7912 Third Ave [79th St]
- **Kelly's Tavern** • 9259 Fourth Ave [93rd St]
- **Kitty Kiernan's** • 9715 Third Ave [97th St]
- **Peggy O'Neill's** • 8123 Fifth Ave [81st St]
- **Salty Dog** • 7509 Fifth Ave [Bay Ridge Pkwy]
- **Speakeasy** • 9427 Fifth Ave [95th St]
- **Wicked Monk** • 8415 Fifth Ave [84th St]

🍴Restaurants

- **Anopoli** • 6920 Third Ave [Bay Ridge Ave]
- **Areo** • 8624 Third Ave [86th St]
- **Arirang Hibachi Steakhouse** •
  8814 Fourth Ave [88th St]
- **Bally Bunion** • 9510 Third Ave [95th St]
- **Banana Leaf** • 6814 Fourth Ave [68th St]
- **Bridgeview Diner** • 9011 Third Ave [90th St] ⏰
- **Canteena** • 8001 Fifth Ave [80th]
- **Casa Pepe** • 114 Bay Ridge Ave [Colonial Rd]
- **Chianti** • 8530 3rd Ave [85th]
- **Chopstix** • 8205 4th Ave [82nd St]
- **Damascus Gate** • 7224 Fifth Ave [72nd St]
- **Embers** • 9519 Third Ave [95th St]
- **Gino's** • 7414 Fifth Ave [74th St]
- **Grandma's Original Pizza** •
  6918 Third Ave [Bay Ridge Ave]
- **Greenhouse Café** • 7717 Third Ave [77th St]
- **Henry Grattan's** • 8814 Third Ave [88th St]
- **Hinsch's Confectionary**•
  8518 Fifth Ave [85th St]
- **Karam** • 8519 Fourth Ave [85th St]
- **La Maison Du Couscous** •
  484 77th St [5th Ave]
- **Lighthouse Café** •
  7506 3rd Ave [Bay Ridge Pkwy]
- **Mambo Italiano** • 8803 Third Ave [88th St]
- **Mazzo Plaza** • 8002 5th Ave [80th St]
- **Mezcals** • 7508 3rd Ave [75th St]
- **Mr Tang** • 7523 Third Ave [Bay Ridge Pkwy]
- **MyThai Café** • 7803 Third Ave [78th St]
- **Nouvelle** • 8716 Third Ave [88th St]
- **Taj Mahal** • 7315 3rd Ave [73rd St]
- **The Pearl Room** • 8201 Third Ave [82nd St]
- **Sancho's** • 7410 Third Ave [74th St]
- **Skinflints** • 7902 Fifth Ave [79th St]
- **Tanoreen** • 7704 Third Ave [77th St]
- **Tuscany Grill** • 8620 Third Ave [86th St]
- **Yiannis Café** •

🛍Shopping

- **Appletree Natural Market** •
  7911 3rd Ave [79th St]
- **Arayssi Bakery** • 7216 Fifth Ave [72nd St]
- **The Bookmark Shoppe** •
  8415 Third Ave [84th St]
- **Century 21** • 472 86th St [4th Ave]
- **Havin' a Party** • 8414 Fifth Ave [84th St]
- **Leske's Bakery** • 7612 5th Ave [76th St]
- **Little Cupcake Bakeshop** •
  9102 3rd Ave [91st St]
- **Modell's** • 531 86th St [5th Ave]
- **Nordic Delicacies** •
  6909 Third Ave [Bay Ridge Ave]
- **Panda Sport** • 9213 Fifth Ave [92nd St]
- **Pretty Girl** • 8501 Fifth Ave [85th St]
- **Village Irish Imports** •
  8508 Third Ave [85th St]

Bay Ridge has ample public transportation, making it very hard to sympathize with all those drivers endlessly circling for a spot to park their Yankee-stickered SUVs. Note that many local restaurants offer high-priced relief in the form of valet parking for dinner guests.

Subways

R . . . . Bay Ridge Avenue
R . . . . 77th Street
R . . . . 86th Street
R . . . . Bay Ridge-95th Street

Car Rental

• **All Car Rent a Car** • 8901 4th Ave [89th St]

Gas Stations

• **BP** • 802 65th St [8th Ave]
• **BP** • 6401 4th Ave [64th St]
• **BP** • 9111 4th Ave [91st St]
• **Exxon** • 605 65th St [6th Ave]
• **Getty** • 8202 Seventh Ave [82nd St]
• **Shell** • 6418 Seventh Ave [64th St]
• **Shell** • 9001 Fourth Ave [90th St]
• **Sunoco** • 805 65th St [8th Ave]

Bensonhurst's Italian community is dwindling as Boro Park expands, but you wouldn't know it to see the annual Santa Rosalia Festival. "The Feast" still draws thousands of hungry *paesans* each summer. Visit well-to-do Dyker Heights in December, when locals' elaborate Christmas decorations draw gawkers galore.

🎯 Bagels

- **13th Avenue Bagels** •
7501 13th Ave [Bay Ridge Pkwy]
- **Bagel Barn** • 1284 65th St [13th Ave]
- **Bagels Plus** •
7501 New Utrecht [Bay Ridge Pkwy]
- **D'Netto's Bagels** • 8308 13th Ave [83rd St]
- **Park Bagels** • 1410 86th St [14th Ave]
- **Tasty Bagels** • 1705 86th St [17th Ave]

💲 Banks

AP • Apple • 1973 86th St [Bay 23rd St]
AP • Apple • 6701 18th Ave [67th St]
AT • Atlantic • 7709 13th Ave [77th St]
BA • Bank of America • 438 86th St [4th Ave]
CF • Carver Federal • 140 58th St [1st Ave]
CH • Chase • 6501 18th Ave [65th St]
CH • Chase • 6701 Bay Pkwy [67th St]
CH • Chase • 8523 20th Ave [85th St]
CI • Citibank • 6414 18th Ave [64th St]
CI • Citibank (ATM) • 266 Cropsey Ave [14th Ave]
CI • Citibank (ATM) • 6409 20th Ave [64th St]
CI • Citibank (ATM) • 6501 Utrecht Ave [65th St]
CO • Commerce • 1301 65th St [13th Ave]
CO • Commerce • 1630 Shore Pkwy [Bay 29th St]
CO • Commerce • 2173 86th St [Bay Pkwy]
CO • Commerce • 9904 4th Ave [99th St]
DI • Dime • 1545 86th St [Bay 11th St]
HS • HSBC • 6102 8th Ave [61st St]
HS • HSBC • 6912 18th Ave [Bay Ridge Ave]
HS • HSBC • 7424 13th Ave [74th St]
NF • North Fork • 6501 11th Ave [65th St]
NF • North Fork •
7120 New Utrecht Ave [71st St]
NF • North Fork • 7401 13th Ave [74th St]
RI • Ridgewood • 7020 13th Ave [70th St]
RI • Ridgewood • 7124 18th Ave [71st St]
SG • Signature • 6321 New Utrecht Ave [63rd St]
SB • Sovereign • 1769 86th St [Bay 17th St]
SB • Sovereign • 2357 86th St [Bay 35th St]
SB • Sovereign • 6424 18th Ave [64th St]
SB • Sovereign (ATM) • 6502 18th Ave [65th St]
SB • Sovereign • 9512 3rd Ave [95th St]
WM • Washington Mutual •
1901 86th St [19th Ave]
WM • Washington Mutual •
7702 13th Ave [77th St]

➕ Emergency Rooms

- **Victory Memorial** • 699 92nd St [7th Ave]

⭕ Landmarks

- **Nellie Bly Amusement Park** •
1824 Shore Pkwy [25th Ave]

📖 Libraries

- **Brooklyn Public** • 1742 86th St [Bay 16th]
- **Brooklyn Public** •
6802 Ft Hamilton Pkwy [68th]
- **Brooklyn Public** • 8202 13th Ave [82nd]

℞ Pharmacies

- **Alleon** • 6823 Ft Hamilton Pkwy [68th St]
- **Be Well Pharmacy** • 8012 20th Ave [80th St]
- **Bi-Wise Pharmacy** • 7407 18th Ave [74th St]
- **Care Pharmacy Plus** • 7010 18th Ave [70th St]
- **CVS** • 6502 18th Ave [65th St]
- **CVS** • 8430 New Utrecht Ave [84th St]
- **Dyker Heights** • 8016 13th Ave [80th St]
- **Eckerd** • 8222 18th Ave [82nd St]
- **Empire Pharmacy** • 1864 86th St [Bay 20th St]
- **Health Treasures** • 8512 20th Ave [85th St]
- **J & L Pharmacy** • 8513 Bay 16th St [86th St]
- **Lifeline Pharmacy** • 7202 13th Ave [72nd St]
- **Park Ridge Pharmacy** •
7426 15th Ave [74th St]
- **Pollina Pharmacy** • 7601 13th Ave [76th St]
- **Quick Stop** • 7210 20th Ave [72nd St]
- **Rite Aid** • 1532 86th St [Bay 11th Ave]
- **Rite Aid** • 2007 86th St [20th Ave]
- **Rite Aid** • 2221 65th St [Bay Pkwy]
- **Rite Aid** • 6423 Fort Hamilton Pkwy [64th St]
- **Rite Aid** • 7009 13th Ave [70th St]
- **Rite Aid** • 7118 3rd Ave [71st St]
- **Rite Aid** • 7501 5th Ave [75th St]
- **Rite Aid** • 8222 18th Ave [82nd St]
- **Rubino Pharmacy** • 6602 17th Ave [66th St]
- **Rx Express Pharmacy** •
6716 18th Ave [67th St]

🚓 Police

- **62nd Precinct** • 1925 Bath Ave [Bay 22nd St]

✉ Post Offices

- **US Post Office** •
301 General Lee Ave [Grimes Rd]
- **US Post Office** • 6618 20th Ave [66th St]

Map 1

Welcome back, Kotter. Too old for a trip to Nellie Bly Park? Hunt for the few grand houses that remain from the original development of Dyker Heights back in the 1890s.

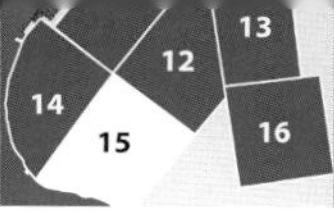

☕ Coffee

- **Dunkin' Donuts** • 1980 86th St [Bay 23rd St]
- **Dunkin' Donuts** • 6502 14th Ave [65th St]
- **Dunkin' Donuts** • 7121 18th Ave [71st St]
- **Dunkin' Donuts** • 8513 18th Ave [85th St]
- **Starbucks** • 1971 86th Ave [Bay 23rd St]
- **Starbucks** • 6423 18th Ave [64th St]

🔧 Hardware Stores

- **18 Avenue Hardware** •
  7324 18th Ave [73rd St]
- **Bath Ave Hardware** •
  1800 Bath Ave [18th Ave]
- **D I Y Supplies** • 1973 Bay Ridge Pkwy [20th St]
- **Karp Hardware** • 6601 18th Ave [66th St]
- **Polstein's Home Center** •
  7615 13th Ave [76th St]
- **Tom's Supplies** • 1872 86th St [Bay 20th St]

🍾 Liquor Stores

- **1 Liquor Store** • 8501 20th Ave [85th St]
- **18th Avenue Liquors** •
  6705 18th Ave [67th St]
- **84 St Beverage Center** •
  1783 84th St [18th Ave]
- **Bensonhurst Discount Liquor** •
  7506 18th Ave [Bay Ridge Pkwy]
- **D'Still Fine Wines & Liquors** •
  7020 New Utrecht Ave [70th St]
- **Dave's Discount Liquor** •
  1698 86th St [17th Ave]
- **Empire Wine & Liquor** •
  6503 11th Ave [65th St]
- **Finest Liquor Mart** •
  7112 Ft Hamilton Pkwy [71st St]
- **Junior's Wines & Liquors** •
  1654 Bath Ave [Bay 14th St]
- **Manna Liquors** • 2002 Cropsey Ave [20th Ave]
- **Murray's Wines & Liquors** •
  7703 13th Ave [77th St]
- **Seaworld Liquors** • 8511 18th Ave [85th St]

🛒 Supermarkets

- **Buy Rite** • 8504 20th Ave [72nd St]
- **C-Town** • 6614 13th Ave [66th St]
- **C-Town** • 7907 13th Ave [79th St]
- **Key Food** • 7000 New Utrecht Ave [70th St]
- **Key Food** • 8772 18th Ave [Bath]
- **Met Food** • 7215 20th Ave [72nd St]
- **New Way** • 7302 18th Ave [73rd St]
- **New Way** • 7423 18th Ave [74th St]

Mangia! Tommaso's is one of the city's great old school Italian joints, with a killer wine list to boot. The Sicilian sandwiches and riceballs at Gino's are good to go, as is any (every?) pastry containing cannoli cream at Villabate's. Relax Uncle Junior-style while spinning the records you scored at SAS.

Restaurants

- **Casa Calamari** • 1801 Bath Ave [18th Ave]
- **Columbus Restaurant & Deli** • 6610 18th Ave [66th St]
- **Gino's Focacceria** • 7118 18th Ave [71st St]
- **Il Colosseo** • 7704 18th Ave [77th St]
- **Outback Steakhouse** • 1475 86th St [Bay 8th St]
- **Shiki** • 1863 86th St [Bay 20th St]
- **Tenzan** • 7116 18th Ave [71st St]
- **Tommaso's** • 1464 86th St [Bay 8th St]
- **Vermicelli House** • 7524 18th Ave [Bay Ridge Pkwy]

Shopping

- **3 Guys from Brooklyn** • 6502 Ft Hamilton Pkwy [65th St]
- **Arcobaleno Italiano** • 7306 18th Ave [73rd St]
- **Lioni Latticini** • 7819 15th Ave [78th St]
- **Pastosa Ravioli** • 7425 New Utrecht Ave [74th St]
- **Queen Ann Ravioli** • 7205 18th Ave [Bay Ridge Pkwy]
- **SAS Italian Records** • 7113 18th Ave [71st St]
- **Sea Breeze** • 8500 18th Ave [85th St]
- **Villabate Pasticceria & Bakery** • 7117 18th Ave [71st St]

Map 13 • Dyker Heights / Bensonhurst

The bus can get you where you need to be, but driving will make it easier to really explore these neighborhoods, especially if you're out to admire the Christmas lights.

14 15 16 12 13

Subways

D M .... 18th Avenue
D M .... 20th Avenue
D M .... 71st Street
D M .... 79th Street
D M N .. New Utrecht Avenue-62nd Street
N .... 18th Avenue
N .... 20th Avenue
N .... Fort Hamilton Parkway

⬤ Car Washes

• **Ace Car Wash** •
  6702 New Utrecht Ave [67th St]
• **Best Car Wash** • 902 65th St [9th Ave]
• **Personal Touch Car Wash** •
  1815 86th St [18th Ave]

🅿 Gas Stations

• **AP Oil** • 1302 65th St [13th Ave]
• **BP** • 6002 18th St [60th St]
• **Citgo** • 8521 Seventh Ave [85th St]
• **Getty** • 1672 86th St [Bay 14th St]
• **Getty** • 6418 Eighth Ave [64th St]
• **Getty** • 7519 18th Ave [Bay Ridge Pkwy]
• **Mobil** • 1420 86th St [14th Ave]
• **Shell** • 1501 86th St [15th Ave]
• **Shell** • 2001 Cropsey Ave [20th Ave]
• **Shell** • 6414 Ft Hamilton Pkwy [64th St]
• **Sunoco** • 1907 Cropsey Ave [19th Ave]
• **Valero** • 1 Bay 13th St [86th St]

Midwood's tree-lined, SUV-laden streets are home to an affluent Orthodox Jewish community that includes many Russian immigrants. Stroll along and observe all the big families living in big homes, then take a tour of the Wyckoff House, the city's oldest structure.

Bagels

- **Avenue M Bagels** • 1712 Avenue M [E 17th St]
- **CPC Bakery** • 1506 Elm Ave [E 15th St]
- **Highway Bagels** • 1921 Kings Hwy [E 19th St]
- **JA Bagels** • 1615 Kings Hwy [E 16th St]
- **Kosher Bagel Hole** • 1423 Ave J [E 14th St]
- **Kosher Bagel Hole** •
  1431 Coney Island Ave [Ave K]
- **My Favorite Bagel** •
  3053 Nostrand Ave [Quentin]
- **Original Brooklyn Bagel** •
  2835 Nostrand Ave [Kings Hwy]
- **Say Bagel and Cheese** • 1
  304 Ave M [E 13th St]
- **Vitale's Pizza** • 397 Ave P [McDonald]
- **Yummy Bagel** • 2932 Ave R [Nostrand]

Banks

AP • Apple • 1321 Kings Hwy [E 13th St]
AP • Apple • 1401 Ave J [E 14th St]
AP • Apple • 1817 Ave M [E 18th St]
AS • Astoria Federal • 1401 Ave M [E 14th St]
BA • Bank of America •
  1502 Kings Hwy [E 15th St]
BA • Bank of America • 2022 Ave U [Ocean Ave]
BK • Berkshire •
  1119 Avenue J [Coney Island Ave]
BK • Berkshire • 1421 Kings Hwy [E 14th St]
CH • Chase • 1501 Ave M [E 15th St]
CH • Chase • 1663 E 17th St [Kings Hwy]
CH • Chase • 1722 Ave U [E 17th St]
CH • Chase (ATM) • Duane Reade •
  1520 Ave J [E 15th St]
CI • Citibank • 1220 Ave J [E 12th St]
CI • Citibank • 1501 Kings Hwy [E 15th St]
CO • Commerce • 1122 Kings Hwy [E 12th St]
CO • Commerce • 1602 Ave U [E 16th St]
DI • Dime • 1600 Ave M [E 16th St]
DI • Dime • 1902 Kings Hwy [E 19th St]
FS • Flushing Savings • 1402 Ave J [E 14th St]
HS • HSBC • 1602 Kings Hwy [E 16th St]
HS • HSBC • 1702 Ave U [E 17th St]
HS • HSBC • 481 Kings Hwy [McDonald Ave]
NF • North Fork • 1226 Kings Hwy [E 12th St]
NF • North Fork • 1620 Ave U [E 16th St]
NF • North Fork • 2123 Ave U [E 21st St]
RS • Roosevelt Savings •
  2925 Ave U [Gravesend Neck Rd]
SB • Sovereign • 1302 Ave J [E 13th St]
SB • Sovereign • 440 Ave P [E 3rd St]
SB • Sovereign • 961 Kings Hwy [E 10th St]
SB • Sovereign (ATM) • CVS •
  2925 Kings Hwy [E 29th St]
WM • Washington Mutual •
  1101 Ave J [Coney Island Ave]
WM • Washington Mutual •
  1521 Kings Hwy [E 15th St]

Landmarks

- **JC Studios** • 1268 E 14th St [Locust]
- **Wyckoff House** (private residence) •
  1669 E 22nd St [Ave P]

Libraries

- **Brooklyn Public** • 975 E 16th St [Ave J]

Pharmacies

- **CVS** • 2925 Kings Hwy [E 29th St]
- **Duane Reade** • 1110 Kings Hwy [Coney Island]
- **Duane Reade** • 1401 Kings Hwy [E 14th St]
- **Duane Reade** • 1417 Ave U [E 14th St]
- **Duane Reade** • 1520 Ave J [E 15th St]
- **Duane Reade** • 2931 Ave U [Nostrand]
- **Duane Reade** • 520 Kings Hwy [E 3rd St]
- **Rite Aid** • 1720 Kings Hwy [E 17th St]
- **Rite Aid** • 2002 Ave U [Ocean]
- **Rite Aid** • 2577 Nostrand Ave [Ave L]
- **Thriftway** • 1909 Kings Hwy [E 19th St]
- **Walgreens** • 946 Kings Hwy [E 10th St]

Post Offices

- **US Post Office** • 1288 Coney Island Ave [Ave I]
- **US Post Office** • 1610 E 19th St [Ave P]
- **US Post Office** • 2302 Ave U [E 23rd St]
- **US Post Office** • 2319 Nostrand Ave [Ave I]

Map

Kosher markets are many here, and bakeries on avenues J and M hold countless Rabbi-approved bagels, bialys, and challahs. On Friday night or Saturday, shoppers should stick to King's Highway because the primarily Orthodox businesses elsewhere will be closed.

Coffee

- **Dunkin' Donuts** • 1410 Ave J [E 14th St]
- **Dunkin' Donuts** • 1422 Kings Hwy [E 14th St]
- **Dunkin' Donuts** • 1510 Elm Ave [Ave M]
- **Dunkin' Donuts** • 1691 E 16th St [Quentin]
- **Dunkin' Donuts** • 1815 Ave U [E 18th St]
- **Dunkin' Donuts** • 2926 Ave I [E 29th St]
- **Milimma's Home Made Food** •
  819 Ave U [E 8th St]

Hardware Stores

- **Avenue U Hardware Corporation** •
  1318 Ave U [E 13th St]
- **Broadmore** • 1317 Ave J [E 13th St]
- **Corner Hardware & Paint** •
  2266 Nostrand Ave [Ave I]
- **Eric Blunbint & Hardware Supply** •
  1229 Ave U [Homecrest Ave]
- **Frankson Hardware** •
  469 Kings Hwy [McDonald]
- **Kings Highway Hardware** •
  1816 Kings Hwy [E 16th St]
- **Midwood Lumber & Millwork** •
  1169 Coney Island Ave [Ave H]
- **York's Hardware Plus** •
  1805 Kings Hwy [E 16th St]

Liquor Stores

- **Ace Wine & Liquor Store** •
  1804 Ave U [E 18th St]
- **Avenue J Wine & Liquor** •
  2388 Nostrand Ave [Ave J]
- **Fullmoon Liquor** •
  2880 Nostrand Ave [Marine]
- **Homecraft Wines & Liquor** •
  1233 Ave U [Homecrest Ave]
- **Kingsway Liquors** •
  1624 Kings Hwy [E 16th St]
- **Liquor Depot** • 824 Kings Hwy [E 8th St]
- **Liquors Galore** • 1418 Ave J [E 14th St]
- **Meyer's Liquor Store** • 1504 Ave M [E 16th St]
- **Midwood Wine & Liquor** •
  1433 Coney Island Ave [Ave K]
- **Orlander Liquors** • 1781 Ocean Ave [Ave M]
- **Tops Liquor Supermarket** •
  2816 Ave U [E 28th St]

Supermarkets

- **Associated Supermarket** •
  1413 Ave J [E 14th St]
- **Associated Supermarket** •
  480 Ave P [E 4th St]
- **Fine Fare** • 406 Ave P [E 2nd St]
- **Key Food** • 2326 Nostrand Ave [Ave I]
- **Met Food** • 1910 Kings Hwy [E 19th St]
- **Shop Rite** • 1080 McDonald Ave [Elmwood]
- **Shop Smart Kosher Supermarket** •
  2640 Nostrand Ave [Ave M]

Map 16 · **Midwood**

Ⓝ

Parkville Ave

Foster Ave

710

13

Brooklyn College

PAGE
142

Walsh Ct

Elmwood Ave

E 7mo

910

710

Avenue H

Wellington Ct

Wall Fort Ct

Campus Rd

E 16th St

E 21st St
E 22nd St
E 23rd St
E 24th St

Bedford Ave

E 27th St
E 28th St
E 29th St

2

Bay Pkwy

McDonald Ave

Dahill Rd

E 3rd St
E 5th St

1118
1122

Avenue I

E 10th St

1290

Avenue J

Cary Ct

E 16th St

E 19th St

1830

1140

E 26th St

Nostrand Ave

4

3

Ocean Pkwy

E 2nd St

A

Washington Cemetery

E 7th St
E 9th St

501

Avenue K

E 12th St
E 13th St
E 15th St
E 16th St

E 18th St
E 19th St

Ocean Ave

1610

1070

1240

1240

E 26th St

1310

1310

1850

1610
1410
1420
1450

1348

1248

410

Avenue M

Ryder Ave

1450

Coney Island Ave

Locust Ave

Chestnut Ave

Elm Ave

Cedar St

Avenue N

Bay Ave

1380

1240

1490

Ocean St

1450

1350

1450

1210

Avenue L

Dahill Rd

1520

1410

Ryder Ave

1510

1520

1510

1450

Avenue O

1450

1450

1450

Bay Ave

1480

Kings Hwy

Avenue P

1660

3460

W 2nd St

Estate Rd

1610

1730

1630

Ocean Pkwy

1640

1630

1640

1750

1770

3810

Germ

Nostrand

Burn

Quentin Rd

Woodside Ave

Quentin Rd

E 10th St

2

1770

1710

1710

B

Kings Hwy

2

Billings Pl

Colin Pl

E 2nd St
E 3rd St
E 4th St
E 5th St

710

1st Ct

1890

2160

1630

1940

1940

Ocean Ave

E 22nd St
Mansfield Pl
Delamere Pl

Bedford Ave

E 27th St
E 29th St

1910

3990

1910

Germ

Kelly Park

Moore Pl

Avenue S

Avenue R

1910

Avenue T

Sloan Pl

W 1st St

Whitney Pl

E 1st St

E 2nd St
E 3rd St
E 4th St
E 5th St

710

1850

Hutchinson Ct
Homecrest Ct

2020

810

Homecrest Ave
E 13th St
E 14th St
E 15th St

E 17th St
E 18th St
E 19th St

Avenue U

3240

Village

1/4 mile

.25 km

Map 1

Basing a whole day around eating DiFara Pizza is justified. Kosher locals prefer Olympic Pita. Chiffon's challah is tops, but Mansoura has the best sweets. Chuckies is to shoes as Eichler's is to Judaica, which is to say that both are awesome.

Movie Theaters

• **Kent Triplex** • 1170 Coney Island Ave [Ave H]

Nightlife

• **Blue Velvet Lounge** • 341 Ave U [West St]

Restaurants

• **Adelman's Kosher Deli** •
1906 Kings Hwy [E 19th St]
• **Anna's Luncheonette** • 2925 Ave I [Nostrand]
• **DiFara** • 1424 Ave J [E 14th St]
• **Essex on Coney** •
1359 Coney Island Ave [Ave J]
• **Jerusalem Steak House** •
533 Kings Hwy [E 3rd St]
• **Kosher Bagel Hole** •
1431 Coney Island Ave [Ave K]
• **La Villita** • 1249 Ave U [Homecrest Ave]
• **Lucky's Diner** • 557 Kings Hwy [E 4th St]
• **Mabat** • 1809 E 7th St [Kings Hwy]
• **Napoli Pizza** • 2270 Nostrand Ave [Ave I]
• **Olympic Pita** • 1419 Coney Island Ave [Ave K]
• **Pizza Time** • 1324 Ave J [E 13th St]
• **Schnitzi** • 1229 Coney Island Ave [Ave J]
• **Sunflower Café** • 1223 Quentin Rd [E 12th St]
• **Taci's Beyti** • 1955 Coney Island Ave [Ave P]
• **Tblisi** • 811 Kings Hwy [E 8th St]
• **Tea for Two** • 547 Kings Hwy [E 4th St]

Shopping

• **Canal Jean Company** •
2236 Nostrand Ave [Ave H]
• **Chiffon Bakery** •
1373 Coney Island Ave [Ave J]
• **Chuckies** • 1304 Kings Hwy [E 13th St]
• **Downtown** • 2502 Ave U [Bedford]
• **Eichler's** • 1401 Coney Island Ave [Ave J]
• **Fish Expo** • 2370 Nostrand Ave [Ave J]
• **Image** • 1310 Kings Hwy [E 13th St]
• **Jinil Au Chocolat** •
1371 Coney Island Ave [Ave J]
• **Mansoura** • 515 Kings Hwy [E 3rd St]
• **Sea Bay** • 1237 Ave U [Homecrest Ave]
• **Wig Showcase** • 820 Kings Hwy [E 8th St]
• **Zelda's Art World** • 2291 Nostrand Ave [Ave I]

Transportaion

Map 16

This is a driving neighborhood with ample parking. The F, B, and Q get by, but the X29 is quickest for commuters. In summertime, hop right on the B49 to Manhattan Beach or the B68 to Brighton Beach.

Subways

B Q	.... Kings Highway
F	.... Avenue I
F	.... Avenue N
F	....................................Avenue P
F	.... Avenue U
F	..............................Bay Parkway
F	.... Kings Highway
Q	.... Avenue H
Q	.... Avenue J
Q	...................................Avenue M
Q	.... Avenue U

Car Rental

- **All Car Rent A Car** •
  1204 Coney Island Ave [Ave I]
- **All Car Rent A Car** •
  2686 Nostrand Ave [Ave M]
- **Eldan Rent A Car** •
  1114 Quentin Rd [Coney Island]
- **Enterprise Rent A Car** •
  1212 Coney Island Ave [Ave I]

Car Washes

- **Dynasty Twenty-One Car Wash** •
  2881 Nostrand Ave [Marine]
- **W&B Gas Enterprises** •
  1775 Coney Island Ave [Ave N]

Gas Stations

- **BP** • 1640 Flatbush Ave [Ave H]
- **BP** • 1775 Coney Island Ave [Ave N]
- **BP** • 1982 Utica Ave [Ave L]
- **Exxon** • 1938 Coney Island Ave [Ave P]
- **Getty** • 2001 Gravesend Neck Rd [Ocean Ave]
- **Mobil** • 1249 Coney Island Ave [Ave I]
- **Mobil** • 1935 Coney Island Ave [Ave P]
- **Mobil** • 2773 Nostrand Ave [Ave N]
- **Mobil** • 5025 Bay Pkwy [E 2nd St]
- **Sunoco** • 1815 Ocean Ave [Ave M]

Overview

Nearly every community of Eastern Brooklyn is surrounded by water, and while you wouldn't exactly get an "Aye, matey" vibe from its inhabitants, this section of the borough is home to over a dozen boating and yacht clubs. In the summer, inlets along Sheepshead Bay, Plum Beach, and Paerdegat Basin become strewn with jet skiers, windsurfers, and the occasional million dollar schooner. Some neighborhoods, such as Canarsie and Marine Park, exude an almost suburban tranquility, while seriously affluent areas like Mill Basin and Manhattan Beach cater to an exclusive crowd that includes State Senator Carl Kruger. Densely populated East New York and Brownsville are packed with drab public housing, though remnants of a former Art Deco glory can be found along Pitkin Avenue. The population is a truly mixed bag, and with Brooklyn's seaside real estate once again on the rise, the nabe can only improve with time.

Transportation

Although the subway extends all the way out to East New York (J Z A C 3) and Canarsie (L), there are many neighborhoods that can be accessed only by bus or car (notably Marine Park, Mill Basin, Bergen Beach, parts of East Flatbush, and the Flatlands). If you need to travel to any of these areas, consult the Brooklyn bus map on the foldout—there are a number of bus routes that will deliver you exactly where you need to go.

Communities

Brooklyn is a borough of individual neighborhoods. The main communities that make up Eastern Brooklyn are:

Bergen Beach (pop. 12,500)
Flatlands (pop. 59,500)
Brownsville (pop. 82,900)
Gerritsen Beach (pop. 6,900)
Canarsie (pop. 89,500)
Gravesend (pop. 93,600)
Cypress Hills (pop. 56,000)
East Flatbush (pop. 181,300)
Marine Park (pop. 20,100)
Mill Basin (pop. 11,800)
East New York (pop. 117,000)
Sheepshead Bay (pop. 127,800)

*Figures based on the 2000 US Census.

Nature

What Eastern Brooklyn lacks in trendiness, it makes up for in scenery. The Eastern Brooklyn shore is lined with more than 3,000 acres of amazing parks that offer a plethora of activities: Nature trails, golf courses, horseback riding, camping, fishing, bird watching, boating, and organized athletics. When you need a break from it all, **Marine Park**, **Floyd Bennett Field**, the **Jamaica Riding Academy**, and **Canarsie Beach Park** provide a nice diversion from city life.

Landmarks

- **Lady Moody House** • 27 Gravesend Neck Rd [McDonald]
- **Old Gravesend Cemetery** • Gravesend Neck Rd b/w McDonald Ave & Van Sicklen St [McDonald]

Nightlife

- **The Wrong Number** • 168 Ave T [W 6th St]

Restaurants

- **Del'Rio Diner** • 166 Kings Hwy [W 12th St]
- **El Greco Diner** • 1821 Emmons Ave [Sheepshead Bay]
- **Frank's Pizza** • 2134 Flatbush Ave, Flatlands [Quentin]
- **Joe's of Avenue U** • 287 Ave U [McDonald]
- **John's Deli** • 2438 Stillwell Ave [Bay 50th]
- **Jordan's Lobster Dock** • 2771 Knapp St, Sheepshead Bay [Harkness]
- **King's Buffet** • 2637 86th St [Ave U]
- **L&B Spumoni Gardens** • 2725 86th St [W 10th St]
- **La Palina** • 159 Ave O [W 5th St]
- **Liman** • 2710 Emmons Ave [E 27th]
- **Mill Basin Kosher Delicatessen** • 5823 Ave T, Mill Basin [E 58th St]
- **Peter Pizza** • 2637 86th St [Ave U]
- **Randazzo's** • 2017 Emmons Ave, Sheepshead Bay [Ocean]
- **Roll-n-Roaster** • 2901 Emmons Ave, Sheepshead Bay [E 29th St]
- **Sahara** • 2337 Coney Island Ave [Ave T]
- **U Shweika** • 2027 Emmons Ave, Sheepshead Bay [Ocean]
- **XO Creperie** • 2027 Emmons Ave [Ocean]

Shopping

- **AKO** • 2184 McDonald Ave [Ave T]
- **Dairy Maid Ravioli** • 216 Ave U [W 5th St]
- **Enterprize** • 1601 Sheepshead Bay Rd [E 16th St]
- **Le Monti** • 2070 McDonald Ave [Ave S]
- **Leohmann's** • 2807 E 21st St [Shore]
- **Meat Supreme** • 181 Ave U [W 6th St]
- **Mini Centro** • 1659 Sheepshead Bay Rd, Sheepshead Bay [Voorhies]
- **Nuts & Candy** • 2079 86th St [Bay 26th]
- **Omni Health** • 265 Ave U [Lake St]
- **Pisa Pork Store** • 306 Kings Hwy [W 6th St]
- **Sheepshead Bay Gourmet** • 1518 Ave Z [E 15th St]

Ahhh, but remember that the city is a funny place
Something like a circus or a sewer…
Coney Island baby
Man, I'd give the whole thing up for you
—Lou Reed, "Coney Island Baby"

Coney Island

No matter what the crowd is like, there is an undeniable nostalgia involved every time you step onto the boardwalk. Whether you're with your kids or trying to reenact your favorite scenes from *The Warriors*, Coney Island is a blast for everyone. Featuring two amusement parks, the **New York Aquarium**, **Sideshows by the Seashore**, the **Coney Island Museum**, **Nathan's Famous** hot dog stand, and **Keyspan Park**—unless you hate fun, you'll find something here to your liking. Though the recent purchase of Coney Island property by a big time developer had Astroland announcing its closure after the 2007 season, it'll be business as usual at least through 2008. Get there before it's history. Literally.

Getting there:
Subway: take the Ⓓ Ⓕ or Ⓝ Ⓠ train to Coney Island/ Stillwell Avenue. For the Aquarium, take the Ⓕ or Ⓠ to W 8th Street/NY Aquarium.
Buses: 🚌 🚌 and 🚌 all go to Coney Island.

Coney Island, USA

Address:	1208 Surf Ave (near W 12th St)
Phone:	718-372-5159
Website:	www.coneyisland.com

Coney Island, USA is the not-for-profit arts organization responsible for maintaining the Coney Island Museum, producing Sideshows by the Seashore, and organizing the annual Mermaid Parade.

The **Coney Island Museum** is open weekends from noon to 5 pm and is free for members but 99 cents for everyone else. Try the distortion mirrors and view other artifacts from the sideshow heyday. The gift shop has capitalized on pretty much every exploitable image available and it's a great spot to pick up some jumbo postcards.

Sideshows by the Seashore remains the only 10-in-1 circus sideshow in the USA. Eak the geek and Insectavora are highlights, and we recommend sipping a cold beer at the Freak Bar in the lobby. From Memorial Day to Labor Day, performances run 2 pm–8 pm on Fridays and 1 pm–11 pm on Saturdays and Sundays, depending on demand. Performances also run (albeit with a reduced cast) on Wednesdays and Thursdays 2 pm–8 pm. Tickets cost $5 for adults and $3 for kids, though "periodic specials" are announced outside if audiences begin to dwindle.

The annual **Mermaid Parade** takes place on the first Saturday after the Summer Solstice. Rain or shine, more freaks than you knew existed strut their stuff down the main drag dressed as… mermaids! Seeing is believing and this is a don't-miss event.

For some of the best thin-crust pizza in Brooklyn go to **Totonno Pizzeria Napolitano**, 1524 Neptune Ave, 718-372-8606.

New York Aquarium

Address:	Surf Ave & W 8th St
Phone:	718-265-FISH
Website:	www.nyaquarium.com

In sobering contrast to the natural environs just footsteps away, the New York Aquarium has a colorful collection of sea life swimming happily in clean tanks. The exhibits strike a nice balance between interesting and educational. The aquarium is open every day of the year from 10 am until 6 pm (Memorial Day–Labor Day) or 4:30 pm (September–May) and remains open for 45 minutes after the last ticket is sold. Entry

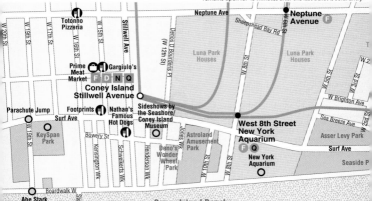

is $12 for adults and $8 for seniors and children 12 and under. Children under 2 are free.

KeySpan Park/Brooklyn Cyclones

Location:	Surf Ave b/w W 16th St & W 19th St
Phone:	718-449-8497
Website:	www.brooklyncyclones.com

After a 44-year absence, professional baseball returned to Brooklyn in 2001 in the shape of the class-A minor league Brooklyn Cyclones (affiliate of the NY Mets). Keyspan's location couldn't be better, allowing any trip to the ballpark to double as a day at the beach or a great first date screaming your brains out and clutching hands on the Cyclones' namesake. On top of that, the team is actually pretty good. Field box seats will only set you back $14 and bleacher seats are $6. You can purchase tickets either on their website or by calling 718-507-TIXX. Go 'Clones!). As a bonus, KeySpan has also started moonlighting as a concert venue, and Daft Punk's laser-enhanced performance was one of NYC's most talked about summer shows.

Astroland Amusement Park

Address:	1000 Surf Ave
Phone:	718-372-0275
Website:	www.astroland.com

Keep your mind off impending doom while in line for the Cyclones by contemplating the historical ride you are about to take. One of the last remaining wooden roller coasters in existence, the Cyclone is the place to be at Astroland. Admission to the park is free and rides range from $2 to $5. An all-day wristband costs $21.99 . Open every day during the summer and on weekends through the cooler months. Keep in mind, there isn't any high-tech DisneyWorld or Six Flags fare here…these are the original rides (with perhaps some of the original carnies still attached). The next day you may feel like you were in a bar fight, but the memories are worth it.

Deno's Wonder Wheel Park

Address:	3059 Denos Vourderis Pl (W 12th St)
Phone:	718-372-2592 or 718-449-8836
Website:	www.wonderwheel.com

A slightly sticky quality adds a touch of authenticity to this 85-year-old amusement park. The Wheel of Wonder is still the major draw and offers a romantic moment well worth the $5 each for the stationary cars. Those looking to have their lives flash before their eyes can wait in a separate line for the "moving cars" and believe us, those things really move. Admission to the park is free and $18 buys 10 kid rides or 5 adult rides.

Brighton Beach

Slightly less frenetic than the Coney Island beach and boardwalk (but only slightly) is nearby Brighton Beach. Named for a resort town on the English Channel, this area is now often referred to as "little Odessa." Russian food, Russian vodka, and Russian-style bathing suits are the name of the game on this sandy stretch. The restaurants on the boardwalk are WAY over-priced—pack a lunch and skip the hassle. And a word to the wise—despite shirtless vendors parading up and down the beach hocking ice cold Coronas with lime—there are also cops on ATV's ready to hand out open container violations, so drink at your own risk! Bear in mind however that this is no white-sandy national park, but still probably your best beach bet by subway. Had enough sun? After the beach, head to the famed restaurant and cabaret, **National** (273 Brighton Beach Ave, 718-646-1225) whose doors whisk you off the street and into Moscow. To access Brighton Beach by subway, take the **B** or the **Q** to the Brighton Beach stop.

36 St Ⓓ Ⓜ Ⓝ Ⓡ

Ⓜ Ⓡ 25 St

Fourth Ave

Ⓟ

Maintenance Entrance

MAP
11

36th St

37th St

34th St

33rd St

32nd St

31st St

30th St

29th St

28th St

27th St

26th St

25th St

24th St

23rd St

22nd St

21st St

20th St

Fifth Ave

Sixth Ave

Lake Ave

Sylvan Ave

Walnut Ave

Community
Mausoleum

Crematory

Chapel

Landscape Ave

Main Entrance

Sylvan
Water

Valley
Water

Willow Ave

Office

Oak Ave

Landscape Ave

Lawn Ave

Sycamore Ave

Bay Side Ave

Arbor Ave

Ⓝ▶

Lake Ave

❷

❾

Highland Ave

Bay View Ave

Battle Ave

Seventh Ave

Tulip Ave

Central Ave

Fern Ave

Battle Hill
(Highest Point
in Brooklyn)

Fern Ave

Seventh Ave

Border Ave

❽

Spruce Ave

Oak Ave

Alger Ave

Greenbough Ave

Pine Ave

Mulberry Ave

❶

62nd St

Border Ave

Eigh

Orchard Ave

Vista Ave

Hemlock Ave

Crescent Ave

❺

Forest Ave

Central Ave

Meadow Ave

Jasmine Ave

Dell
Water

Vale Ave

❸

Border Ave

Crescent
Water

Dale Ave

Union Ave

Locust Ave

Southwood Ave

Dell Ave

Linden Ave

Ninth Ave Er

Summit Ave

Vernal Ave

Southwood Ave

Vista Ave

Oakwood Ave

Birch Ave

❼

Atlantic Ave

Grove Ave

Elm Ave

20th St

Ninth Ave

37th St

Border Ave

Cypress Ave

Locust Ave The Catacombs

Grove Ave

❹

Sassafras Ave

❻

Vine Ave

Cypress Ave

Atlantic Ave

Ocean Ave

Crestview
Mausoleum

Hillside Ave

Tent

❿

Hillside
Mausoleum

Terrace Pl

Fir Ave

Sassafras Ave

Fir Ave

Beech Ave

Border Ave

Seeley St

Vanderbilt St

Ft Hamilton Pkwy

Eastern Entrance

McDonald Ave

E 2nd St

E 3rd St

MAP
12

Greenwood Ave

General Information

NFT Maps: 11 & 12
Main Entrance: Fifth Ave & 25th St
Phone: 718-768-7300
Website: www.green-wood.com
Subway: **M R** to 25th St; **D** to Ninth Ave;
                 F to Ft Hamilton Pkwy

Overview

When Green-Wood Cemetery opened in 1838, it was the largest outdoor park in all of New York City. With its winding paths, rolling hills, Victorian sculpture, and manmade lakes, this lush 478-acre cemetery inspired a contest to create a park in Manhattan—Central Park. The winning design, by Frederick Law Olmstead and Calvert Vaux, was based on Green-Wood. Today the picturesque grounds are dotted with the mausoleums and tombstones of nearly 600,000 people and counting, including several famous figures (see below). As a member of the Audubon Cooperative, this cemetery is a wildlife sanctuary and a haven for bird-watching. Green-Wood is also home to 220-foot Battle Hill, the highest point in all of Brooklyn. During the Revolutionary War, 400 Maryland soldiers held off the British Army here, allowing the rest of George Washington's troops to survive and fight another day. There are memorials to Revolutionary and Civil War dead at the summit that afford incredible views of lower Manhattan and New York Harbor. If you're craving some peace and solitude in the outdoors, this is the perfect retreat.

Visiting

The administrative offices are open Monday through Saturday 8 am–5 pm. The cemetery itself is open to the public every day and can be accessed from three different points:

• Main Entrance (Fifth Avenue & 25th Street): Open everyday 8 am–5 pm (7 am–7 pm in the summer).
• Ninth Avenue Entrance (Ninth Avenue & 20th Street): Open 8 am–4pm on weekends only.
• Eastern Entrance (Fort Hamilton Parkway & Chester Avenue): Open 8 am–4pm on weekends only.

For the most impressive entry into the cemetery, we recommend walking through the main entrance gate. Designed by Richard Upjohn in 1860, this brownstone Gothic revival gate is embellished with four carved panels portraying scenes of death and resurrection—a great way to kick off your grim excursion.

Walking Tours

Three distinct walking tour routes provide unique commentary on the history of the cemetery and its interred. Check the website for schedules. Tours usually last about 2½ hours and cost $10 per person. We highly recommend the Special Halloween Tour, which includes local ghost stories and tales of murder for $15. These popular tours (scheduled around Halloween), are first-come, first-served, so arrive early.

Famous Graves

1. **Leonard Bernstein** – composer, conductor.
2. **Horace Greeley** – founder of the *New Yorker* and the *New York Tribune*.
3. **"Boss" Tweed** – corrupt politician.
4. **Susan Smith McKinney-Steward** – first black female doctor in New York
5. **Samuel F.B. Morse** – inventor of the telegraph.
6. **John Michel Basquiat** – graffiti artist and painter.
7. **Peter Cooper** – founder of Cooper Union; inventor of Jell-O.
8. **Joey "Crazy Joe" Gallo** – mobster killed in Umberto's Clam House.
9. **DeWitt Clinton** – politician; brain behind the Erie Canal.
10. **Henry Ward Beecher** – abolitionist.

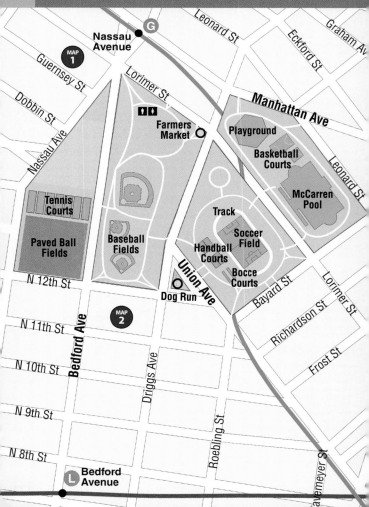

Overview

McCarren Park is not easy on the eyes, but it's getting easier. Serving Greenpoint and Williamsburg, this 35-acre park reflects both the industrial and increasingly condo-ified surroundings of the neighborhood The grass is brown or even nonexistent in many patches, the graffiti-laden McCarren Pool has been re-imagined as a performance venue, and cars race through the park on three streets. However, McCarren Park is all about *function*, not form. When the sun is shining, the park is packed with a wide cross-section of people enjoying this rare open space. It is a much needed sports and social hub in a part of Brooklyn that has very little parkland. Besides, where else can you play kickball in the shadow of the Empire State Building while still being within walking distance of the local dive bar selling cheap beer in styrofoam cups?

How to Get There

The easiest way to access the park is by walking, biking, or taking the subway. Take the 🄛 train to the Bedford Avenue stop or the 🄖 train to the Nassau Avenue stop. The 61 Bus also runs right through the park along Bedford Avenue. Parking can usually be found fairly easily in the surrounding blocks.

Activities

Public space is a limited commodity for folks in Greenpoint and Williamsburg, so the locals take full advantage of McCarren Park. There are several facilities for sports, including seven tennis courts, a soccer field, five ball fields (although two "fields" are made of asphalt), and a running track. There are also handball, basketball, and two nice bocce courts. The Vincent V. Abate Playground is a great place to take the kids and includes animal-shaped fountains for summer cooling. Other activities include sunbathing, picnicking, and people-watching from the numerous benches. On Sunday afternoons you'll find Billyburg hipsters in ironically designed uniforms hanging out and playing kickball. There is a decent year-round farmers market at the corner of Driggs Avenue and Lorimer Street every Saturday from 8 am to 3 pm. The park stays open until 1 am, and it is a fine place to check out the view of the Manhattan skyline on a summer evening.

The McCarren Pool

The McCarren Pool is a dilapidated yet beautiful Art Deco landmark on the rebound. There is an excellent view of the interior of the pool from the Vincent V. Abate Playground. Opened in 1936, the pool accommodated an astounding 6,800 swimmers. It quickly became a popular destination for all of Brooklyn. It closed in the 1980s after a long decline. Various ideas have been proposed to restore the pool, but none have advanced past the preliminary planning stages. However, there is hope. Noemi LaFrance's dance company held a successful performance in the summer of 2005 that opened the space to the public for the first time in many years. For the past couple summers, free weekly 'Pool Parties' featuring indie rock bands (JellyNYC) and somewhat pricey big-name concerts (Live Nation) were so well attended you could've finished *Beowulf* while waiting in line for beer. Even without a full renovation, the pool is now a prime summer destination for events featuring music, film, and dodgeball. All seasons could be covered if a proposed ice-skating rink becomes a reality. Stay tuned.

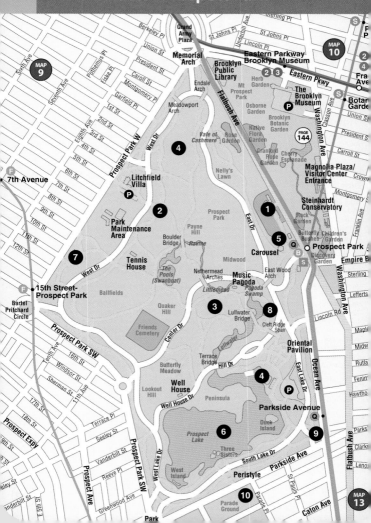

General Information

NFT Maps: 9, 10, 13
Address: 95 Prospect Park W
Phone: 718-965-8951
Events: 718-965-8999
Website: www.prospectpark.org

Overview

Visit Prospect Park on a sunny Saturday and you'll witness thousands of people barbequing, biking, fishing, sunbathing, flying kites, and playing ball games. Designed by famed landscape architects Frederick Law Olmstead and Calvert Vaux (more well-known as the team behind Central Park in Manhattan), the park is the 585-acre home to Long Meadow, Brooklyn's only forest, and the relatively enormous Prospect Lake. In winter, smart locals know to eschew Manhattan's overcrowded and overpriced Rockefeller Center and ice skate at Wollman Rink for less than half the price. Prospect Park is also proud to have the first urban Audubon Center, housed in a brand-new building that opened in 2002.

Getting There:

Depending on where in the park you're visiting, subway lines ②
③ ④ ⑤ ⑧ ⓠ and ⓣ stop around the perimeter. If you drive, there is limited parking available in the park at the Wollman Center (use the Parkside/Ocean Avenue entrance), Bartel-Pritchard Circle, and Litchfield Villa (enter at 3rd Street).

1. Prospect Park Zoo/Wildlife Center

Address: 450 Flatbush Ave
Phone: 718-399-7339
Website: ww.prospectparkzoo.com
Subway: ⓑ ⓠ ⓢ to Prospect Park

The Prospect Park Zoo boasts more than 80 different species of animals in environments mirroring their natural habitats. Open 365 days a year, the zoo opens at 10 am and closes at 5 pm on weekdays, 5:30 pm on weekends from April to October. November to March, the Zoo is open from 10 am to 4:30 pm daily. Admission is $6 for adults, $2 for children aged 3–12, and $2.25 for seniors. Free parking is available on Flatbush Avenue and the park is handicapped-accessible. Eating options are limited to vending machines, but there are plenty of outdoor picnic tables for those who take their own lunch. Purchases at the gift shop contribute to the maintenance of the park.

2. Picnic House

After a year-long renovation, the Picnic House reopened in 2005 and is now better than ever. To reach it, enter the park at 3rd Street and Prospect Park West and head southeast towards the Long Meadow. The Picnic House is available for rent to the public (718-287-6215) and, in addition to its magnificent view of the Long Meadow, features an open interior of 3600 square-feet, a raised stage, fireplace, piano, and restrooms.

3. Long Meadow and Nethermead

The two largest open areas of the park, Long Meadow and Nethermead, play host to group picnics, ball-playing, frisbee-throwing, kite-flying, strolling, lazing about, and everything else people do in big green spaces.

4. Wollman Center and Rink

Located near the Lincoln Road entrance, the Wollman Center and Rink offers ice skating from late November to March and pedal boating from mid-May to mid-October. It costs adults $5 to skate, $3 for seniors and children under 14, and $5.50 for skate rentals. Pedal boating will set you back $15 per hour, plus a $10 refundable deposit.

5. Lefferts Historic House

Lefferts Historic House is located on Flatbush, near Empire Boulevard between the zoo and the Carousel (open April to October, $1.50 per ride). The house is used primarily as a children's museum and aims to impart knowledge about America's history through crafts, workshops, storytelling, displays, and a variety of hands-on activities, like candle-making and butter-churning. The house is open to the public April-November, Thursday through Sunday 12 pm–5 pm, December–March 12 pm–4 pm on weekends and school holidays only, and admission is always free.

6. Prospect Lake

In addition to pedal boat rides, the Lake also accommodates anglers, but don't expect to catch your evening's dinner—there is a 'catch and release' rule that helps to ensure the healthiness of the fish population. Macy's holds a fishing contest every July for kids 14 and under at the rustic shelter located near the Wollman Rink.

7. The Bandshell

Each summer, the Bandshell hosts the Celebrate Brooklyn! Performing Arts Festival, which organizes performances in music, dance, film, and spoken word from June through August. For a $3 suggested donation, this is an inexpensive way to enjoy the Brooklyn arts in the summer months. Check the website for performance details at www.brooklynx.org/celebrate.

8. The Boathouse and Camperdown Elm

One of New York's first landmarks, this majestic building houses the nation's first urban Audubon Center. In addition to exhibits, hands-on activities, and an environmental reference library, the Audubon Center also provides nature trail maps so you can take a self-guided tour of some of the most beautiful areas of the park. The space is also available for rental (718-287-6215).

If you decide against the self-guided tour, at least check out the Camperdown Elm (the result of grafting a Scotch Elm onto an American Elm), a prime example of the exquisite European trees in Prospect Park. You can find it on the southeast side of the Boathouse.

9. Drum Circle

Totally cool, and regularly scheduled—every Sunday from 2 pm to dusk, April–October. Bring your bongos!

10. Parade Grounds

Across Parkside Avenue on the southeast corner of the park, the Parade Grounds offer playing fields and an all-new tennis center, complete with pro shop, clubhouse, locker rooms, a café, and even tennis lessons. The tennis center (718-436-2500) is open daily from 7 am until midnight.

Brooklyn Museum & Botanic Garden

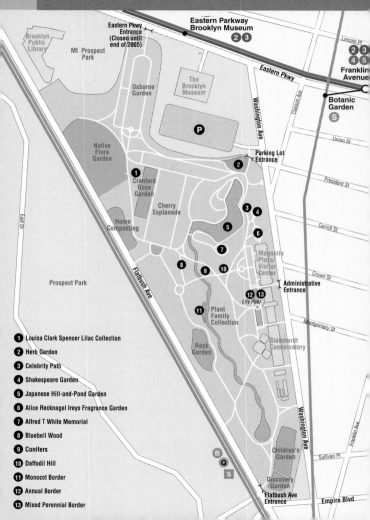

Brooklyn Public Library

Mt Prospect Park

Eastern Pkwy Entrance (Closed until end of 2005)

Eastern Parkway Brooklyn Museum

2 3

Lincoln Pl

2 3

4 5

Franklin Avenue

Eastern Pkwy

Washington Ave

Classon Ave

Botanic Garden

S

Osborne Garden

The Brooklyn Museum

P

Union St

Native Flora Garden

Cranford Rose Garden

1

Parking Lot Entrance

2

President St

Cherry Esplanade

Home Composting

3 4

Carroll St

5

6

7

8

9

10

Crown St

Magnolia Plaza/ Visitor Center

Administrative Entrance

Prospect Park

Flatbush Ave

East Dr

11

Plant Family Collection

12 13

Lily Pool

Montgomery St

Rock Garden

Steinhardt Conservatory

B

Children's Garden

Washington Ave

Franklin Ave

Q

S

Discovery Garden

Sullivan Pl

Flatbush Ave Entrance

Empire Blvd

1 Louisa Clark Spencer Lilac Collection
2 Herb Garden
3 Celebrity Path
4 Shakespeare Garden
5 Japanese Hill-and-Pond Garden
6 Alice Recknagel Ireys Fragrance Garden
7 Alfred T White Memorial
8 Bluebell Wood
9 Conifers
10 Daffodil Hill
11 Monocot Border
12 Annual Border
13 Mixed Perennial Border

Brooklyn Botanic Garden

NFT Maps:	9 & 10
Address:	1000 Washington Ave
Phone:	718-623-7200
Website:	www.bbg.org
Subway:	B Q to Prospect Park; 2 3 to Eastern Pkwy/Brooklyn Museum

Literally rising from the ashes (it was built on the site of a late 1800s ash dump), the Brooklyn Botanic Garden houses a number of diverse gardens, including the Plant Family Collection, Japanese Hill-and-Pond Garden, the Cranford Rose Garden, the Native Flora Garden, as well as the extraordinary Steinhardt Conservatory. Special events include the lovely Sakura Matsuri (Cherry Blossom Festival) in the spring, a lush, Asian flower market and indoor festival celebrating the Lunar New Year, plus plant sales, lectures, and changing exhibits. There is also a charming Children's Garden, offering tours and events just for kids. A welcome oasis from the bustling city, the garden is open to the public Tuesday to Friday, from 8 am on weekdays and 10 am on weekends. The gardens close at 4:30 pm from November to March, and at 6 pm from April to October.

Admission is free on Saturdays 10 am to 12 noon and on weekdays from mid-November to the end of February. Otherwise, entrance fees are $5 per adult, $3 for seniors and students (seniors are free on Fridays), and zilch if you're under 16 years of age. If you visit a lot, you can pick yourself up a "Frequent Visitor Pass," which allows unlimited entry for a year and costs $20 for individuals and $30 for two adults.

While you're there, be sure to check out the Terrace Cafe, serving gourmet lunches and drinks outdoors in the warmer months and in the Conservatory in the winter months.

Brooklyn Museum

NFT Map:	9
Address:	200 Eastern Pkwy
Phone:	718-638-5000
Website:	www.brooklynmuseum.org
Subway:	2 3 to Eastern Pkwy/Brooklyn Museum

In an effort to triple its annual attendance, the Brooklyn Museum recently underwent a $63 million face-lift. The renovations include a new ultramodern glass entrance, complete with minimalist water fountains and a sleek new name and logo. (The "of Art" was officially dropped in 2004.) The museum, which anywhere else would be considered a must-see, has always struggled to lure visitors from Manhattan. Maybe the shiny new galleries and innovative exhibits will help. Recent highlights have included the hyper-realist sculptures of Ron Mueck, Brooklyn landscapes by Francis Guy, and other borough-centric shows; the museum's permanent collection of Egyptian artifacts is one of world's most extensive. The second largest art museum in New York City, the space boasts an outdoor sculpture garden, an appealing mix of wares in its museum shop, and a newly revamped café serving gourmet snacks.

Admission is an $8 contribution for adults, $4 for students, seniors, and Metrocard carriers, and free for members and children under 12. The museum, café, and shops are closed on Monday and Tuesday, open Wednesday to Friday 10 am–5 pm, and weekends 11 am–6 pm. Museum libraries and archives are open by appointment only. If you're up for a double dose of culture and nature, you can buy a combination "Art & Garden Ticket" for the museum and Botanic Garden. Tickets can be purchased only at the museum and cost $11 for adults and $6 for "older adults" and students. Parking at the museum will cost you $3 for the first hour, and $2 each additional hour.

The "First Saturday" series is a popular program of free art and entertainment held during the evening of the first Saturday of every month. These Target-sponsored events feature live music, performance art, lectures, and dance parties set in the elegant Beaux-Arts Court with a cash bar and café. On "First Saturdays," there is $4 flat rate parking starting at 5 pm, and the museum closes at 11 pm. The museum also offers free "Arty Facts" workshops and activities for kids ages 4–7, every weekend from October to June. The Gallery/Studio program provides a variety of cool art classes for children and adults, including free work-study courses for teens.

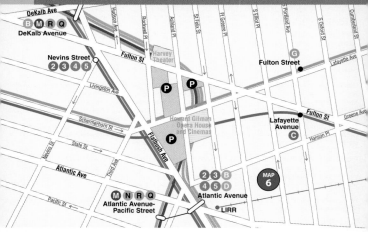

Harvey Theater

Howard Gilman Opera House

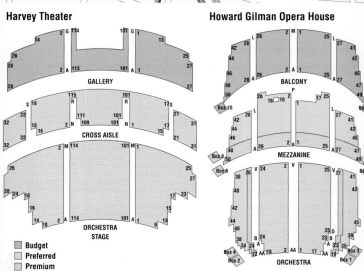

- Budget
- Preferred
- Premium

General Information

NFT Map:	6
Gilman Opera House:	30 Lafayette Ave
Harvey Theater:	651 Fulton St
Box Office Phone:	718-636-4100
Box Office Hours:	by phone, Mon-Fri: 10 am-6 pm, Sat: 12 noon-6 pm
	in person, Mon-Sat: 12 noon-6 pm
Website:	www.bam.org
Subway to Opera House:	② ③ ④ ⑤ Q D M N R to Atlantic Avenue
Subway to Harvey Theater:	② ③ ④ ⑤ to Nevins Street

Overview

Historic Fort Greene is home to the world famous Brooklyn Academy of Music, better known to locals as BAM. A brilliant, thriving, urban arts center, BAM brings domestic and international performing arts and film to Brooklyn by way of two theaters (the Harvey Theater and Howard Gilman Opera House), the BAM Rose Cinemas, and the BAMcafé. For theater and dance buffs, BAM presents two main seasons annually—the *Spring Season* and the *Next Wave Festival*—both of which are three-month celebrations of cutting-edge dance, theater, music, and opera. Live performances at the BAMcafé happen year-round, as do BAMcinématek presentations at the BAM Rose Cinemas. Visit the BAM website for a comprehensive calendar of events and ticket information. A word of warning: If you're buying tickets for performances at the Harvey, be prepared to either spend a little extra on decent seats, or take a cushion with you to prevent fanny fatigue in the cheap seats (something akin to Jeremy Irons' various "medical instruments" in *Dead Ringers*).

Seeing Stuff at BAM

With BAM, "hit or miss" is taken to a new level—ridiculously god-awful Shakespeare adaptations are presented right after the most exquisitely beautiful dance performances. However, it's rarely just boring at BAM—so we definitely recommend going at least a few times to check out the scene. One great way to get your feet wet is at the BAMcinématek series, where showings of first-run films and classic screenings are $10—or just $7 for Cinema Club Members. Another good bargain is the subscription option—you buy at least four different performances from either the Spring Season or the Next Wave and get a good discount for each in the process. The public spaces are cool and the stripped-down Harvey Theater is a must-see (though we reiterate: Pay extra for the good seats!).

Here are the main spaces of BAM:

The Howard Gilman Opera House—The main space. A beautiful setting for music, dance, and just about anything else. Recommended.

The Harvey Theater—As we mentioned, horrific seating upstairs, but a great stripped-to-the-bones renovation makes it look utterly cool. The site of many of BAM's theater performances.

The BAM Rose Cinemas—Great first-run movies, excellent documentaries, revivals, and festivals, good seating, and munchies like everywhere else. A recent partnership with Sundance has made BAM an even more popular destination for film. Not quite Park City, but with Sundance premier films, documentaries, readings, and shorts, it's not too shabby.

BAMcafé—More than just for noshing, the café now hosts the "Dinner and a Reading" series and has free music on many nights.

The Mark Morris Dance Center—It's not officially part of BAM, but it's right across the street and looks cool. Sign up for a class and release your inner Twyla (or Mark, in this case).

How to Get Tickets

Buy individual tickets through the BAM website or by calling the box office. BAM Subscription packages offer a 20% discount when you purchase the same number of tickets for four or more BAM performances. Friend of BAM memberships are also available. Packages start at $75 and benefits include priority notice of upcoming shows and events, no handling fees on ticket purchases, invitations to working rehearsals, reservation privileges at the BAMcafé, and access to the exclusive Natman Room member lounge.

↑ Brooklyn Bridge

↑ Manhattan Bridge

Tillary St

New York City College of Technology

New York City College of Technology

George Westinghouse High School

11 Metrotech Center

DoITT

E-911

NYC Police Academy

Gold St

Prince St

Johnson St

Tech Pl

Brooklyn Family Court

330 Jay Street

6 MetroTech Center

Polytechnic University Dibner Library

PAGE 152

NYC Fire Department EMS

Empire Blue Cross & Blue Shield

Student Union

New York Marriott at the Brooklyn Bridge

Jacobs Academic/Athletic Building

Polytechnic University Rogers Hall

MetroTech Commons

15 MetroTech Center

Myrtle Ave

Brooklyn Renaissance Plaza

Adams St

1 MetroTech Center

KeySpan

2 MetroTech Center

JP Morgan Chase & Co

P

Flatbush Ave

NYC Transit

Bear Stearns & Company

JP Morgan Chase & Co

JP Morgan Chase & Co

MetroTech BID Office

345 Adams Street

Brooklyn Friends School

Old Fire Dept Headquarters

Helen Keller Services for the Blind

Verizon

Verizon

St Boniface Church & Rectory

Institute of Design & Construction

Old American Telegraph and Telephone Building

A C F
Jay Street Borough Hall

Pearl St

Jay St

M N R
Lawrence Avenue

Willoughby St

St Joseph High School

P

P

MAP 5

HRA

P

Parking Garage

P

Red Hook Ln

Smith St

Lawrence St

Bridge St

Duffield St

Albee Square W

Fleet St

Fulton Mall

Gallatin Pl

Bridge St

Hoyt Pl

2 3
Hoyt Street

Elm Pl

Bond St

Livingston St

Schermerhorn St

Educational Buildings
Office Buildings
Cultural and Institutional
Parking

General Information

NFT Map: 5
Address: 12 MetroTech Ctr/330 Jay St
Website: www.metrotechbid.org
Subway: Ⓐ Ⓒ Ⓕ to Jay Street/Borough Hall;
Ⓜ Ⓝ Ⓡ to Lawrence Street;
② ③ to Hoyt Street

Overview

The MetroTech Center is a 16-acre commercial/governmental/educational/cultural/yuppie pedestrian entity adjacent to Borough Hall in Downtown Brooklyn. Built on what was one of the earliest settled ambits in Brooklyn, the factories, frame houses, and shops that used to occupy the ten-block neighborhood were leveled to make way for the MetroTech project in the '70s. Envisioned as a center of research and technology to rival California's Silicon Valley, New York's Polytechnic University signed on as the project's sponsor and remains an integral focus of MetroTech's continued expansion. Needless to say, it is but a faint shadow of Silicon Valley.

Today, the MetroTech Commons—located between Jay Street and Duffield Street—provides the area with a necessary verdant refuge from the surrounding cement, exhibiting proof of the urban center's successful development. The compound is home to such prestigious blue-chip companies as Bear Stearns & Company, KeySpan Energy, JP Morgan Chase, and Chase Manhattan Bank. The public tenants that also reside within the hyper-sterile universe include the New York City Fire Department's central data processing center, the MTA, and the city's Department of Information and Telecommunications Technology, as well as the New York State Supreme Court and Kings County Family Court.

Several scholastic institutions including Polytechnic University, the New York City College of Technology, Brooklyn Friends School, St. Joseph High School, and the Helen Keller Services for the Blind are all located within the campus. There's even a hotel (New York Marriott Brooklyn Hotel) and a church (St. Boniface Church). Empire Blue Cross and Blue Shield is housed at 9 MetroTech Center South, a 19-story edifice that was the first commercial office building constructed in New York City after September 11th, 2001.

In 1990, four historic houses were moved from their Johnson Street homes to now-permanent residences on nearby Duffield Street. Along with Brooklyn's Old Fire Department Headquarters on Jay Street, Poly's Student Center (a renovated Episcopal Church originally built in 1847) right on the Commons, and the beautiful Old American Telegraph & Telephone building on Willoughby Street, the transplanted buildings are part of MetroTech's effort to preserve the community's historic architecture. In an effort to support local emerging artists, the

Commons features rotating outdoor art exhibitions as part of the Public Art Fund. Participants are encouraged to respond to the exhibition space and the surrounding downtown area in their work. The Commons also hosts to several cultural events throughout the year, including the Festival of Traditional Music and the BAM Rhythm & Blues Festival.

The MetroTech Center has played a key role in the revitalization (read: gentrification) of downtown Brooklyn over the last decade, attracting thousands of new businesses and jobs to the area. That said, there are still many local activists who strongly oppose what they call the "Manhattanization" of downtown Brooklyn. If MetroTech's developer, Bruce Ratner, continues with his plans to reshape downtown Brooklyn (see Atlantic Yards), the opposition's voice will likely grow louder.

Schools

Brooklyn Friends School • 375 Pearl St • 718-852-1029
George Westinghouse Information Technology High School • 105 Tech Pl • 718-625-6130
Helen Keller Services for the Blind • 57 Willoughby St • 718-522-2122
Institute of Design & Construction • 141 Willoughby St • 718-855-3661
New York City College of Technology • 300 Jay St • 718-260-5500
Polytechnic University • 6 Metrotech Ctr • 718-260-3600
St Joseph High School • 80 Willoughby St • 718-624-3618

Big Business

Bear, Stearns & Company • 1 MetroTech Ctr • 212-272-1000
Brooklyn Renaissance Plaza • 333-335 Adams St • 718-263-3800
Chase Manhattan Bank • 4 MetroTech Ctr • 718-935-9935
Empire Blue Cross and Blue Shield • 9 Metrotech Ctr • 718-510-8015
JP Morgan Chase & Co • 3 MetroTech Ctr • 718-858-9593
KeySpan Energy • 1 MetroTech Ctr • 718-403-1000
New York Marriott at the Brooklyn Bridge • 333 Adams St • 718-246-7000
Verizon • 7 & 8 MetroTech Ctr • 718-890-1550

1. Brooklyn Bridge

NFT Map: 5

At the time of its construction in 1883, this was the world's longest suspension bridge. Today, it is still widely celebrated for its structural functionality and beauty, and crossing the Brooklyn Bridge remains a quintessential New York experience. We recommend you stroll across by foot from Manhattan and reward yourself with lunch at Patsy Grimaldi's upon arrival.

2. Brooklyn Heights Promenade

NFT Map: 5

This 1,826-foot promenade undoubtedly boasts the best views of lower Manhattan (unless you live in one of the houses behind it). In addition to the skyline, the path offers spectacular vistas of the Statue of Liberty, the Brooklyn Bridge, and the boat traffic in New York Harbor. There are also plenty of benches on which to rest your weary bones and take it all in. The serenity of the path is an engineering triumph considering it's right next to the BQE.

3. Dyker Beach Golf Course

NFT Foldout: G1

Okay, so it's not the best course you've ever played, but considering its location and price, the DBGC is an attractive choice for urban golfers. The course has a good mix of difficult and easy holes and great views of the Verrazano Bridge. For more information, call 718-836-9722.

4. Empire-Fulton Ferry State Park

NFT Map: 5

This little hideaway is nestled between the Brooklyn and Manhattan Bridges and offers dramatic views of lower Manhattan and the underbellies of both bridges. This is also one of the only parks in which you can see the river lapping an actual shore. Every summer, the park is the site of an outdoor sculpture gallery. And, for Brooklynites in love, this is the choice destination to pitch your wedding tent. No pets, bikes, or alcohol allowed.

5. Floyd Bennett Field

NFT Foldout: G6

Formerly marshland, this plot of land has been used for a variety of purposes: Garbage dump, glue factory, municipal airport, and naval base. Today Floyd Bennett Field is part of the Gateway National Recreation Area. At 1,500 acres, this park is hardly ever crowded and contains nature trails, two public campgrounds, a wildlife refuge and grassland bioreserve, and breathtaking views of the bay. FBF is quite expansive, so be sure to take some form of wheels to explore the grounds.

6. Marine Park

NFT Foldout: G5

Marine Park, connected to Floyd Bennett Field, is another great getaway in Eastern Brooklyn. This 798-acre park offers nature trails through the salt marshes, fishing, a running track, the Marine Park Golf Course (the largest in Brooklyn), and organized athletics (most notably baseball). Marine Park is also a haven for bird-watching enthusiasts—over one hundred species of birds have been spotted in this area.

7. Fort Greene Park

NFT Map: 6

The oldest park in Brooklyn, this hilly Olmsted and Vaux park (the same duo that designed Central Park) is a sanctuary for the residents of Fort Greene. During the summer, Fort Greene Park hosts a series of outdoor films and free concerts. The park also offers a farmers market every Saturday on the corner of Washington Park and DeKalb Avenue. www.fortgreenepark.org.

8. Brooklyn Brewery

NFT Map: 2

Since 1987 this independent brewery has been cranking out top-notch beers. Free tours of the brewery's Williamsburg digs happen on Saturdays, every hour on the hour 1 pm–4 pm. And did we mention the free samples at tour's end? The brewery also offers a happy hour every Friday night 6 pm–11 pm (take your own eats!) and organizes the annual Brooklyn Beerfest every September. 718-486-7422; www.brooklynbrewery.com.

9. Piers in Red Hook

NFT Map: 8

Two points of interest here. For gawking purposes only—head over to Red Hook's Brooklyn Cruise Terminal to catch *The Queen Mary 2*, the largest ocean liner doing the transatlantic run these days. If "The Mary" is there, you don't really need an address, you'll see 'er. Secondly, and worth more than just a stare—check out Louis Valentino Jr. Park and Pier, located at the western end of Coffey Street in Red Hook. This pier is great to check out at dusk for a romantic stroll. And if it ever does actually happen, this will be THE place to see The Statue of Liberty come alive and attack Manhattan (i.e. great views).

Brooklyn College at CUNY

NFT Maps:	13 & 16
Address:	2900 Bedford Ave
Phone:	718-951-5000
Website:	www.brooklyn.cuny.edu
Subway:	**2** **5** to Brooklyn College/ Flatbush Ave

Brooklyn College is a part of the City University of New York, the nation's leading public urban university. CUNY comprises eleven senior colleges, six community colleges, a graduate school, a law school, and a medical school. BC was recently ranked by the *Princeton Review* as the third "best value" college in the US based on its quality academics and low tuitions.

Brooklyn Law School

NFT Map:	5
Address:	250 Joralemon St
Phone:	718-625-2200
Website:	www.brooklaw.edu
Subway:	**2** **3** **4** **5** to Borough Hall; **M** **R** to Court St; **A** **C** **F** to Jay St

Brooklyn Law School first opened its doors in 1901 with 18 students. Today, the school has an enrollment of over 1,400. It is headquartered at 250 Joralemon Street and One Boerum Place, the intersection of the landmark Brooklyn Heights Historic District, the Brooklyn Civic Center, and Downtown Brooklyn.

Long Island University - Brooklyn Campus

NFT Map:	5
Address:	1 University Plz
Phone:	718-488-1011
Website:	www.brooklyn.liu.edu
Subway:	**2** **3** **4** **5** to Nevins St; **M** **R** to DeKalb Ave; **A** **C** **G** to Hoyt-Schermerhorn

LIU offers more than 160 programs of study to undergraduate and graduate students within the Conolly College of Arts and Sciences, School of Business, Public Administration and Information Sciences, School of Education, School of Health Professions, School of Nursing, and the Arnold & Marie Schwartz College of Pharmacy and Health Sciences.

Polytechnic University

NFT Map:	5
Address:	6 MetroTech Ctr
Phone:	718-260-3600
Website:	www.poly.edu
Subway:	**A** **C** **F** to Jay St; **2** **3** **4** **5** to Borough Hall; **M** **R** to Lawrence St/MetroTech; **B** **Q** to DeKalb Ave

Polytechnic University is New York City's leading educational resource in science and technology education and research. A private, co-educational institution, Polytechnic offers degrees in electrical engineering, polymer chemistry, aerospace, and microwave engineering. Currently, it is a leader in telecommunications, information science, and technology management.

Pratt Institute

NFT Map:	6
Address:	200 Willoughby Ave
Phone:	718-636-3600
Website:	www.pratt.edu
Subway:	**G** to Clinton-Washington

Pratt Institute is an undergraduate and graduate institution that includes the School of Architecture, School of Art and Design, School of Information and Library Science, School of Liberal Arts and Sciences, and Center for Continuing Education and Professional Studies. Pratt's grounds are endlessly fascinating and beautifully landscaped, featuring a burgeoning collection of outdoor sculpture. Improvements to the campus are all an effort to help garner more contributions to elevate the school's infrastructure and educational programs to the same high level.

SUNY Downstate Medical Center

NFT Map:	10
Address:	450 Clarkson Ave
Phone:	718-270-1000
Website:	www.downstate.edu
Subway:	**2** **5** to Winthrop St

Formally known as The State University of New York Health Science Center at Brooklyn, the center is better known to locals as SUNY Downstate Medical Center. The original school of medicine was founded as the Long Island College Hospital in 1860, one of the first institutions to recognize that medical students should be trained in the field as well as in university lecture halls. SUNY Downstate encompasses a College of Medicine, College of Health Related Professions, College of Nursing, School of Graduate Studies, and University Hospital of Brooklyn.

General Info

Prospect Park Horseback Riding:	www.prospectpark.org/acti/main.cfm?target=horse
Gowanus Dredgers Canoe Club:	www.waterfrontmuseum.org/dredgers
Brooklyn Kickball League:	www.brooklynkickball.com
NYC Park Facilities:	www.nycgovparks.org/sub_things_to_do/facilities.php
NYC Marathon:	www.nycmarathon.org

Nothing beats a summer evening at a Cyclones game on Coney Island. But if you'd rather participate than watch, from dark billiard halls to transcendent yoga studios, Brooklyn has it all. Some highlights include horseback riding in Prospect Park, bocce tournaments in Marine Park in summer or Union Hall in winter, or for the truly adventurous, kayaking the Gowanus Canal. Until McCarren pool is filled with water instead of drugged-out hipsters, the **Metropolitan Pool (Map 2)** in Williamsburg is a steal at $75 per year. If you have a need to relive your childhood, join the Brooklyn Kickball League. For all you Anglophiles, Brooklyn even has three cricket fields. Don't miss the NYC Marathon every November, which runs right through the heart of Brooklyn. Brooklynites stumble out of bed to heartily cheer on runners from around the globe. Finally, don't forget to save your money for season tickets to the Brooklyn Nets, who are tentatively scheduled to move into a controversial new arena (named after a British banking conglomerate, of course) by 2010 at the earliest. Until then, cheer on the Cyclones and show some Brooklyn spirit.

Golf

Driving Range	Address	Phone	Fees	Map
Brooklyn Sports Center	3200 Flatbush Ave	718-253-6816	$10 for 150 balls, $12 for 285 balls	p74

Golf Courses	Address	Phone	Fees	Map
Dyker Beach Golf Course	86th St & Seventh Ave	718-836-9722	Weekend fees $17/early, twilight/$38 morning and afternoon; weekday fees $16–$27, non-residents add $8	15

Swimming

Metropolitan Rec Center	261 Bedford Ave	718-599-5707	Year-round	Indoor	2
Bushwick Houses	Flushing Ave & Humboldt St	718-452-2116	June–Labor Day	Outdoor	3
Commodore Barry Swimming Pool	Flushing Ave & Park Ave	718-243-2593	June–Labor Day	Outdoor	5
PS 20 Playground	225 Adelphi St	718-625-6101	June–Labor Day	Outdoor	6
JHS 57/ HS 26	117 Stuyvesant Ave	718-452-0519	June–Labor Day	Outdoor	7
Kosciusko	Kosciusko b/w Marcy & DeKalb	718-622-5271	June–Labor Day	Outdoor	7
Douglass and Degraw	Third Ave & Nevins St	718-625-3268		Outdoor	8
Red Hook Pool	155 Bay St	718-722-3211	June–Labor Day	Outdoor	8
Sunset Swimming Pool	Seventh Ave & 43rd St	718-965-6578	July–Labor Day	Outdoor	11

Sports · **Tennis**

General Information

• Website: www.nycgovparks.org
Permit Locations: The Arsenal, 830 5th Ave @ 64th St; Paragon Sporting Goods Store, 867 Broadway & 18th St

Overview

There are a decent number of courts in Brooklyn, but they vary greatly in quality. If you're anal (like us), always carry some rope with you so you can strap down the center of the net to a reasonable height—it's usually the first thing to go (with the actual net itself being second) on non-maintained courts. Juxtaposed with all this is one of the crown jewels of NYC tennis, the **Prospect Park Tennis Center (Map 13)**, on the corner of Parkside Avenue and Coney Island Avenue in the Parade Grounds just across the street from Prospect Park itself. The center has a bunch of well-maintained Har-Tru (green clay for you bashers) courts as well as a few hard courts. You can reserve courts in advance with a credit card, take lessons, play competitively, and chill out at the café. In winter the center puts a bubble over the courts so you can play year-round—and permits aren't required for the winter season, so just bring your credit card. Check out www.prospectpark.org for more information on rates, lessons, etc.

Getting a Permit

The tennis season, according to the NYC Parks Department, lasts from April 7 to November 18. Permits are good for use until the end of the season at all public courts in all boroughs, and are good for one hour of singles or two hours of doubles play. Fees are:

Juniors (17 yrs and under) $10	Adults (18–61 yrs) $100
Senior Citizens (62 yrs and over) $20	Single-play tickets $7

Tennis

	Address	Phone	Type—Fees	Map
McCarren Park	Driggs Ave & Lorimer St	718-965-6580	Outdoor, 7 courts, hard surface, lessons offered	2
Ft Greene Park	DeKalb Ave & S Portland Ave	718-722-3218	Outdoor, 6 courts, hard surface	6
Decatur Playground	Decatur St b/w Marcus Garvey Blvd & Lewis Ave	718-965-6502	Outdoor, 1 court, hard surface	7
Jackie Robinson	Malcolm X Blvd & Chauncey St	718-439-4298	Outdoor, 4 courts, hard surface	7
One Van Voorhes Park	Pacific St & Hicks St	718-722-3213	Outdoor, 2 courts, hard surface	8
Gravesend Playground	18th Ave & 56th St	718-965-6502	Outdoor, 8 courts, hard surface	12
Prospect Park Tennis Center	95 Prospect Park W Marcus Garvey Blvd & Lewis Ave	718-436-2500	Outdoor, lessons offered $30–$66 per hour per court	13
Ft Hamilton High School Playground	Colonial Rd & 83rd St	718-439-4295	Outdoor, 4 courts, hard surface	14
JJ Carty	95th St & Ft Hamilton Pkwy	718-439-4298	Outdoor, 10 courts, hard surface, lessons offered	14
Leif Ericsson Park	Eighth Ave & 66th St	718-439-4295	Outdoor, 9 courts, hard surface, lessons offered	14
McKinley Park	Seventh Ave & 75th St	718-439-4299	Outdoor, 8 courts, hard surface, lessons offered	14
Shore Road Playground	Shore Rd & 95th St	718-439-4295	Outdoor, 4 courts, hard surface	14
Lucille Ferrier-Bay	Bay 8th St & Cropsey Ave	718-439-4295	Outdoor, 9 courts, hard surface, lessons offered	15
Breakpoint Tennis Center in Bensonhurst	9000 Bay Pkwy	718-372-6878	Indoor, 8 courts, hard surface, lessons offered $25–$56 per hour per court	16
Friends Field	Ave L & E 4th St	718-965-6502	Outdoor, 2 courts, hard surface	16
Kelly Playground	Ave S & E 14th St	718-946-1373	Outdoor, 7 courts, hard surface	16
McDonald Avenue Playground	McDonald Ave & Ave S	718-946-1373	Outdoor, 7 courts, hard surface	16

Bowling

Bowling fans of all stripes welcomed **The Gutter (Map 2)** to Williamsburg in 2007, the first bowling alley to open in the borough in nearly fifty years. It's a vintage style bowling alley with great brews on tap—what could be better? The Brooklyn Bowling scene boasts a couple of gems. **Melody Lanes (Map 11)** features 26 lanes, electronic scoring, bumpers, an internet jukebox, pro shop, birthday package deals, snack counter, and a dark bar replete with colorful bartenders serving up pitchers of beer and life advice. Melody Lanes will provide everything you could hope for in an old-school bowling experience. Another bowling hot spot is the much larger, much flashier **Maple Lanes (Map 12)**. On Fridays and Saturdays, Maple Lanes features a live DJ, raffles, and a phenomenal Cosmic Bowl—complete with disco balls and dance club lighting. There are 48 lanes, so if the Cosmic Bowl is too wild, standard bowling is available for the tamer set. With a full bar and specials like Sunday Dollar Mania (9:30 pm–close; $6 cover and $1 for each game) and International Bowling Karaoke Superstar (the name says it all), Maple Lanes is definitely worth a night out. They have a slick website to boot: www.bowlmaple.com.

Bowling	Address	Phone	Fees	Map
The Gutter	200 N 14th St	718-387-3585	$6.00–$7.00 per game, $2.00 for shoe rental	2
Melody Lanes	461 37th St	718-832-2695	$5.50–$7.00 per game, $3.50 for shoe rental	11
Maple Lanes	1570 60th St	718-331-9000	$4.50–$6.50 per game, $4.25 for shoe rental	12
Gil Hodges Lanes	6161 Strickland Ave	718-763-3333	$6.00–$8.00 per game, $4.25 for shoe rental	p74
Shell Lanes	1 Bouck Ct	718-336-6700	$3.25–$5.25 per game, $3.50 for shoe rental	p74

Yoga

Yoga	Address	Phone	URL	Map
Bikram Yoga Williamsburg	108 N 7th St	718-218-9556		2
Go Yoga	112 N 6th St	718-486-5602	www.goyoga.ws	2
Greenhouse Holistic & Wellness Center	88 Roebling St	718-599-3113	www.greenhouseholistic.com	2
The Well	25 Broadway	718-387-7570	www.thewellwilliamsburgh.com	2
Bikram Yoga Brooklyn Heights	106 Montague St, 2nd Fl	718-797-2100	www.bikramyogabrooklyn.com	5
Dahn Yoga Brooklyn Heights	130 Clinton St	718-254-8833	www.dahnyoga.com	5
White Wave Dance Studio	25 Jay St	718-855-8822	www.whitewavedance.com	5
Yoga People Brooklyn Heights	157 Remsen St	718-522-9642	www.yoga-people.com	5
Lucky Lotus Yoga	184 DeKalb Ave	718-522-7119		6
Area Yoga	320 Court St	718-797-3699	www.areabrooklyn.com	8
Area Yoga & Baby	320 Court St	718-246-9453	www.areabrooklyn.com	8
Bija	237 Columbia St	718-360-4552	www.bijabrooklyn.com	8
Vayu Yoga Center	259 Columbia St	718-403-0305	www.vayuyoga.com	8
Yoga Center of Brooklyn	474 Smith St	718-834-6067	www.brooklynyoga.com	8
Jaya Yoga & Wellness Center	1626 Eighth Ave	718-788-8788	www.jayayogacenter.com	9
Kundalini Yoga	473 13th St	718-832-1446	www.kundaliniyogaparkslope.com	9
Mind-Body Balance Yoga & Healing Arts	759 President St	718-636-3950		9
Park Slope Yoga Center	792 Union St, 2nd Fl	718-789-2288	www.parkslopeyoga.com	9
Shambhala Yoga & Dance Center	348 St Marks Ave	718-622-9956		9
Spoke the Hub	748 Union St	718-408-3234		9
Yogasana Center for Yoga	90 Fifth Ave	718-789-7255		9
Dahn Yoga Bay Ridge	8206 Third Ave	718-765-0099	www.dahnyoga.com	14
Body and Soul Central	1123 McDonald Ave	718-421-5766	www.body-and-soul-central.com	16
Yoga Spot	1219 Quentin Rd	718-339-6425	www.yogaspotny.com	16

Gyms	Address	Phone	Map
Aay Fitness	283 Ave O	718-627-4442	16
Absolute Power	750 Grand St	718-387-4711	3
Absolute Power Fitness Center	5313 Fifth Ave	718-567-8848	11
Bally's	2163 Tilden Ave	718-703-6700	13
Bally's	1921 86th St	718-266-6300	15
Bally's	2032 Coney Island Ave	718-376-9444	16
Body Elite	348 Court St	718-935-0088	8
Body Reserve	207 Fifth Ave	718-789-7009	9
Church Avenue Fitness	2228 Church Ave	718-941-1200	13
Crunch	691 Fulton St	718-797-9464	6
Crunch	330 Flatbush Ave	718-783-5152	9
Curves (women only)	128 Norman Ave	718-383-0838	1
Curves (women only)	580 Grand St	718-218-8981	2
Curves (women only)	1707 Broadway	718-443-6666	4
Curves (women only)	52 Court St	718-237-9394	5
Curves (women only)	408 Myrtle Ave	718-488-8444	6
Curves (women only)	1542 Fulton St	718-771-0097	7
Curves (women only)	515 Court St	718-852-8777	8
Curves (women only)	317 Flatbush Ave	718-230-9777	9
Curves (women only)	375 9th St	718-788-0003	9
Curves (women only)	6215 Fifth Ave	718-492-7121	11
Curves (women only)	4416 Ft Hamilton Pkwy	718-853-6173	12
Curves (women only)	793 Flatbush Ave	718-282-5822	13
Curves (women only)	7409 Third Ave	718-238-4523	14
Curves (women only)	9801 Fourth Ave	718-680-7975	14
Curves (women only)	7203 20th Ave	718-232-6306	15
Curves (women only)	7304 13th Ave	718-833-4222	15
Curves (women only)	1127 McDonald Ave	718-377-3290	16
Curves (women only)	2645 Nostrand Ave	718-692-2950	16
Curves (women only)	2724 Ave U	718-743-1632	16
Dolphin Fitness Club	316 Bay Ridge Pkwy	718-491-2200	14
Dolphin Fitness Club	8701 Fourth Ave	718-680-5500	14
Dolphin Fitness Club	1645 86th St	718-236-5999	15
Eastern Athletic Club	333 Adams St	718-330-0007	5
Eastern Athletic Club	43 Clark St	718-625-0500	5
Eastern Athletic Club	17 Eastern Pkwy	718-789-4600	9
Empire Fitness Clubs	2825 Nostrand Ave	718-677-1400	16
Equinox Fitness Clubs	104 Joralemon St	718-522-7533	5
Exodus Fitness	510 Metropolitan Ave	718-599-1073	2
Fitness Xpress	286 Warren St	718-237-1127	8
Frenchie's Gymnasium	303 Broadway	718-384-9461	2
Gold's Gym	85 Livingston St	718-596-4653	5
Harbor Fitness	191 15th St	718-965-6200	9
Harbor Fitness	9215 Fourth Ave	718-238-9400	14
Hollywood Fitness (women only)	7414 13th Ave	718-238-1700	15
Kensington Aerobics & Fitness	202 Caton Ave	718-854-8300	13
Kosher Gym	1800 Coney Island Ave	718-376-3535	16
Lucille Roberts Health Club (women only)	540 Fulton St	718-624-4300	6
Lucille Roberts Health Club (women only)	927 Flatbush Ave	718-469-7272	13
Lucille Roberts Health Club (women only)	430 89th St	718-680-8200	14
Lucille Roberts Health Club (women only)	925 Kings Hwy	718-339-0990	16
Maxim Health and Fitness	193 N 9th St	718-486-0630	2
Metropolitan Pool Recreation Center	261 Bedford Ave	718-599-5707	2
New York Sports Club	179 Remsen St	718-246-0606	5
New York Sports Club	110 Boerum Pl	718-643-4400	8
New York Sports Club	324 9th St	718-768-0880	9
New York Sports Club	7118 Third Ave	718-921-5300	14
Otom Fitness Center	169 Calyer St	718-383-2800	1
Richie's Gym	6 Stanwix St	718-666-4485	3
Richie's Gym	5119 Fourth Ave	718-567-7387	11
The Slope	808 Union St	718-783-4343	9
YMCA	125 Humboldt St	718-782-3000	3

Gyms

Gyms	Address	Phone	Map
YMCA	1121 Bedford Ave	718-789-1497	7
YMCA	225 Atlantic Ave	718-625-3136	8
YMCA	357 9th St	718-768-7100	9
YMCA	1401 Flatbush Ave	718-469-8100	13
YMCA Greenpoint	99 Meserole Ave	718-912-2260	1
YWCA (women only)	30 Third Ave	718-875-1190	6

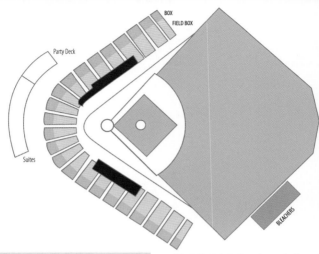

General Information

Website: www.brooklyncyclones.com
Location: 1904 Surf Ave
Phone: 718-449-8497

Overview

Since 2001, KeySpan Park has been the home of the Brooklyn Cyclones, a Class-A minor league affiliate of the New York Mets. With tickets for games as low as $5, you can take your whole family, stuff them full of hot dogs, beer, and pretzels, and still pay less than half of what you'd pay at Shea or Yankee Stadium. The crowd at KeySpan (given its location) couldn't be anything but colorful, and the 'Clones keep things lively and competitive, having clinched four division championships since their inception. Mascots Sandy the Seagull and PeeWee (the Seagull) will keep kids and adults alike enamored with their crazy antics. Imagine the crack of the bat, the roar of the crowd, the holy toots of the calliope mixed with screams from the Cyclone's namesake a mere block away, all this cowering in the shadow of the Parachute Drop. This is American baseball—enough to make Ken Burns weep or bring to mind the immortal words of Roy Hobbs: "My dad…I love baseball."

The 7,500-seat stadium also doubles as a concert venue and has hosted bands such as Daft Punk, the White Stripes,

and Bjork. The Park also hosts the two-day "Across the Narrows" concerts in conjunction with Richmond County Ballpark in Staten Island. Dig it!

How To Get There—Driving

The Belt Parkway to Ocean Parkway S is the quickest route. Stay on Ocean Parkway to Surf Avenue. The stadium is on the south side of Surf Avenue between W 17th and W 19th streets. Parking for all Cyclones games is available in a lot right next to the park. If you're allergic to the Belt, you can take Ocean Avenue from the Prospect Park Expressway all the way to Surf Avenue, but we guarantee it won't be quicker, just different.

How To Get There—Mass Transit

Take the ⓓ, Ⓝ, Ⓕ, or Ⓠ train down to the Coney Island/Stillwell Avenue stop, or ride the 🚌, 🚌, or 🚌 bus, or the Coney Island–bound 🚌 bus to Stillwell Avenue and Surf Avenue. KeySpan Park is just a few blocks west along Surf Avenue using either one.

How To Get Tickets

You can order individual or season tickets for Cyclones games online through the website, in person at the box office, or over the phone.

When most people think of bicycling in Brooklyn, pizza delivery is probably the first thing that comes to mind. To others, it's just a bad excuse to wear spandex. Surprisingly, Brooklyn actually has a rich biking history and culture. The country's first officially designated bike path opened in 1895 along Ocean Parkway in Brooklyn.

Today, bicycling is booming in Brooklyn. Whether they are atop vintage Schwinns, fancy mountain bikes, fold-up bikes, toy bikes, custom-made stainless –steel bikes, or six–foot tall mutant bikes, thousands of Brooklynites now rely on bikes as their main mode of transport. Just be careful weaving in and out of traffic going the wrong way on a one-way street coming home from a bar at 3 am. If you are going to partake in these kinds of adventures, please at least adhere to some biking laws. Notably, don't ride on the sidewalks and make sure you have a white headlight and a red tail light for evening riding. Also, put aside your vanity and wear a helmet. Your skull and brain will thank you. And don't forget to buy the biggest bike chain you can find—if you park your bike on the street, someone will mess with it at some point. You can see the evidence strewn across Brooklyn in the form of single tires and rusted cut chains clinging to trees and poles. That being said, there are plenty of great bike rides in the BK. Zipping around Prospect Park is always fun. From there you can take the path along Olmstead-designed Ocean Parkway to the Coney Island boardwalk. Biking the famous boardwalk is highly recommended; just make sure you go between 5 am and 10 am to avoid the chance of being ticketed. There is a beautiful ride along the Shore Parkway Greenway on a dedicated bike path. On parts of this trip, you will hardly realize that you are still in Brooklyn. There are also some excellent annual bike events that take place in Brooklyn, including the Tour de Brooklyn, sponsored by Transportation Alternatives. For those of you with a more underground biking inclination, follow the tell-tale markings for Critical Mass spray-painted along the Williamsburg Bridge or surf the web to find some bike jousting events under the BQE. There are many bike shops scattered throughout Brooklyn that offer repair and sales services. If you need to rent a bike, take advantage of the reasonable rates at Spokes and Strings in Williamsburg.

Biking around Brooklyn will give you a deeper affection for this great borough. It will also make you truly appreciate the deliveryman's harrowing journeys to get your pizza to your apartment. If it arrives with the cheese still intact, make sure to tip extra next time.

General Information

Bicycle Defense Fund:
www.bicycledefensefund.org
Brooklyn Greenway Initiative:
www.brooklyngreenway.org
Five Borough Bicycle Club:
www.5bbc.org
NYC Parks:
www.nycgovparks.org
NYC City Bike Network Development:
www.nyc.gov/html/dcp/html/bike
NYC DOT:
www.nyc.gov/html/dot/html/bikeped/
bikemain.html
NYBC—New York Bicycling Coalition:
www.nybc.net
Right of Way:
www.rightofway.org
Time's Up:
www.times-up.org
Transportation Alternatives:
www.transalt.org

A Few Bike Shops…

Bay Ridge Bicycle World:
8916 Third Ave, 718-238-1118
Bicycle Station:
560 Vanderbilt Ave, 718-638-0300
Brooklyn Heights Bike Shoppe:
278 Atlantic Ave, 718-625-9633
Dixon's Bike Shop:
792 Union St, 718-636-0067
Recycle-A-Bicycle:
35 Pearl St, 718-858-2972
www.recycleabicycle.org
Roy's Sheepshead Cycles:
2679 Coney Island Ave, 718-646-9430
Spokes and Strings:
140 Havemeyer St, 718-599-2409

Transit · **Bridges & Tunnels**

Henry Hudson Bridge 12

THE BRONX

George Washington Bridge 1

Throgs Neck Bridge 14

Bronx-Whitestone Bridge 13

East River

Triborough Bridge 11

MANHATTAN

Hudson River

Lincoln Tunnel 2

Queensboro Bridge 10

Holland Tunnel 3

Queens Midtown Tunnel 9

QUEENS

Williamsburg Bridge

La Guardia Airport

Manhattan Bridge 7 6

Brooklyn Battery Tunnel 5

Brooklyn Bridge

JFK Airport

NEW JERSEY

BROOKLYN

Upper New York Bay

Cross Bay Veterans Memorial Bridge 15

Bayonne Bridge 17

Marine Parkway Gil Hodges Memorial Bridge 16

Goethals Bridge 18

Verrazano-Narrows Bridge 4

STATEN ISLAND

Jamaica Bay

Lower New York Bay

Free Harlem River Crossings

- A Broadway Bridge
- B University Heights Bridge
- C Washington Bridge
- D A Hamilton Bridge
- E Macombs Dam Bridge
- F 145th St Bridge
- G Madison Ave Bridge
- H 3rd Ave Bridge
- I Willis Ave Bridge

By Foot or Bike

Each day, nearly 4,000 cyclists cross the Brooklyn, Manhattan, and Williamsburg bridges. There's really no more convenient or scenic way to commute to work (or colder, in winter). Each bridge is distinct, with its own unique structure, aesthetic, and even passengers.

• Brooklyn Bridge

The most famous of them all, and the most easily recognizable, it is New York's Golden Gate. Separate bicycle and pedestrian lanes run down the center, with the bicycle lane on the north side and the pedestrian lane on the south. Because of the bridge's landmark appeal, both lanes are often clogged by picture-taking tourists, so cyclists need to stay alert. Rollerbladers and skateboarders must watch themselves over some of the bumpy wooden planks. For the most part, the bridge is level, and the ride is smooth and enjoyable.

Brooklyn Access: Ramp at Adams St & Tillary St or stairs at Cadman Plz E & Prospect St in DUMBO
Manhattan Access: Chambers St & Centre St

• Manhattan Bridge

The last of the three bridges to have bike and pedestrian paths installed. The bicycle lane is on the north side of the bridge, and the pedestrian lane is on the south side. The enforced separation allows cyclists to pedal worry-free, with no dawdling walkers in sight. Pedestrians, in return, don't have to stress about getting run over. One annoyance, which affects only those on foot, is the entrance on the Brooklyn side. To access this, one must climb a steep set of stairs, which is particularly hard on those with strollers or suitcases. Bikers, however, have no stairs to contend with, and can enter and leave Brooklyn without a care.

Brooklyn Access: Jay St & Sands St
Manhattan Access: Bike Lane – Canal St & Forsyth St
Pedestrian Lane – Bowery, just south of Canal St

• Williamsburg Bridge

The bridge of the chosen people (Jews and well-off hipsters), with the biggest bike/pedestrian path of all three. The northern lane is 12 feet wide and the southern lane is 8 feet wide, and both are shared by cyclists and pedestrians. Usually, only one of the paths is open at any given time. When entering or exiting the bridge on both sides, the gradient is quite steep. Going up can be a workout, and going down, depending on how "extreme" you are, can either be exhilarating or scary.

Brooklyn Access: North Entrance – Driggs Ave, right by the Washington Plz
South Entrance – Bedford Ave b/w S 5th & S 6th Sts
Manhattan Access: Delancey St & Clinton St/Suf-folk St

Driving Across the Bridges

Rush-hour traffic is notoriously awful on all of these bridges. Listen to 1010 WINS or Newsradio 880 for the latest updates.

• Brooklyn Bridge

No commercial vehicles are allowed (including your U-Haul rental van, newbie!). With the fewest amount of traffic lanes (6), delays are sometimes unavoidable. If you're coming into Manhattan, you've got easy access to the FDR Drive north, but reaching the BQE on the reverse route is a pain in the ass. Currently the NYPD thinks it's interesting to block one lane of traffic in either direction during rush hour for "security" reasons.

• Manhattan Bridge

Commercial vehicles are permitted. Seven lanes of traffic allow for a reasonable commute. The newly reconstructed lower roadway provides three extra lanes into Manhattan and back into Brooklyn between 5 am and 3 pm. A lane for high-occupancy vehicles (it pays to bring a friend!) has been established for upper roadway drivers between 6 and 10 am on weekdays. The bridge places you directly onto major streets in Manhattan (Canal) and Brooklyn (Flatbush). However, connecting to speedier thoroughfares on both sides, including the FDR and BQE, is far from convenient.

• Williamsburg Bridge

Commercial vehicles are permitted across the Williamsburg Bridge, and the eight traffic lanes are generally fast-flowing. Reaching the Queens-bound BQE on the Brooklyn side is butter. On the Manhattan side, you'll end up on the traffic mess that is Delancey Street. Good luck.

• Brooklyn-Battery Tunnel

Gridlock can be intense, and you have to pay a toll ($4.50), but isn't it worth it to ride the longest underwater vehicular tunnel in North America? It's also damn convenient. On the Manhattan side you'll end up directly on the West Side Highway (with an option to immediately make a left so you can loop under Battery Park and be on the FDR in seconds), and on the Brooklyn side you'll find yourself smack dab on the BQE. Take the tunnel if you need to go to Coney Island, the Verrazano Bridge, JFK, or the ever-popular Home Depot.

• Verrazano Bridge

Giovanni da Verrazano, the first European to enter New York Harbor, would probably turn over in his grave if he knew his name was associated with a bridge that's best known for its traffic and for charging a fee ($9) to enter Staten Island (it's at least free going back to Brooklyn). But the efficiency factor is high, especially if you're looking to head to the Jersey Shore, Washington DC, Colonial Williamsburg, and other points south.

Getting to Brooklyn

It is a decision fraught with peril: Manhattan Bridge vs. Brooklyn Bridge? Brooklyn Bridge vs. Brooklyn–Battery Tunnel? Verrazano Bridge vs. well, nothing?

Consequently, listening to traffic updates (such as 1010 WINS) is the way to go. Because traffic is usually fairly heavy, stations are lax about mentioning buildup on the East River crossings. But if there's a major accident or bridge closure and you tune in, you can be sailing over an alternate bridge with a big smile on your face.

Most of the time, we do think it's worth the $4.50 (unless you're driving back and forth four times a day) to take the Brooklyn-Battery Tunnel. The tunnel gives you instant access to both the West Side Highway and FDR Drive in Manhattan, or the Gowanus Expressway and the Carroll Gardens/Park Slope/Sunset Park area in Brooklyn.

As for the bridges, the Williamsburg to Brooklyn will only give you direct access to the BQE heading towards Queens—for south Brooklyn–bound access to the BQE, you'll encounter some annoying traffic lights. The same southbound BQE access problem exists from both the Manhattan and Brooklyn bridges.

Getting Around Brooklyn

With no highway that actually runs *through* Brooklyn, you've simply got to suck it up if you're heading to Canarsie or the Rockaways. Pick your poison: The Belt Parkway, a route with innumerable slowdowns that takes you 15 miles out of your way but avoids surface roads with traffic lights, or Flatbush Avenue, a direct line from the Manhattan Bridge with one lane for traffic and one lane for double-parked cars and many, many traffic lights.

The same dilemma exists for getting out to eastern Brooklyn and southern Nassau County. The alternative to the Belt Parkway is Atlantic Avenue, which moves more fluidly than Flatbush, especially once you get out past Utica Avenue. You'll experience slowdowns on the Belt Parkway around the Verrazano Bridge, Coney Island, JFK, and other random locations, but it is still usually the fastest, albeit longest, route.

For trips to northwestern Brooklyn, the best options are the BQE north to Williamsburg or Greenpoint or the "coastal route" of Flushing to Kent to Franklin.

The route you choose will depend on your desire to avoid traffic and look at Hasidim standing on street corners (corner of Kent & Flushing), or get the nice city views while waiting in traffic (BQE just south of Kosciuszko Bridge).

The strange thing is that even with the hassle of driving in Brooklyn, it's often much easier than trying to train or bus it when traveling throughout the borough. A straphanger from the Slope has to take an Odyssean journey into the city and back again just to get to Williamsburg a mere 5 miles away—so if you have access to a car, it's probably worth it. Remember that driving in Brooklyn is all about attitude. Keep your wits about you, look out for unparking cars and psychotic livery drivers, and rediscover the true use of your horn—as an additional appendage.

A Few Tips

Most of these tips are probably not worth a damn, but they seem to work for us…
- For northwestern Brooklyn, Kent Street is a good way to save time if you don't want to deal with the BQE.
- Fourth Avenue is a good alternative north/south between Bay Ridge and Park Slope/Carroll Gardens/Atlantic Avenue.
- 9th Street is a quick through-street east over the Gowanus Canal from Carroll Gardens to Park Slope.
- Don't ask us to choose between McDonald Avenue, Ocean Parkway, Coney Island Avenue, and Ocean Avenue when traveling north/south between Prospect Park and Coney Island/Brighton Beach—they can all suck.
- Metropolitan Avenue is a wonderfully scenic way to get to central Queens if you're not in a hurry.
- Traffic on the Gowanus heading towards the Brooklyn-Battery Tunnel always looks like a nightmare, but most of it is not tunnel traffic—get in the far left lane as early as possible to avoid BQE traffic.
- The Pulaski Bridge is a much better way to cross between Queens and Brooklyn than the Kosciusko Bridge, but where does that get you?

Parking in Brooklyn is pretty straightforward—most folks just park on the street, unless they're lucky enough to have their own garage. Street parking is relatively easy in places like Clinton Hill and Greenpoint, and maddening in more densely populated areas like Park Slope, where the only solution is to become one of those parallel-parking ninjas who can shrink their cars to fit any available spot. Here's a tip: When leaving your car overnight, try to avoid parking alongside a park, as these secluded areas seem to invite break-ins (of course, that's why you can usually find a spot there).

The chief nemesis of street parking is street cleaning: The city will tow your car or slap you with a nasty ticket if you're in the wrong place at the wrong time. Posted signs will alert you to street cleaning times. During these times, the alternate side parking rules dictate that you may double park along the opposite side of the street (e.g. If there is no parking on the north side of the street 11–2 on Thursdays, then during that time it is permissible to double park along the south side of that same street). You'll get the hang of this slightly confusing yet strangely graceful system soon if you haven't already. But just in case, you can always check the www.nyc.gov/html/dot/html/motorist/scrintro.html for rules, exceptions, and suspensions. The best tip we can give you is to always have a few dollars' worth of quarters with you—you can usually find commercial spots in Brooklyn, but the parking meter nazis are never far away.

The only area where parking is truly a grind is downtown. Unofficially, you can try the lot at the Brooklyn Bridge Marriott, which charges $14 a day and sometimes accommodates non-guests. Below is a list of some of the key parking lots/garages in the downtown area:

Downtown Parking Lots / Garages

- **Adams Parking** · 66 Adams St
- **Albee Square Parking** · 420 Albee Sq
- **Central Parking** · 9 Metrotech Center
- **Central Parking** · 15 Hoyt St
- **Central Parking** · 71 Schermerhorn St
- **Central Parking** · 75 Henry St
- **Central Parking** · 85 Livingston St
- **Central Parking** · 333 Adams St
- **Central Parking** · 351 Jay St
- **College Place Enterprises** · 48 Love Ln
- **Edison Parkfast** · 71 Smith St
- **Edison Parkfast** · 160 Livingston St
- **Edison Parkfast** · 203 Jay St
- **Flatbridge Car Park** · 120 Concord St
- **One Pierrepont Plaza Garage** · 300 Cadman Plaza W
- **Willoughby Street Parking** · 120 Willoughby St

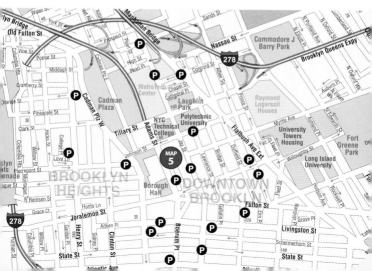

Transit · JFK Airport

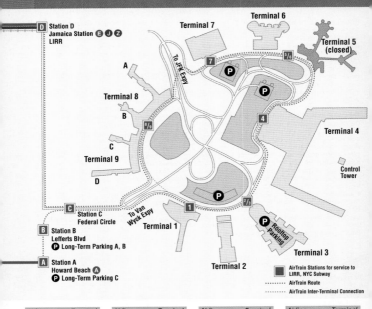

Airline	Terminal
Aer Lingus	4
Aeroflot	1
Aerolineas Argentinas	4
Aero Mexico	1
Aerosvit Ukrainian	4
Air Canada	7
Air China	1
Air France	1
Air India	4
Air Jamaica	4
AirPlus Comet	1
Air Tahiti Nui	4
Alitalia	1
Allegro (seasonal)	4
American	8
American Eagle	8
ANA	7
Asiana	4
Austrian Airlines	1
Avianca	4
Azteca	4
Biman Bangladesh	4
British Airways	7

Airline	Terminal
BWIA	4
Cathay Pacific	7
Cayman Airways	1
China Airlines	1
China Eastern	1
Comair	3
Constellation	4
Continental	4
Continental Express	4
Corsair (seasonal)	4
Copa Airlines	4
Czech Airlines	4
Delta	3
Egypt Air	4
El Al	4
Emirates	4
EOS	4
Etihad	4
Eurofly	4
Finnair	8
Flyglobespan	4
Harmony	4

Airline	Terminal
Iberia	7
Icelandair	7
Israir	4
Japan Airlines	1
Jet Airways	8
Jetblue(San Juan)	4
JetBlue Airways	6
KLM	4
Korean Air	1
Kuwait Airways	4
Lacsa	4
Lan Chile	4
Lan Ecuador	4
Lan Peru	4
LOT	4
LTU	4
Lufthansa	1
Malev Hungarian	8
Max Jet	4
Mexicana	4
Miami Air (charter)	4
North American	4
Northwest	4
Olympic	1

Airline	Terminal
Pakistan	4
Qantas	7
Royal Air Maroc	1
Royal Jordanian	4
Saudi Arabian Airlines	1
Singapore	4
South African	4
SN Brussels Airlines	8
Sun Country	4
Swiss International	1
TACA International	4
TAM	4
Thai Airways	4
Travel Span	4
Turkish	1
United Airlines	7
US Airways/ America West	7
USA 3000	4
US Helicopter	3
Uzbekistan	4
Varig	4
Virgin American	4
Virgin Atlantic	4
Zoom Airlines	4

General Information

Address:	JFK Expy
	Jamaica, NY 11430
Phone:	718-244-4444
Lost & Found:	718-244-4225
Website:	www.kennedyairport.com
AirTrain:	www.airtrainjfk.com
AirTrain Phone:	718-570-1048
Long Island Rail Road:	www.mta.info/lirr

Overview

JFK, once known as Idlewild Airport, is the international air passenger gateway to the United States. It's long been an onus to Knickerbockers due to the fact that it's the farthest of the three airports from the city. However, for Brooklyners it's convenient (because it's close) and a good reason to take a short trip to Queens (as if you haven't already got a good reason). For Brooklyn's international jetsetters, JFK is their pivot since Newark is two boroughs and a pallid state away, and LaGuardia paves tarmac for flights over our land of liberty, alone. With the addition of the AirTrain, taking the subway to JFK has become a breeze if you have a stale two hours to kill.

Rental Cars (On-Airport)

The rental car offices are all located along the Van Wyck Expressway near the entrance to the airport. Just follow the ubiquitous signs. The AirTrain also stops at the rental car lot at Station C, Federal Circle.

1 · **Avis** · 718-244-5406 or 800-230-4898
2 · **Budget** · 718-656-6010 or 800-527-0700
3 · **Dollar** · 718-656-2400 or 800-800-4000
4 · **Enterprise** · 718-659-1200 or 800-RENT-A-CAR
5 · **Hertz** · 718-656-7600 or 800-654-3131
6 · **National** · 718-632-8300 or 800-CAR-RENTAL

Hotels

Crown Plaza JFK · 151-20 Baisley Blvd · 718-489-1000
Comfort Inn JFK · 144-36 153rd Ln · 718-977-0001
Double Tree Club Hotel · 135-30 140th St · 718-276-2188
Holiday Inn JFK Airport · 144-02 135th Ave · 718-659-0200
Ramada Plaza Hotel · Van Wyck Expy · 718-995-9000

Car Services & Taxis

Taxis in Brooklyn to and from the airport do not cost a flat fee like they do to Manhattan. The meter is turned on and you pray that the driver knows the shortest and quickest route (usually Atlantic Avenue to Conduit Boulevard). As a result, the fare can and shall vary greatly depending on where your trip originates in Brooklyn. However, catching a yellow cab in Brooklyn can be tricky, and the majority of Brooklyners rely on car services. Most car services charge around $30 to $35 for a ride from Brooklyn to JFK. But there are some deals out there, so calling around may save you some hard–earned cash. Be SURE to agree on a price ahead of time.

For a listing of Brooklyn car services see page 171.

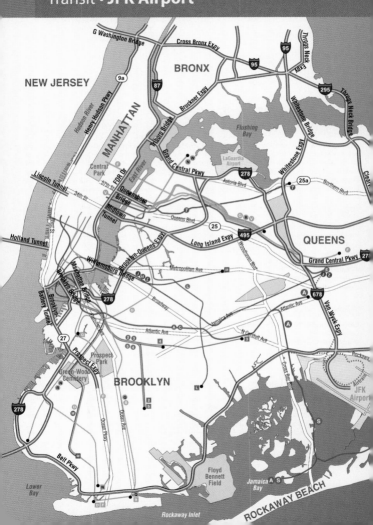

How to Get There—Driving

You can take the corroded pave of the Belt Parkway or the Van Wyck. Stay at home if 'round rush hour—you'll be squandering hours of your life. If the brake-wearing bliss of stop-and-go highway traffic irks you, you might entertain an alternate route using local roads, like Atlantic Avenue in Brooklyn, and drive east until you hit Conduit Avenue. Follow this straight to JFK—it's direct and fairly simple. JFK also has two AM frequencies solely devoted to keeping you versed in all of the airport's endeavors that may affect traffic. Tune into 1630AM for general airport information and 1700AM for construction updates en route to your next flight. It may aid in alleviating the headache you're bound to acquire, anyway.

How to Get There—Mass Transit

The subway + AirTrain, while not the best, is really the cheapest option for patient and attentive Brooklyners. You avoid traffic, save a bouquet of bills, and get to spend some time catching up on your favorite book. The trip will only set you back $7 and there is no one to tip. However, do make sure to check the MTA website or station posters ahead of time for service delays. The Far Rockaway Ⓐ train connects to the AirTrain at the Howard Beach/JFK stop (be certain to board the correct A; there are two; NOT toward Ozone Park). Remain alert when nearing. The Ⓙ Ⓩ line also conveniently connects to the AirTrain at the Sutphin Blvd-Archer Ave stop. Another, though lesser practiced for fantastic reasons, subway option is to take the ⓷ train to New Lots Ave and catch the Ⓑ bus to JFK. This saves a few bucks, but requires the intangible cost of spending well-being as well as requiring you to haul your own luggage onto the bus. Finally, you might choose to take the LIRR doing so will ensure your trip will progress a lot quicker. Do beware, not all trains stop at Jamaica, so double check the LIRR schedule before departing.

Parking

Daily rates for the Central Terminal Area lots are $3 for the first half-hour, $6 for up to one hour, and $3 for every hour after that up to $30 per day. Long-term parking costs $15 for the first 24 hours, and $5 for each 8-hour period thereafter. Be warned, though, many of the ongoing construction projects at JFK affect both their short-term and long-term lots, so be sure to allow extra time for unpleasant surprises. For updated parking availability, call 718-244-4080.

Transit · LaGuardia Airport

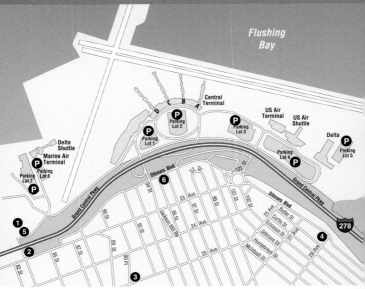

Airline	Terminal
Air Canada	A
Air Tran	B
American	D
American Eagle	C
ATA	B
Canjet	A
Colgan	US Airways
Comair	Delta
Continental	A
Continental Express	A
Delta	Delta
Delta Shuttle	Marine
Frontier Airlines	A
JetBlue	A,B
Midwest Express	B
Northwest	Delta
Spirit	B
United	C
United Express	C
US Airways	US Airways
US Airways Express	US Airways
US Airways Shuttle	US Air Shuttle

General Information

Address:	LaGuardia Airport
	Flushing, NY 11371
Recorded Information:	718-533-3400
Lost & Found:	718-533-3988
Police:	718-533-3900
Website:	www.laguardiaairport.com

Overview

Welcome to Queens' other airport. It is so tiny compared to JFK, it feels like a glorified bus station. The best thing we can say about LaGuardia is that it's named for a most excellent former New York City mayor, Fiorello LaGuardia. Although LaGuardia has improved in recent years, it still has a long way to go before it can hold its own against the nation's other airports. Although LaGuardia remains inconvenient to public transportation, especially from Brooklyn, it's still closer than Newark and much easier to navigate than JFK.

How to Get There—Driving

If it is not jammed, take the BQE to Grand Central Parkway right to the airport. Alternatively, you can take the BQE to Exit 38/Northern Blvd, then follow Northern Boulevard to 94th Street, where you take a left. This will lead directly to the airport.

How to Get There—Mass Transit

For those Brooklynites dependent on their Metrocard, getting to LaGuardia is a long haul. Thanks to poor urban planning, there is no direct subway connection to LaGuardia. That leaves the illustrious 60 bus as the airport's public transportation lifeline. You can hook up with the 60 in upper Manhattan on the ❶ ❷ ❸ Ⓐ Ⓒ ❹ ❺ ❻ and Ⓓ lines. You can also catch it by taking the Ⓝ Ⓦ train to Astoria Blvd in Queens. The one small benefit is that it will take you right to your terminal—not a bad deal for $2. If it is the evening (9 pm–5:30 am) or weekends, a more creative way to get there is to take the lovely Ⓖ train to Jackson Heights-Roosevelt Avenue in Queens, where you can connect to the ⬛ and ⬛ buses operated by Triboro Coach. The Ⓖ train and bus schedule can be erratic and do not stop at all terminals, so check their website, www.triborocoach.com, for appropriate information. Or better yet, just see the next section.

How to Get There—Really

Two words: Car service. Call them, they'll pick you up at your door and drop you at the terminal. If you have the extra cash, it is certainly worth it. Most trips from Brooklyn are in the $25 to $35 range. See page 171 for car service listings.

Parking

Daily parking rates at LaGuardia cost $3 for the first half-hour, $6 for up to one hour, $3 for every hour thereafter, and up to $30 per day. Long-term parking is $30 for each of the first two days, then $5 for each 8-hour period thereafter (though only in Lot 3). Another option is independent parking lots, such as Clarion Airport Parking (Ditmars Blvd & 94th St, 718-335-6713) and AviStar (23rd Ave & 90th St, 800-621-PARK).

They run their own shuttle buses from their lots, and they usually charge $14–$17 per day. If all the parking garages onsite are full, follow the "P" signs to the airport exit and park in one of the off-airport locations.

Rental Cars

1 · **Avis** · LGA · 800-230-4898
2 · **Budget** · 83-34 23rd Ave · 800-527-0700
3 · **Dollar** · 90-05 25th Ave · 800-800-4000
4 · **Enterprise** · 104-04 Ditmars Blvd · 718-457-2900
5 · **Hertz** · LGA · 800-654-3131
6 · **National** · Ditmars Blvd & 95th St · 800-227-7368

Hotels

Clarion · 94-00 Ditmars Blvd · 718-335-1200
Courtyard · 90-10 Grand Central Pkwy · 718-446-4800
Crowne Plaza · 104-04 Ditmars Blvd · 718-457-6300
Eden Park Hotel · 113-10 Corona Ave · 718-699-4500
LaGuardia Marriott · 102-05 Ditmars Blvd · 718-565-8900
Paris Suites · 109-17 Horace Harding Expy · 718-760-2820
Sheraton · 135-20 39th Ave · 718-460-6666
Wyndham Garden · 100-15 Ditmars Blvd · 718-426-1500

Map 1 · Greenpoint

America United	718-349-5900
Java Car Service	718-383-5600
Malone Car Service	718-383-1500
McGuinness Car Service	718-383-6556

Map 2 · Williamsburg

Brooklyn Car Service	718-384-7070
Metro-Line Car Service	718-388-1800
Mobil Car Service	718-349-7111
The New Brooklyn Car Service	718-388-2828
Northside Car Service	718-387-2222

Map 3 · East Williamsburg

Bushwick Car Service	718-386-5002
New Eastern Car & Limousine Service	718-387-0222

Map 4 · Bushwick

Freedom Limousine & Car Service	718-452-5400
New Ridgewood Car Service	718-456-0777
New York Limo & Car Service	718-455-1010

Map 5 · Brooklyn Heights / DUMBO / Downtown

Cadman Express	718-858-7771
Clinton Car & Limo Service	718-522-4474
Promenade Car Service PCS Limousine	718-858-6666
Prominent Car & Limo Service	718-855-7900
River Car & Limousine Service	718-852-3333

Map 6 · Fort Greene / Clinton Hill

Cypress Car Service	718-398-7900
New Bell Car Service	718-230-4499
Pratt Car Service	718-789-4900
Trans Academy Car & Limousine Service	718-875-5800
United Express Car & Limo Service	718-452-4000

Map 7 · Bedford-Stuyvesant

Brown & Brown	718-574-4900

Map 8 · BoCoCa / Red Hook

Bergen Car Service	718-855-1400
Cobble Hill Car Service	718-643-1113
Court Express	718-237-8888
Eastern Car Service	718-499-6227
Golden Express Car Service	718-797-0777
Jerusalem Car Service	718-522-2111
Timely Car Service	718-852-6688
Trans Union Car Service	718-858-8889

Map 9 · Park Slope / Prospect Heights / Windsor Terrace

11th Street Car Service	718-499-3800
Arecibo Car Service	718-783-6465
Castle Car Service	718-499-9333
Continental Car Service	718-499-0909
Evelyn Car Service	718-230-7800
Family Car Service	718-596-0664
International Car Service	718-230-0808
Legends Car & Limousine Service	718-643-6635
Monaco Car Service	718-230-0202
Pacific Express Car Service	718-488-0000
Seventh Avenue Car Service	718-965-4242

Map 10 · Prospect-Lefferts Gardens / Crown Heights

Bedstar Car Service	718-771-2299
Econo Express Car Service	718-493-1133
Transportation Unlimited Car Service	718-363-1000

Map 11 · Sunset Park / Green-Wood Heights

Bell Car Service	718-833-2929
Elegant Car Service	718-833-6262
Mega Car Service Corporation	718-633-2020
Puebla Express Car Service	718-633-4400

Map 12 • Borough Park

Aemunah Car Service	718-633-3135
American Car Service	718-238-4558
Aviv-Express Car & Limousine Service	718-338-8888
Church Avenue Car Service	718-633-4444
Empire Car and Limousine Service	718-972-7212
Golden Express Car Service	718-972-6666
Haimish Car Service	718-972-5151
Jay's Car Service	718-236-5900
Keshet Car Service	718-854-8200
Khageirekh Car Service	718-438-5400
Munkacs Car Service	718-854-4700
New Mazel Car Messenger Service	718-871-9000

Map 13 • Kensington / Ditmas Park / Windsor Terrace

California Car Service	718-282-4444
Five Star Car Service	718-940-0044
Hummingbird Car Service	718-856-6155
Marlboro Car Service	718-434-4141
Mex Express Car Service	718-941-5200
New American Car & Limousine Service	718-972-7979
On Your Way Car Service	718-675-3333
Ontime Car Service	718-891-2600
Rachel's Car Service	718-972-2223
US Express Car & Limousine Service	718-633-4800

Map 14 • Bay Ridge

Alexandria Limo & Car Service	718-491-3111
Apple Express	718-836-8200
Bridgeview Car Service	718-833-3015
Dyker	718-833-3838
Harbor View Car Service	718-680-2500
Marine Limousine & Car Service	718-680-0003
Max Car & Limousine Service	718-921-3399
Ridge Car Service	718-748-4444
Sam's Car Services & Limo	718-238-8888
Your Car Service	718-680-2900

Map 15 • Dyker Heights / Bensonhurst

AR Car & Limo	718-236-8881
Car Service 69	718-234-6666
Gal Hana Car Service	718-491-5900
L&Y Car & Limousine Service	718-837-6464
Libby's Car Service	718-232-2435
Strictly Car Service	718-256-4225
Tripp Car Service	718-256-2190

Map 16 • Midwood

Ascona Car Service	718-336-5353
Best Way Car Service	718-252-6363
ELAT Car & Limousine Service	718-339-5111
Jaffa Car Service	718-376-6400
Jilly's Car Service	718-859-8300
Monte's Car Service	718-258-2880
Rechev Car Service	718-338-2003
TOV (Too) Car & Limousine Service	718-375-8877

Month	Event	Information
January	New Year's Fireworks	*Prospect Park* B-side fireworks in the park.
January	New Year's Day Dip	*Coney Island* The Polar Bears come out and play.
February	Chinese New Year Celebration	*Sunset Park* An annual festival featuring singing, dancing, and fireworks.
March	Brooklyn Irish-American Parade	*Prospect Park* Irish Pride. www.brooklynirishamericanparade.com
March	Opening Day in Prospect Park	*Prospect Park* Lefferts Historic House and the 1912 carousel open for the season
March–April	Central Brooklyn Jazz Festival	*various locations* Event is hosted by the Central Brooklyn Jazz Consortium and musicians from all over the country attend. 718-875-1016
April	Brooklyn Underground Film Festival	*Brooklyn Lyceum* Film Festival of emerging radical global prices films. www.brooklynunderground.org
April	Earth Day Weekend Celebration	*Prospect Park* Various events in Prospect Park honoring Baby Blue.
May	BayFest/Blessing of the Fleet	*Sheepshead Bay* Celebrating the working fishing village of the neighborhood.
May	Brooklyn Bridge Day Parade	*Brooklyn Bridge* Commemorates the bridge's anniversary.
May	Brooklyn Designs	*DUMBO* Furniture designers show off their creations.
May	Haitian-American Independence	*Nostrand Avenue, Empire Blvd – Foster Ave* Haitian Pride Day Parade.
May	Norwegian-American Parade	*Bay Ridge* Even the Vikings get their own parade. www.may17paradeny.com/
May	SONYA Art Studio Stroll	*various locations* The South of the Navy Yard Artists hold an annual event to show artist studios. www.sonyaonline.org
May–June	BWAC Pier Show	*Red Hook* Contemporary art exhibit featuring work by Brooklyn artists. www.bwac.org
Summer	Celebrate Brooklyn	*Prospect Park* Brooklyn's long-running, outdoor, summer-long performing arts festival. www.celebratebrooklyn.com
Summer	Rooftop Films	*Various Locations* Snuggle up on the romantic rooftops of Brooklyn.
June	Brooklyn Cyclones Opening Day	*Keyspan Park* Brooklyn's own start another season.
June	Brooklyn Pride Parade & Festival	*Park Slope* Celebrate gay pride. www.brooklynpride.org
June	Mermaid Parade	*Coney Island* Slap on your fins and celebrate summer. www.coneyisland.com
June	Smith Street Fun Day	*Carroll Gardens* Smith Street vendors sell their wares at reduced rates.
June	Brooklyn International Film Festival	*Brooklyn Museum* International, competitive festival for and by independent film makers. www.wbff.org
July 4th wknd	International African Arts Festival	*Commodore Barry Park* Outdoor cultural festival with live performances, marketplace, and kids events. www.internationalafricanartsfestival.com
July 4th wknd	Fulton Art Fair	*Fulton Park* Public viewing of fine arts and crafts, dance, comedy, drama, and music performances. www.fultonartfair.com
July	The Feast of Giglio	*Williamsburg* Italian festival with parades and food.
July	Nathan's Hot Dog Eating Contest	*Coney Island* The one and only.
July	Siren Festival	*Coney Island* Great live music for free.
July/August	Martin Luther King Jr. Concert Series	*Wingate Field* R&B, Gospel, and Carribean music.
July/August	Seaside Summer Concert Series	*Coney Island* Classic Rock, Oldies, and "Salsa by the Sea".
August	Brighton Jubilee	*Brighton Beach* A sea of crafts and food.
September	Atlantic Antic	*Atlantic Avenue* Huge street fair.
September	Brooklyn BeerFest	*Williamsburg* Brooklyn's answer to Octoberfest.
September	Brooklyn Book Festival	*Borough Hall* Look for the NFT table. www.brooklynbookfestival.org
September	Harvest Fair	*Botanic Gardens* Celebrate the start of autumn with live music and square dancing.

Month	Event	Information
September	Santa Rosalia Festival	*Bensonhurst* Celebration of Italian food (rivals San Gennaro).
September	West Indian Day Parade	*Eastern Parkway* West Indian pride. Lots of good food.
October	DUMBO Art Center Festival	*DUMBO* Art all over the place.
October	Gowanus Open Studio Tour	*Carroll Gardens* Check out lots of cool art for free.
October	Brooklyn Eats	*Brooklyn Marriott Hotel* Annual tasting event featuring food, beer, wine, and beverages from Brooklyn. www.brooklyneats.com
October	Halloween Tours	*Greenwood Cemetery* Get spooked.
October	Ragamuffin Parade	*Bay Ridge* Watch the kiddies parade in their costumes.

Don't let it ever be said that Brooklyn lets a festival go unnoticed. Borough Of Brooklyn: http://www.visitbrooklyn.org/calendar.html. Check out their full calendar if you yearn for more!

Brooklyn Timeline

1609: Henry Hudson explores Coney Island.
1646: Town of Breuckelen chartered by Dutch West India Company.
1776: The Battle of Brooklyn results in British victory.
1814: Steamboat service begins from DUMBO to Manhattan.
1834: City of Brooklyn is chartered.
1849: The Great Cholera Epidemic begins and Brooklyn Borough Hall opens.
1855: Walt Whitman publishes *Leaves of Grass*.
1868: Prospect Park completed.
1871: East River freezes and thousands stream across to Manhattan for the day.
1883: Brooklyn Bridge opens with a one-cent toll.
1887: Peter Luger launches New York's best steakhouse.
1890: Brooklyn candy store owner invents the egg cream, which contains neither egg nor cream.
1896: The borough's first free library begins service at Pratt Institute, with an interior designed by Tiffany's.
1898: In a close vote, residents approve a merger with the City of Greater New York
       (a.k.a. "Great Mistake of 1898").
1899: Brooklyn Children's Museum opens to become world's first museum dedicated to kids.
1902: Air conditioner invented by Willis Carrier, thereby allowing future elderly Brooklynites to flee to Florida.
1913: Subway deal completed that will extend lines to outer Brooklyn and spur massive development.
1914: Topless bathing at Coney Island leads to arrest of 50 men.
1916: Nathan's sells its first nickel hot dog.
1928: Brooklyn Paramount Theatre opens as world's first cinema dedicated to talking pictures.
1930: Brooklyn residential population surpasses Manhattan's.
1933: G line begins service between Brooklyn and Queens. The first train should be pulling in shortly.
1939: Brooklynite Alex Steinweiss designs the first-ever album cover.
1947: Jackie Robinson bravely joins the Dodgers, breaking the MLB's color barrier.
1954: The BQE rips apart Brooklyn, but offers sweeping views of Manhattan to truck drivers
       (Thank you again, Mr. Moses).
1955: Dodgers win the World Series against the Yankees, setting off the biggest street party in Brooklyn's
       history.
1957: Dodgers run off to LA. Depression/nostalgia engulfs Brooklyn to this day.
1960: Airplane crashes in Park Slope, killing 90.
1964: Verrazano Narrows Bridge crowned longest suspension bridge in the world.
1968: Brooklynite Shirley Chisholm becomes the first black woman elected to Congress.
1969: First annual West Indian Carnival.
1973: Park Slope Food Co-op founded.
1976: Rheingold and Schaefer breweries shut down in Brooklyn.
1983: Next Wave festival debuts at Brooklyn Academy of Music.
1987: MetroTech Center finishes development in downtown Brooklyn.
1988: Coney Island's Cyclone, the iconic roller coaster, named an official NYC landmark.
1991: Crown Heights riots rage for three days.
1995: Brooklyn Brewery starts producing tasty microbrews.
2001: Brooklyn Metropolitan Detention Center holds numerous immigrants indefinitely after 9/11.
2002: Nation's first urban Audubon center opens in Prospect Park.
2004: *NFT Brooklyn* published to joy of new Brooklynites looking for an ATM and liquor store in their new 'hood.
2005: "Leaving Brooklyn – Oy Vey!" sign erected on Williamsburg Bridge
2007: Legendary pizzeria DiFara's shut down temporarily by the DOH.
2008: Final summer of Coney Island's famed Astroland? Stay tuned.

Websites

www.abrooklynlife.com • Living it up in Brooklyn.
www.bedstuyblog.com • All things Bed-Stuy.
www.bklyn-genealogy-info.com • Old School website on obscure Brooklyn.
www.brooklyn.about.com • Edited by an avid Brooklynphile.
www.brooklyn.net • America's most creative diasporic culture captured in a website.
www.brooklyn-usa.org • Website of the Brooklyn Borough President with tons of info.
www.brooklyneagle.com • Only daily newspaper devoted to Brooklyn.
www.brooklynheightsblog.com Chronicling America's first suburbs
www.brooklynhistory.org • Website of the Brooklyn Historical Society.
www.brooklynparrots.com • Blog dedicated to Brooklyn's wild monk parrots.
www.brooklynvegan.com • Music, photos, and news from a vegan. In Brooklyn.
www.brownstoner.com • An unhealthy obsession with historic Brooklyn brownstones.
www.clintonhillblog.com • All things Clinton Hill.
www.dailyslope.com • All things Park Slope.
www.freewilliamsburg.com • Essential guide to Brooklyn's hippest 'hood.
www.gowanuslounge.blogspot.com Musings about life in post-industrial Brooklyn
www.newyorkshitty.com All things Greenpoint and beyond.
www.onlytheblogknowsbrooklyn.typepad.com • Park Slope and beyond.

Essential Brooklyn Books

Leaves of Grass, Walt Whitman, 1855
A Tree Grows in Brooklyn, Betty Smith, 1943
The Assistant, Bernard Malamud, 1957
Last Exit to Brooklyn, Hubert Selby, 1964
The Chosen, Chaim Potok, 1967
Boys of Summer, Roger Kahn, 1972
The Gift, Pete Hamill, 1973
The Great Bridge, David McCullough, 1983
The Neighborhoods of Brooklyn, Kenneth Jackson and John Manbeck, 1998
Motherless Brooklyn, Jonathan Lethem, 1999
Brooklyn Dreams, J. M. DeMatteis and Glenn Barr, 2003
Brooklyn Noir, Tim McLoughlin, 2004
Dew Breaker, Edwidge Danticat, 2004
The Brooklyn Follies, Paul Auster, 2005

Essential Brooklyn Songs

"Brooklyn Bridge," Frank Sinatra, 1946
"The Bridge," Sonny Rollins, 1962
"Brooklyn Roads," Neil Diamond, 1970
"No Sleep 'Till Brooklyn," The Beastie Boys, 1986
"Brooklyn Blues," Barry Manilow, 1987
"Brooklyn," Mos Def, 1999

Essential Brooklyn Movies

Arsenic and Old Lace (1944)
The Kid From Brooklyn (1946)
It Happened in Brooklyn (1947)
Bela Lugosi Meets a Brooklyn Gorilla (1952)
A View from the Bridge (1961)
The Landlord (1970)
The Gang that Couldn't Shoot Straight (1971)
The French Connection (1971)
Education of Sonny Carson (1974)
The Super Cops (1974)
The Lords of Flatbush (1975)
Dog Day Afternoon (1975)
Saturday Night Fever (1977)
The Sentinel (1977)
Nunzio (1978)
The Warriors (1979)
Turk 182! (1985)
Brighton Beach Memoirs (1986)
Moonstruck (1987)
Do the Right Thing (1989)
Last Exit to Brooklyn (1989)
Goodfellas (1990)
Straight Out Of Brooklyn (1991)
Crooklyn (1994)
Little Odessa (1994)
Smoke/Blue in the Face (1995)
Someone Else's America (1995)
Vampire in Brooklyn (1995)
The Search For One-Eyed Jimmy (1996)
Soul in the Hole (1997)
Pi (1998)
Girlfight (2000)
Requiem for a Dream (2000)
Everyday People (2004)
The Squid and the Whale (2005)
Block Party (2005)
Half Nelson (2006)

Map 1 • Greenpoint

Automotive High	50 Bedford Ave
PS 110 The Monitor	124 Monitor St
PS 31 Samuel F Dupont	75 Meserole Ave
PS 34 Oliver H Perry	131 Norman Ave
St Stanislaus Kostka	10 Newell St

Map 2 • Williamsburg

Bais Yakov of Khal Adas Yereim	563 Bedford Ave
Be'Ikvei Hatzoin	31 Division Ave
Beth Chana	204 Keap St
Beth Chana	620 Bedford Ave
Bnos Chayil	345 Hewes St
Bnos Yaakov Education Center	274 Keap St
Bnos Yakov School for Girls	62 Harrison Ave
El Puente Academy for Peace & Justice	183 S 3rd St
Harry Van Arsdale High	257 N 6th St
Jewish Center for Special Education	430 Kent Ave
JHS 126 John Ericsson	424 Leonard St
JHS 50 John D Wells	183 S 3rd St
Juan Morel Campos Secondary	215 Heyward St
Kedishas Naftoli	117 Keap St
Mesivta Nachlas Yacov-A Yerim	185 Wilson St
Mesivta Tifereth Zvi Spinka	199 Lee Ave
Northside Catholic Academy	10 Withers St
Nuestros Ninos Child Development	384 S 4th St
PS 16 Leonard Dunkly	157 Wilson St
PS 17 Henry D Woodworth	208 N 5th St
PS 19 Roberto Clemente	325 S 3rd St
PS 319	360 Keap St
PS 380 John Wayne	370 Marcy Ave
PS 84 Jose De Diego	250 Berry St
St Peter & Pauls	288 Berry St
St Vincent de Paul RC	180 N 7th St
Talmud Torah Dnitra	712 Wythe Ave
Talmud Torah of Kasho	324 Penn St
Talmud Torah Toldois Yakov Yos	105 Heyward St
Transfiguration	250 Hooper St
United Talmudical Academy	227 Marcy Ave
United Talmudical Academy	590 Bedford Ave
United Talmudical Academy	82 Lee Ave
United Talmudical Academy-Will	212 Williamsburg St E
Williamsburg High School of Architecture & Design	257 N 6th St
Williamsburg Prep	257 N 6th St
Yeshiva Ateres Tzvi	162 Ross St
Yeshiva Beth Joseph Zvi Dushinsky	135 Ross St
Yeshiva Beth Yitchak Dspinka	575 Bedford Ave
Yeshiva Bnai Yesucher	467 Bedford Ave
Yeshiva Bnos Ahavas	12 Franklin Ave
Yeshiva Chasdei Tzvi	219 Keap St
Yeshiva Gedolah Ohr Yisroel	281 Rutledge St
Yeshiva Jesode Hatorah	505 Bedford Ave
Yeshiva Kehilath Yaakov	206 Wilson St
Yeshiva & Mesivta Arugath	40 Lynch St
Yeshiva Ohel Shaim	128 Hewes St
Yeshiva Tzemach Tzadik Viznitz	186 Ross St

Map 3 • East Williamsburg

Beginning with Children Charter	11 Bartlett St
Boricua College	9 Graham Ave
Brooklyn Temple	3 Lewis Ave
Bushwick Leaders High	797 Bushwick Ave
Central Brooklyn SDA	130 Boerum St
Cong Ahavas Shulem Dna Tiferes Bnos	545 Broadway
Enterprise, Business and Technology High	850 Grand St
IS 347 School of Humanities	35 Starr St
IS 349 Math, Science, and Technology	35 Starr St
JHS 318 Eugenio Maria Dehostos	101 Walton St
JHS 49 William J Gaynor	223 Graham Ave
MS 577	320 Manhattan Ave
MS 582	207 Bushwick Ave
Progress High School for Professional Careers	850 Grand St
PS 120 Carlos Tapia	18 Beaver St
PS 132 Conselyea	320 Manhattan Ave
PS 145 Andrew Jackson	100 Noll St
PS 147 Issac Remsen	325 Bushwick Ave
PS 18 Edward Bush	101 Maujer St
PS 196 Ten Eyck	207 Bushwick Ave
PS 250 George H Lindsay	108 Montrose Ave
PS 257 John F Hylan	60 Cook St
PS 373 Brooklyn Transition Center	185 Ellery St
PS 59 William Floyd	211 Throop Ave
School for Legal Studies	850 Grand St
School of Legal Studies	850 Grand St
St Cecilia	1-15 Monitor St
St John the Evangelist	195 Maujer St
St Joseph and Dominic Catholic Academy	140 Montrose Ave
St Mark's Lutheran	626 Bushwick Ave
St Nicholas Elementary	287 Powers St
United Talmudical Academy	110 Throop Ave

Map 4 • Bushwick

Academy of Urban Planning	400 Irving Ave
Acorn High School for Social Justice	1396 Broadway
All City Leadership Secondary	1474 Gates Ave
Bushwick Community High	231 Palmetto St
Bushwick School for Social Justice	400 Irving Ave
Charles Churn Christian Academy	1052 Greene Ave
EBC High School for Public Service	1155 DeKalb Ave
JHS 162 The Willoughby	1390 Willoughby Ave
JHS 291 Roland Hayes	231 Palmetto St
JHS 296 The Halsey	125 Covert St
JHS 383 Phillippa Schuyler	1300 Greene Ave
New York Harbor	400 Irving Ave
PS 106 Edward Everett Hale	1314 Putnam Ave
PS 116 Elizabeth L Farrell	515 Knickerbocker Ave
PS 123 Suydam	100 Irving Ave
PS 151 Lyndon B Johnson	763 Knickerbocker Ave
PS 274 Kosciusko	800 Bushwick Ave
PS 299 Thomas Waren Field	88 Woodbine St
PS 376	194 Harman St
PS 377 Alejandrina B Degautier	200 Woodbine St
PS 45 Horace E Greene	84 Schaefer St

PS 5 Dr Ronald McNair	820 Hancock St
PS 75 Mayda Cortiella	95 Grove St
PS 86 The Irvington	220 Irving Ave
St Brigid	438 Grove St
St Elizabeth Seton	751 Knickerbocker Ave
St Frances Cabrini	181 Suydam St
St Mark's Lutheran	66 Weirfield

Map 5 • Brooklyn Heights / DUMBO / Downtown

A Fantis Parochial	195 State St
Brooklyn Friends	375 Pearl St
Brooklyn International High	49 Flatbush Ave Ext
Brooklyn Law	250 Joralemon St
Freedom Academy	116 Nassau St
George Westinghouse Career and Technical Education High	105 Tech Pl
Institute of Design & Construction	141 Willoughby St
Long Island University	1 University Plz
NYC Technical College	300 Jay St
Pacific High	112 Schermerhorn St
Packer Collegiate Institute	170 Joralemon St
Polytechnic University	6 Metrotech Ctr
PS 287 Bailey K Ashford	50 Navy St
PS 307 Daniel Hale Williams	209 York St
PS 369 Coy L Cox	383 State St
PS 67 Charles A Dorsey	51 St Edwards St
PS 8 Robert Fulton	37 Hicks St
Satellite West Middle	209 York St
Science Skills High	49 Flatbush Ave Ext
St Ann's	124 Henry St
St Ann's	129 Pierrepont St
St Charles Borromeo	23 Sidney Pl
St Francis College	180 Remsen St
St Joseph High	80 Willoughby St
The Urban Assembly School for Law & Justice	50 Navy St
The Urban Assembly School of Music & Art	49 Flatbush Ave Ext

Map 6 • Fort Greene / Clinton Hill

Benjamin Banneker Academy	71 Clinton Ave
Bethel Elementary	457 Grand Ave
Bishop Loughlin Memorial High	357 Clermont Ave
Bnei Shimon Yisroel of Sopron	18 Warsoff Pl
Bnos Square of Williamsburg	2 Franklin Ave
Brooklyn Preparatory High	300 Willoughby Ave
Brooklyn Technical High	29 Ft Greene Pl
Francis Scott Key Junior High	300 Willoughby Ave
Hanson Place Elementary	38 Lafayette Ave
Hensen Preparatory	144 St Felix St
Hychel Hatorah	70 Franklin Ave
JHS 113	300 Adelphi St
JHS 265 Susan S McKinney	101 Park Ave
Metropolitan Corporate Academy High	362 Schermerhorn St
Pratt Institute	200 Willoughby Ave

PS 11 Purvis J Behan	419 Waverly Pl
PS 157 Benjamin Franklin	850 Kent Ave
PS 20 Clinton Hill	225 Adelphi St
PS 256 Benjamin Banneker	114 Kosciusko St
PS 270 Johann Dekalb	241 Emerson Pl
PS 297 Abraham Stockton	700 Park Ave
PS 46 Edward C Blum	100 Clermont Ave
PS 54 Samuel C Barnes	195 Sandford St
PS 56 Lewis H Latimer	170 Gates Ave
PS 753 School for Career Development	510 Clermont Ave
Queen of All Saints	300 Vanderbilt Ave
Satellite Three	170 Gates Ave
St Joseph's College	245 Clinton Ave
Talmud Torah Toldos Hillel-Krasna	35 Hewes St
United Talmudical Academy	45 Williamsburg St W

Map 7 • Bedford-Stuyvesant

Bedford Academy High	1119 Bedford Ave
Bethel Christian Academy	344 Tompkins Ave
Boys & Girls High	1700 Fulton St
Bridge Street Prep	277 Stuyvesant Ave
Brooklyn Academy High	832 Marcy Ave
Brooklyn Excelsior Charter	856 Quincy St
Clara Muhammad School of Masjid Khalifah	1174 Bedford Ave
College of New Rochelle	1368 Fulton St
Concord Elementary Day	833 Dr G C Taylor Blvd
Dr CR Johnson Christian Academy	600 Lafayette Ave
Empire State College	20 New York Ave
Frederick Douglass Academy IV	1014 Lafayette Ave
JHS 258 David Ruggles	141 Macon St
JHS 33 Mark Hopkins	70 Tompkins Ave
JHS 57 Whitelaw Reid	125 Stuyvesant Ave
MS 143 Performing & Fine Arts	800 Gates Ave
MS 267 Math, Science & Tech	800 Gates Ave
Mt Pisgah Christian Academy	760 DeKalb Ave
PS 21 Crispus Attucks	180 Chauncey St
PS 23 Carter C Woodson	545 Willoughby Ave
PS 25 Eubie Blake	787 Lafayette Ave
PS 26 Jesse Owens	1014 Lafayette Ave
PS 262 El Hajj Malik Shabazz	500 Macon St
PS 3 The Bedford Village	50 Jefferson Ave
PS 304 Casimir Pulaski	280 Hart St
PS 305 Dr Peter Ray	344 Monroe St
PS 308 Clara Cardwell	616 Quincy St
PS 309 George E Wibecan	794 Monroe St
PS 35 Stephen Decatur	272 McDonough St
PS 44 Marcus Garvey	432 Monroe St
PS 81 Thaddeus Stevens	990 DeKalb Ave
PS 93 William H Prescott	31 New York Ave
School of Business, Finance and Entrepreneurship	125 Stuyvesant Ave
St John the Baptist	82 Lewis Ave
Tabernacle Elementary	264 Lexington Ave
The Urban Assembly School for the Urban Environment	70 Tompkins Ave
Williston Academy	1 Jefferson Ave

177

General Information • **Schools**

Map 8 • BoCoCa / Red Hook

Agnes Y Humphrey School for Leadership	27 Huntington St
Brooklyn School for Global Studies	284 Baltic St
Brooklyn Secondary School for Collaborative Studies	610 Henry St
Cobble Hill School for American Studies	347 Baltic St
Hannah Senesh	215 Pacific St
Mary McDowell Center for Learning	20 Bergen St
New Horizons	317 Hoyt St
PS 146	610 Henry St
PS 15 Patrick F Daly	71 Sullivan St
PS 261 Philp Livingston	314 Pacific St
PS 29 John M Harrigan	425 Henry St
PS 38 The Pacific	450 Pacific St
PS 58 The Carroll School	330 Smith St
School for International Research	284 Baltic St
School for International Studies	284 Baltic St
South Brooklyn Community High	173 Conover St
The Sterling	299 Pacific St

Map 9 • Park Slope / Prospect Heights / Windsor Terrace

Acorn High	561 Grand Ave
Al-Madinah	383 Third Ave
Berkeley-Carroll	181 Lincoln Pl
Brooklyn Conservatory of Music	58 Seventh Ave
Brooklyn Free School	120 16th St
Brooklyn High School of the Arts	345 Dean St
Cathedral	910 Union St
Holy Name	241 Prospect Park W
IS 340	227 Sterling Pl
JHS 266 Park Place Community	62 Park Pl
Magnet School of Math, Sciencey & Design Technolog	511 Seventh Ave
The Math & Science Exploratory School	345 Dean St
Montessori School of NY	105 Eighth Ave
MS 51 William Alexander	350 Fifth Ave
MS 571	80 Underhill Ave
New Voices	330 18th St
Park Slope Christian Academy	98 Fifth Ave
Poly Prep--Lower	50 Prospect Park W
PS 107 John W Kimball	1301 Eighth Ave
PS 124 Silas B Dutcher	515 Fourth Ave
PS 133 William A Butler	375 Butler St
PS 154 Magnet School for Science & Technology	1625 11th Ave
PS 22	443 St Marks Ave
PS 282 Park Slope	180 Sixth Ave
PS 295/MS 827	330 18th St
PS 321 William Penn	180 Seventh Ave
PS 372 The Children's School	512 Carroll St
PS 39 Henry Bristow	417 Sixth Ave
PS 77K Special Education School	62 Park Pl
PS 9 Teunis G Bergen	80 Underhill Ave
Rivendell	421 7th St

Secondary School for Journalism	237 Seventh Ave
Secondary School for Law (HS 462)	237 Seventh Ave
Secondary School for Research	237 Seventh Ave
Soterios Ellenas Parochial	224 18th St
St Francis Xavier	763 President St
St Saviour Elementary	701 Eighth Ave
St Saviour High	588 6th St
St Thomas Aquinas	211 8th St

Map 10 • Prospect-Lefferts Gardens / Crown Heights

Arista Prep	275 Kingston Ave
Arista Prep	755 Eastern Pkwy
Beth Rivkah	470 Lefferts Ave
Beth Rivkah High	310 Crown St
Brooklyn Academy of Science and the Environment	883 Classon Ave
Brooklyn Jesuit Prep	560 Sterling Pl
Clara Barton High	901 Classon Ave
Cush Campus	221 Kingston Ave
Darchai Menachem	823 Eastern Pkwy
Educational Inst Oholei Torah	667 Eastern Pkwy
Elijah Stroud Middle	750 Classon Ave
Epiphany Lutheran Elementary	721 Lincoln Pl
Full Gospel Christian Academy	836 Franklin Ave
Hebron SDA Bilingual	920 Park Pl
International Arts Business School	600 Kingston Ave
International High School at Prospect Heights	883 Classon Ave
Irving	402 Fenimore St
John Dinkins School of Arts	395 Maple St
John Hus Moravian	153 Ocean Ave
League School	567 Kingston Ave
Lubavitcher Yeshiva	570 Crown St
MACADEMY	1313 Union St
Machon Chana	433 Crown St
Medgar Evers College	1650 Bedford Ave
Middle College High at Medgar Evers	1186 Carroll St
MS 2	655 Parkside Ave
MS 61 Gladstone H Atwell	400 Empire Blvd
Paul Robeson High	150 Albany Ave
PS 138 Brooklyn	760 Prospect Pl
PS 161 The Crown School	330 Crown St
PS 241 Emma L Johnston	976 President St
PS 289 George V Brower	900 St Marks Ave
PS 316 Elijah Stroud	750 Classon Ave
PS 375 Jackie Robinson	46 McKeever Pl
PS 397 Foster-Laurie	490 Fenimore St
PS 92 Adrian Hegeman	601 Parkside Ave
School for Democracy and Leadership	600 Kingston Ave
School for Human Rights	600 Kingston Ave
St Francis De Sales School for the Deaf	260 Eastern Pkwy
St Francis of Assisi	400 Lincoln Rd
St Gregory the Great Elementary	991 St Johns Pl
St Mark's	1346 President St
SUNY Downstate Medical Center	450 Clarkson Ave
United Lubavitcher Yeshivoth	885 Eastern Pkwy

WEB Dubois Academic High	402 Eastern Pkwy
Yeshiva Chanoch Lenaar	876 Eastern Pkwy

Map 11 • Sunset Park / Green-Wood Heights

Al Madrasa Al Islamiya	5224 Third Ave
Al-Noor	675 Fourth Ave
Bay Ridge Christian Academy	6324 Seventh Ave
Hellenic Classical Charter	646 Fifth Ave
IS 136 Charles O Dewey	4004 Fourth Ave
JHS 220 John J Pershing	4812 Ninth Ave
JHS 88 Peter Rouget	544 Seventh Ave
Our Lady of Perpetual Help	5902 Sixth Ave
PS 1 The Bergen	309 47th St
PS 169 Sunset Park	4305 Seventh Ave
PS 172	825 Fourth Ave
PS 24	427 38th St
PS 371 Lillian L Rashkis	355 37th St
PS 506 School of Journalism and Technology	330 59th St
PS 69 Vincent D Grippo	884 63rd St
PS 94 The Henry Longfellow	5010 Sixth Ave
St Agatha's	736 48th St
St Michael	4222 Fourth Ave
Sunset Park Prep	4004 Fourth Ave
Tomer Dvora	4500 Ninth Ave
Yeshiva Machzikel Hadas	695 Sixth Ave

Map 12 • Borough Park

Bais Brocho of Karlin Stolin	4314 10th Ave
Bais Ruchel School of Boro Park	5301 14th Ave
Bais Sarah-Educ School for Girls	1363 50th St
Bais Yaakov D'Gur High	1975 51st St
Bais Yaakov D'Khal Adas Yereim	1169 43rd St
Bais Yaakov of Brooklyn	1362 49th St
Beth Jacob High	4421 15th Ave
Beth Jacob of Boro Park	1371 46th St
Bnos Zion of Bobov	5000 14th Ave
Franklin Delano Roosevelt High	5800 20th Ave
Hebrew Academy for Special Children	5902 14th Ave
Holy Spirit	1668 46th St
JHS 223 The Montauk School	4200 16th Ave
Martin De Porres High	500 19th St
Mosdos Bnos Frima	1377 42nd St
Mosdos Chasidei SQ-TYY Boro Park	1373 43rd St
PS 105 The Blythebourne	1031 59th St
PS 121 Nelson A Rockefeller	5301 20th Ave
PS 131	4305 Ft Hamilton Pkwy
PS 160 William T Sampson	5105 Ft Hamilton Pkwy
PS 164 Caesar Rodney	4211 14th Ave
PS 180 Homewood	5601 16th Ave
PS 192	4715 18th Ave
PS 230 Doris L Cohen	1 Albermarle Rd
PS 48 Mapelton	6015 18th Ave
St Catharine of Alexandria	1053 41st St
Tiferes Bais Yaakov High	4508 16th Ave
Tomer Devora High School for Girls	5801 16th Ave
United Talmudical Academy	5411 Ft Hamilton Pkwy

Viznitzer Chaider Tiferes Yisroel	1424 43rd St
Yeshiva Bais Yitzchok	1413 45th St
Yeshiva Beis Meir (Boys)	1327 38th St
Yeshiva Beth Hillel of Krasna	1364 42nd St
Yeshiva Beth Hillel of Krasna	1371 42nd St
Yeshiva Boyan	1205 44th St
Yeshiva Ch San Sofer	1876 50th St
Yeshiva Derech Chaim	1573 39th St
Yeshiva Imrei Yosef Spinka	5801 15th Ave
Yeshiva Karlin Stolin	1818 54th St
Yeshiva Kehilath Yakov	4706 10th Ave
Yeshiva Machzikei Hadas	1601 42nd St
Yeshiva Tiferes Bunim	5202 13th Ave
Yeshiva Tifereth Elimelech	1650 56th St
Yeshiva Toras Chesed	5506 16th Ave
Yeshiva Yesode Hatorah	1350 50th St
Yeshivas Novominsk-Kol Yehuda	1569 47th St
Yeshivat Ohel Torah	1760 53rd St

Map 13 • Kensington / Ditmas Park / Windsor Terrace

Bais Yaakov D'Rav Meir High	85 Parkville Ave
Bais Yaakov of 18th Ave	4419 18th Ave
Bnos Yerushalayim	600 McDonald Ave
Brooklyn College	2900 Bedford Ave
Brooklyn College Academy	2900 Bedford Ave
Cortelyou Early Childhood Cent	1110 Cortelyou Rd
Cycle Educ Center	2414 Church Ave
Erasmus High	911 Flatbush Ave
Flatbush Catholic Academy	2520 Church Ave
Get Set Kindergarten	2301 Snyder Ave
Holy Innocents	249 E 17th St
Immaculate Heart of Mary	3002 Ft Hamilton Pkwy
IS 246 Walt Whitman	72 Veronica Pl
JHS 62 The Ditmas	700 Cortelyou Rd
K134	4001 18th Ave
Midwood High	2839 Bedford Ave
Our Lady of Refuge	1087 Ocean Ave
PS 130 The Parkside	70 Ocean Pkwy
PS 139 Alexine A Fenty	330 Rugby Rd
PS 179 Kensington	202 Ave C
PS 217 Colonel David Marcus	1100 Newkirk Ave
PS 245	49 E 17th St
PS 249 The Caton School	18 Marlborough Rd
PS 269 Nostrand	1957 Nostrand Ave
PS 315	2310 Glenwood Rd
PS 399 Stanley Eugene Clark	2707 Albemarle Rd
PS 6	43 Snyder Ave
School of Science and Technology	725 E 23rd St
Shaare Torah Girls Elementary	222 Ocean Pkwy
St Jerome	465 E 29th St
St Rose of Lima Elementary	259 Parkville Ave
UCP NYC Brooklyn Childrens Pro	160 Lawrence Ave
Yeshiva Ketana of Bensonhurst	953 Coney Island Ave
Yeshiva Torah Temimah	555 Ocean Pkwy
Yeshiva Torah Vodaath	425 E Ninth St
Yeshivat Shaare Torah Girls' D	500 Church Ave

General Information · **Schools**

Map 14 · Bay Ridge

Bay Ridge Prep High	7420 Fourth Ave
Bay Ridge Prep--Lower	8101 Ridge Blvd
Fontbonne Hall	9901 Shore Rd
Fort Hamilton High	8301 Shore Rd
High School of Telecommunications	350 67th St
Holy Cross Parochial	8502 Ridge Blvd
IS 30 Mary White Ovington	415 Ovington Ave
Lutheran Elementary	440 Ovington Ave
New Hope Christian Academy	257 Bay Ridge Ave
Our Lady of Angels	337 74th St
Poly Prep Country Day	9216 Seventh Ave
PS 102 The Bayview	211 72nd St
PS 170 Lexington	7109 Sixth Ave
PS 185 Walter Kassenbrock	8601 Ridge Blvd
PS / IS 104 The Fort Hamilton School	9115 Fifth Ave
St Anselm's	365 83rd St
Visitation Academy	8902 Ridge Blvd
Xaverian High	7100 Shore Rd

Map 15 · Dyker Heights / Bensonhurst

IS 187	1171 65th St
JHS 201 Dyker Heights	8010 12th Ave
JHS 227 Edward B Shallow	6500 16 Ave
JHS 259 William McKinley	7301 Ft Hamilton Pkwy
Leif Ericsson	1037 72nd St
New Utrecht High	1601 80th St
Our Lady of Guadalupe	1518 73rd St
PS 112 Lefferts Park	7115 15th Ave
PS 163 Bath Beach	1664 Benson Ave
PS 176 Ovington	1225 69th St
PS 186 Dr Irving A Gladstone	7601 19th Ave
PS 200 Benson	1940 Benson Ave
PS 204 Vince Lombardi	8101 15th Ave
PS 205 Clarion	6701 20 Ave
PS 229 Dyker	1400 Benson Ave
Regina Pacis	1201 66th St
St Bernadette's	1313 83rd St
St Finbar	1825 Bath Ave
St Frances Cabrini	21 Bay 11th St
St Patrick	401 97th St
Tiferes Miriam High School for Girls	6510 17th Ave

Map 16 · Midwood

Andries Hudde	2500 Nostrand Ave
Bais Yaakov Academy	1213 Elm Ave
Bet Yaakov Ateret Torah	1750 E 4th St
Bet Yakov Ateret Torah High	1649 E 13th St
Bnos Yisroel School for Girls	1401 Kings Hwy
Edward R Murrow High	1600 Ave L
IS 381	1599 E 22nd St
James Madison High	3787 Bedford Ave
Lev Bais Yaakov	1033 E 22nd St
Lubavitcher School Chabad	841 Ocean Pkwy
Masores Bais Yaakov	1395 Ocean Ave
Midwood Catholic Academy	1340 E 29th St

Mirrer Yeshiva	1795 Ocean Pkwy
Nefesh Academy	1750 E 18th St
Prospect Park Bnos Leah High	1601 Ave R
Prospect Park Yeshiva	1784 E 17th St
PS 193 Gil Hodges	2515 Ave L
PS 197	1599 E 22nd St
PS 199 Frederick Wachtel	1100 Elm Ave
PS 215 Morris H Weiss	415 Ave S
PS 238 Anne Sullivan	1633 E 8th St
PS 99 Isaac Asimov	1120 E 10th St
Shaare Torah	1680 Coney Island Ave
Shulamith School for Girls	1277 E 14th St
St Edmund Elementary	1902 Ave T
St Ephrem	7415 Ft Hamilton Pkwy
Sts Simon & Jude Elementary	294 Ave T
Three Hierarchs Parochial	1724 Ave P
Windmill Montessori	1317 Ave T
Yeshiva Ahavas Torah	2961 Nostrand Ave
Yeshiva of Brooklyn	1470 Ocean Pkwy
Yeshiva of Brooklyn Boy's Div	1200 Ocean Pkwy
Yeshiva of Flatbush-Joel Braverman H	1609 Ave J
Yeshiva Ohr Shraga D'Veretzky	1102 Ave L
Yeshiva Rabbi Chaim Berlin	1310 Ave I
Yeshiva Ruach Chaim	2294 Nostrand Ave
Yeshiva Vyelipol	860 E 27th St
Yeshivah of Flatbush Elementary	919 E 10th St
Yeshivat Mizrachi L'Banim	2810 Nostrand Ave

General Information · **Copy Shops**

Map 1 · Greenpoint

Insta-Press	10 Bedford Ave	718-389-3223

Map 2 · Williamsburg

Internet Garage	218 Bedford Ave	718-486-0059
The UPS Store	144 N 7th St	718-218-6440

Map 5 · Brooklyn Heights / DUMBO / Downtown

Long Island Copy & Printing	394 Flatbush Ave Ext	718-501-0019
Copyrite	45 Washington St	718-243-0959
C Two Copy Center	90 Livingston St	718-797-9700
Superior Copy Center	90 Livingston St	718-797-9701
Brooklyn Progress Blue Printing	193 Joralemon St	718-875-0696
FedEx Kinko's	16 Court St	718-852-5631
The UPS Store	93 Montague St	718-802-0900

Map 6 · Fort Greene / Clinton Hill

Save Mor Copy Center	25 Flatbush Ave	718-624-6136

Map 8 · BoCoCa / Red Hook

Copy Cottage	249 Smith St	718-237-8267

Map 9 · Park Slope / Prospect Heights / Windsor Terrace

Park Slope Typing Service & Copy Center	123 Seventh Ave	718-783-0268
Seventh Avenue Copy & Office Supply	315 Seventh Ave	718-965-2707
Graphicolor Corporation	89 Fifth Ave	718-398-8745
Mail Boxes of Park Slope	328 Flatbush Ave	718-857-5858
Office Max	625 Atlantic Ave	718-783-2614
Staples	348 Fourth Ave	718-222-5732
The UPS Store	320 Seventh Ave	718-499-0464
The UPS Store	315 Flatbush Ave	718-701-5294

Map 10 · Prospect-Lefferts Gardens / Crown Heights

Sondam Copy & Business Services	1657 Bedford Ave	718-467-2011
Vaad Printing	788 Eastern Pkwy	718-774-7200
Island Tee Shirts And Copy Center	803 Nostrand Ave	718-756-3306

Map 11 · Sunset Park / Green-Wood Heights

One Stop Blueprinting	4202 Third Ave	718-499-6466

Map 12 · Borough Park

M&S Copy Center	4401 15th Ave	718-972-4806
Copy Graph	4403 14th Ave	718-436-3800

Map 13 · Kensington / Ditmas Park / Windsor Terrace

Far Better Printing & Copy Center	43 Hillel Pl	718-859-3137
Printech Media	619 Church Ave	718-437-2737
Staples	1011 Flatbush Ave	718-703-0979

Map 14 · Bay Ridge

Staples	9319 Fifth Ave	718-833-1270
The UPS Store	8225 Fifth Ave	718-680-8225
The UPS Store	9322 Third Ave	718-759-9100
Action Photocopy	511 Bay Ridge Pkwy	212-410-0404
The UPS Store	7103 Third Ave	718-238-1805

Map 15 · Dyker Heights / Bensonhurst

On the Spot Printing	1916 86th St	718-232-2000

Map 16 · Midwood

Ink Shop	1958 Coney Island Ave	718-627-1020
Mail N Pack	1412 Ave M	718-376-6245
Command Copy	1918 Ave M	718-339-2244
Advance Copies	1417 Ave J	718-677-9781
Staples	1880 Coney Island Ave	718-376-8336
PIP Printing	1323 E 15th St	718-627-6177

Map 1 • Greenpoint

Self-service	66 Meserole Ave	Wed 6:45 PM
Self-service	1155 Manhattan Ave	Wed 6:30 PM
Self-service	557 Leonard St	Wed 6:30 PM
Self-service	79 Bridgewater St	Wed 6:30 PM
P&P Shipping & Handling	790 Manhattan Ave	Wed 5:30 PM

Map 2 • Williamsburg

Self-service	129 S 8th St	Wed 7:00 PM
Self-service	134 Broadway	Wed 7:00 PM
Self-service	185 Marcy Ave	Wed 7:00 PM
Champion Wireless	190 Bedford Ave	Wed 7:00 PM
Self-service	263 S 4th St	Wed 7:00 PM
Self-service	11 Harrison Ave	Wed 6:45 PM
FedEx Authorized Ship Center	442 Lorimer St	Wed 5:30 PM

Map 3 • East Williamsburg

Self-service	303 Johnson Ave	Wed 7:15 PM
Office 11211	331 Graham Ave	Wed 6:30 PM
Self-service	395 Graham Ave	Wed 6:30 PM
Parcel Plus	402 Graham Ave	Wed 6:00 PM

Map 4 • Bushwick

Sandbox Pack & Ship	1446 Myrtle Ave	Wed 6:30 PM

Map 5 • Brooklyn Heights / DUMBO / Downtown

Self-service	3 Chase Metrotech Center	Wed 8:15 PM
Self-service	20 Jay St	Wed 7:45 PM
Self-service	45 Main St	Wed 7:45 PM
Self-service	50 Washington St	Wed 7:45 PM
Self-service	57 Front St	Wed 7:45 PM
Self-service	16 Court St	Wed 7:30 PM
Self-service	4 Chase Metrotech Center	Wed 7:30 PM
Self-service	142 Joralemon St	Wed 7:15 PM
Self-service	225 Cadman Plaza E	Wed 7:15 PM
United Shipping Agency	16 Court St	Wed 7:00 PM
FedEx Kinko's Office & Print Center	16 Court St	Wed 7:00 PM
Self-service	63 Flushing Ave	Wed 7:00 PM
Shippers Express	41 Schermerhorn St	Wed 6:00 PM
Copy Rite	45 Washington St	Wed 5:00 PM

Map 6 • Fort Greene / Clinton Hill

Dickerson And Associates	115 S Oxford St	Wed 7:00 PM
Self-service	15 Washington Ave	Wed 7:00 PM
Packing Source	257 Nostrand Ave	Wed 5:00 PM

Map 7 • Bedford-Stuyvesant

Self-service	1368 Fulton St	Wed 4:00 PM

Map 8 • BoCoCa / Red Hook

Self-service	51 20th St	Wed 8:45 PM
FedEx Express Ship Center	51 20th St	Wed 8:45 PM
Self-service	615 Clinton St	Wed 7:15 PM
Self-service	540 Court St	Wed 6:15 PM
Copy Cottage	249 Smith St	Wed 6:00 PM
Cobble Hill Mailing	495 Henry St	Wed 6:00 PM
Smalls It / Dba Sandbox	141 Smith St	Wed 5:00 PM

Map 9 • Park Slope / Prospect Heights / Windsor Terrace

Self-service	227 4th Ave	Wed 7:15 PM
Self-service	279 9th St	Wed 7:15 PM
Self-service	625 Atlantic Ave	Wed 7:15 PM
Park Slope Copy Center	123 7th Ave	Wed 6:00 PM
Mailboxes On Fifth	172 5th Ave	Wed 6:00 PM
Mailboxes Of Park Slope	328 Flatbush Ave	Wed 6:00 PM
552 Atlantic Corp	552 Atlantic Ave	Wed 6:00 PM
Active Transport Services	285 5th Ave	Wed 4:00 PM
Self-service	557 Atlantic Ave	Wed 4:00 PM

Map 10 • Prospect-Lefferts Gardens / Crown Heights

Self-service	315 Empire Blvd	Wed 6:30 PM
M&E Enterprises	476 Albany Ave	Wed 6:30 PM
Exprss Mail	327 Empire Blvd	Wed 6:00 PM
Mo-betta Ventures	1647 Bedford Ave	Wed 5:30 PM
Kaydmailboxetc	521 Rogers Ave	Wed 5:00 PM
Self-service	866 Eastern Pkwy	Wed 3:30 PM

Map 11 • Sunset Park / Green-Wood Heights

Self-service	140 58th St	Wed 7:45 PM
Self-service	225 25th St	Wed 7:15 PM
Self-service	5600 First Ave	Wed 7:15 PM
Self-service	900 3rd Ave	Wed 7:00 PM
Americomp Technology	5202 8th Ave	Wed 6:00 PM
JP Cellular	5222 8th Ave	Wed 5:30 PM

Map 12 · Borough Park

Self-service	4626 18th Ave	Wed 7:30 PM
Self-service	1200 51st St	Wed 7:15 PM
Self-service	1312 44th St	Wed 7:00 PM
Self-service	4510 16th Ave	Wed 7:00 PM
Self-service	5014 16th Ave	Wed 7:00 PM
Self-service	5811 16th Ave	Wed 7:00 PM
Self-service	1450 37th St	Wed 6:45 PM
Self-service	1333 60th St	Wed 6:30 PM
Brooklyn Mailing Center	1274 49th St	Wed 6:00 PM
Mr Mailman	1303 53rd St	Wed 6:00 PM
Talk About Shipping	4403 15th Ave	Wed 4:00 PM

Map 13 · Kensington / Ditmas Park / Windsor Terrace

Self-service	419 Mcdonald Ave	Wed 7:00 PM
Metropolis Multi Service	1398 Flatbush Ave	Wed 6:00 PM
Xpress Mail Svc Ctr	3001 Church Ave	Wed 5:00 PM
Supreme Shipping	921 Coney Island Ave	Wed 4:30 PM

Map 14 · Bay Ridge

NYC Postal Services	6904 Colonial Rd	Wed 7:00 PM
Self-service	8801 5th Ave	Wed 7:00 PM
Self-service	9319 5th Ave	Wed 6:45 PM
Global Express Service	7013 Ft Hamilton Pkwy	Wed 6:30 PM
Self-service	9710 3rd Ave	Wed 6:30 PM
Shiprite	7304 5th Ave	Wed 5:15 PM
Bay Ridge Mail Station	9728 Third Ave	Wed 5:00 PM

Map 15 · Dyker Heights / Bensonhurst

Self-service	6618 20th Ave	Wed 7:15 PM
Silver Rod Shipping	6402 18th Ave	Wed 7:00 PM
Self-service	1865 Benson Ave	Wed 6:45 PM
Self-service	7502 13th Ave	Wed 6:45 PM
Self-service	1475 86th St	Wed 6:30 PM
Self-service	7302 13th Ave	Wed 6:30 PM
FedEx Authorized Ship Center	7622 13th Ave	Wed 6:30 PM
Postal Plaza	2220 65th St	Wed 5:30 PM
The Fast Mail Station	7816 New Utrecht Ave	Wed 5:30 PM
The Shipping Depot	6801 20th Ave	Wed 5:00 PM

Map 16 · Midwood

Self-service	1288 Coney Island Ave	Wed 7:00 PM
Self-service	1639 E 13th St	Wed 7:00 PM
Self-service	2319 Nostrand Ave	Wed 7:00 PM
Self-service	1608 E 19th St	Wed 6:45 PM
Mailbox Plus Of Midwood	1375 Coney Island Ave	Wed 6:30 PM
Self-service	2302 Ave U	Wed 6:30 PM
Five Star Global	2010 Coney Island Ave	Wed 6:00 PM
Mail-n-pack	1412 Ave M	Wed 5:30 PM
Mail Drop Corporation	1204 Ave U	Wed 5:00 PM
Smalls It / Dba Sandbox	1704 Flatbush Ave	Wed 5:00 PM
Best Mail & Copy Center	2920 Ave R	Wed 5:00 PM
E-z Photo	1673 E 16th St	Wed 4:30 PM

Hospitals / Police / Libraries

Emergency Rooms

	Address	Phone	Map
Woodhull	760 Broadway St	718-963-8000	3
Wyckoff Heights Medical Center	374 Stockholm St	718-963-7272	4
Brooklyn Hospital Center	121 DeKalb Ave	718-250-8000	6
Long Island College	339 Hicks St	718-780-1000	8
New York Methodist	506 6th St	718-780-3000	9
Downstate Medical Center	450 Clarkson Ave	718-270-1000	10
Interfaith Medical Center	1545 Atlantic Ave	718-613-4000	10
Kings County	451 Clarkson Ave	718-245-3131	10
Lutheran Medical Center	150 55th St	718-630-7000	11
Maimonides Medical Center	4802 Tenth Ave	718-283-6000	12
Victory Memorial	699 92nd St	718-567-1234	15

Other Hospitals

	Address	Phone	Map
NY State VA Medical Center	800 Poly Pl	718-836-6600	15

Police

	Address	Phone	Map
94th Precinct	100 Meserole Ave	718-383-3879	1
90th Precinct	211 Union Ave	718-963-5311	2
Police Service Area 3	25 Central Ave	718-386-5357	3
83rd Precinct	480 Knickerbocker Ave	718-574-1605	4
84th Precinct	301 Gold St	718-875-6811	5
88th Precinct	298 Classon Ave	718-636-6511	6
79th Precinct	263 Tompkins Ave	718-636-6611	7
81st Precinct	30 Ralph Ave	718-574-0411	7
76th Precinct	191 Union St	718-834-3211	8
78th Precinct	65 Sixth Ave	718-636-6411	9
71st Precinct	421 Empire Blvd	718-735-0511	10
72nd Precinct	830 Fourth Ave	718-965-6311	11
66th Precinct	5822 16th Ave	718-851-5611	12
67th Precinct	2820 Snyder Ave	718-287-3211	13
70th Precinct	154 Lawrence Ave	718-851-5511	13
68th Precinct	333 65th St	718-439-4211	14
62nd Precinct	1925 Bath Ave	718-236-2611	15

Public Libraries

		Phone	Map			Address	Phone	Map
Brooklyn Public	107 Norman Ave	718-349-8504	1	Brooklyn Public	Grand Army Plz		718-230-2100	9
Brooklyn Public	240 Division Ave	718-302-3485	2	Library (Central Branch)				
Brooklyn Public	81 Devoe St	718-486-3365	2	Brooklyn Public	725 St Marks Ave	718-773-7208	10
Brooklyn Public	340 Bushwick Ave	718-602-1348	3	Brooklyn Public	560 New York Ave	718-773-1180	10
Brooklyn Public	790 Bushwick Ave	718-455-3898	4	Brooklyn Public	5108 Fourth Ave	718-567-2806	11
Brooklyn Public	360 Irving Ave	718-628-8378	4	Brooklyn Public	1265 43rd St	718-437-4085	12
Brooklyn Public	8 Thomas S Boyland St	718-573-5224	4	Brooklyn Public	1702 60th St	718-256-2117	12
Brooklyn Public	280 Cadman Plz W	718-623-7100	5	Brooklyn Public	2035 Nostrand Ave	718-421-1159	13
Brooklyn Public	93 St Edwards St	718-935-0244	6	Brooklyn Public	160 E 5th St	718-686-9707	13
Brooklyn Public	25 Fourth Ave	718-638-1531	6	Brooklyn Public	1305 Cortelyou Rd	718-693-7763	13
Brooklyn Public	380 Washington Ave	718-398-8713	6	Brooklyn Public	22 Linden Blvd	718-856-0813	13
Brooklyn Public	617 DeKalb Ave	718-935-0032	7	Brooklyn Public	410 Ditmas Ave	718-435-9431	13
Brooklyn Public	496 Franklin Ave	718-623-0012	7	Brooklyn Public	7223 Ridge Blvd	718-748-5709	14
Brooklyn Public	361 Lewis Ave	718-573-5606	7	Brooklyn Public	9424 Fourth Ave	718-748-6919	14
Macon Branch				Brooklyn Public	1742 86th St	718-236-4086	15
Brooklyn Public	396 Clinton St	718-596-6972	8	Brooklyn Public	6802 Ft Hamilton Pkwy	718-748-8001	15
Brooklyn Public	7 Wolcott St	718-935-0203	8	Brooklyn Public	8202 13th Ave	718-748-6261	15
Brooklyn Public	431 Sixth Ave	718-832-1853	9	Brooklyn Public	975 E 16th St	718-252-0967	16

Other Libraries

	Address	Phone	Map
Brooklyn Bar Association Foundation	123 Remsen St	718-624-0875	5
Brooklyn Law Library	250 Joralemon St	718-780-7973	5
New York State Supreme Court	360 Adams St	347-296-1144	5
Brooklyn Hospital Medical	121 DeKalb Ave	718-250-6944	6

General Information · **Hotels**

Although the borough is not really a hotbed for tourism yet, these listings should prove useful to adventurous out-of-town guests, or those seeking less adventurous inner-borough "romantic getaways." In the case of the latter, see the hotels with hourly rates. Prices are ballpark estimates and subject to change—go to one of the many middle-man websites (Hotels.com, Expedia, Hotwire, etc.) to find the best bargains. Brooklyn's bed & breakfast options are the classiest of the bunch.

Map 1 · Greenpoint

	Address	Phone	Rate
YMCA	99 Meserole Ave	718-389-3700	43

Map 2 · Williamsburg

Glenwood Hostel	339 Broadway	718-387-7858	30

Map 3 · East Williamsburg

Bushwick Hotel	171 Bushwick Ave	718-386-1801	140

Map 4 · Bushwick

Hotel Neptune	1461 Broadway	718-455-1500	75
Kings Hotel Apartments	1078 Bushwick Ave	718-452-9743	130
Red Carpet Inn	980 Wyckoff Ave	718-417-4111	120

Map 5 · Brooklyn Heights / DUMBO / Downtown

Awesome Bed & Breakfast	136 Lawrence St	718-858-4859	130
Hotel Princess	211 Schermerhorn St	718-468-3565	85
Marriott New York at the Brooklyn Bridge	333 Adams St	718-246-7000	300

Map 6 · Fort Greene / Clinton Hill

Prince Lefferts Hotel	127 Lefferts Pl	718-783-2984	85
Regina's New York Bed & Breakfast	16 Ft Greene Pl	718-834-9253	120
Washington Hotel	400 Washington Ave	718-783-9545	95

Map 8 · BoCoCa / Red Hook

Brooklyn Motor Inn	140 Hamilton Ave	718-875-2500	110
Union Street Bed & Breakfast	405 Union St	718-852-8406	125

Map 9 · Park Slope / Prospect Heights / Windsor Terrace

Bed & Breakfast Marisa	288 Park Pl	718-398-4185	125
Holiday Inn Express Brooklyn	625 Union St	718-797-1133	170

Map 11 · Sunset Park / Green-Wood Heights

Days Inn Brooklyn	437 39th St	718-853-4141	109

Map 12 · Borough Park

Mosaic Suites	4320 16th Ave	718-972-4377	55
Park House Hotel	1206 48th St	718-871-8100	149

Map 13 · Kensington / Ditmas Park / Windsor Terrace

Bibi's Garden B&B	762 Westminster Rd	718-434-3119	120
Dekoven Suites	30 Dekoven Ct	718-421-1052	130
Honey's B&B	770 Westminster Rd	718-434-7628	95
The Strange Dog Inn	51 Dekoven Ct	718-338-7051	195

Map 14 · Bay Ridge

Best Western	8315 Fourth Ave	718-238-3737	150
Prince Hotel	315 93rd St	718-748-8995	75

Map 16 · Midwood

Midwood Suites	1078 E 15th St	718-253-9535	99

They may not make the itinerary of the casual tourist, but Brooklyn is still home to some stupendous destinations. You often simply look up and realize that you are standing at the oldest, biggest, or first... something. Amazing unique sights around every corner define a native's Brooklyn. And many of the families that built these landmarks still live amongst them. Take that, Manhattan!

Best Views

One of the best things about Brooklyn is how underrated it is. Try the **Beard Street Pier (Map 8)** in way-out Red Hook for a stunning view of the Statue of Liberty and Lower Manhattan, sans crowds no matter what the season. For an incredible vista, visit the Shore Parkway Greenway, a waterfront bike and pedestrian trail that you can enter from Owls Head Park (Map 14) in Bay Ridge. The **Empire-Fulton Ferry State Park (Map 5)**, located on the water in DUMBO, leads a bevy of scenic vistas near downtown Brooklyn, and it has a few patches of green grass to boot. On the **Brooklyn Heights Promenade (Map 5)** there may be a few more people, though for a sunset or sunny afternoon it's the best panorama around. The pedestrian pathway across the **Manhattan Bridge (Map 5)** is another destination often overshadowed by its more famous neighbor. The views of the river and the shimmering Financial District are just as good as those from the **Brooklyn Bridge (Map 5)**, and you can also see the **Jetsons Building (Map 5)** on the Brooklyn side, variously lit depending on the whims of its owners. The **Williamsburg Bridge (Map 2)** also offers exciting views of the city (as well as hipsters in oversized sunglasses). Heading toward Queens on the BQE you'll have to cross the **Kosciusko Bridge (Foldout A5)**, named for a Polish general who fought in the Revolutionary War. While keeping your eyes on the road, take a quick glimpse towards Midtown from one of the borough's highest points.

Architecture

Brooklyn has its own "Arc de Triomphe" at **Grand Army Plaza (Map 9)**, formally named the Soldiers' and Sailors' Arch. It, too, clogs traffic around its gigantic rotary, and marks the way to both the **Brooklyn Museum (Map 10)** and the **Brooklyn Botanic Gardens (Map 9)**, two venerable architectural marvels. Both have a very antique air about them, though the museum steps have been renovated in

a somewhat futuristic fashion. The arch also houses the must-see **New York Puppet Library (Map 9)**, open only on Saturdays in the summer. Even Paris can't top that. Prospect Park West runs along the most expensive side of the park where turn-of-the-century homes that might redefine some people's concept of Brooklyn still stand. In north Brooklyn, the **Williamsburg Savings Bank (Map 6)** with its gigantic golden dome is similarly opulent.

Historical

In Bed-Stuy, the **Akwaaba Mansion (Map 7)** is an example of the area's early glory, and many of the surrounding brownstones follow in its stylistic footsteps. Back in Walt Whitman's old neighborhood in Fort Greene is the Pratt Institute where university buildings include a former shoe factory, several original sealed subway tunnels, and a working **Power Plant (Map 6)**. Litchfield Villa (p.143) is an Italian-style castle just across 5th Street in Prospect Park. Some historic farmhouses worth visiting include the Lefferts House (p.143) in the "Children's Corner" of Prospect Park, and the **Lott House (Eastern Brooklyn)** on E 36th Street in Marine Park. Both were built in the 18th century and now look slightly odd in their respective neighborhoods, having remained wholly untouched for years. Way before real estate developers began pillaging Brooklyn, the Vikings may have done some speculation of their own as commemorated by the **Leif Ericsson Runestone (Map 14)**. And speaking of dead people, **Green-Wood Cemetery (Map 11)** in Sunset Park has more famous corpses than you can shake a stick at, and is also beautiful in a somber sort of way.

Out of the Ordinary

Broken Angel (Map 6) is a funky, free-form private residence that will soon be transformed into expensive condos (like everything else in Brooklyn). **Junior's Restaurant (Map 5)** is a mecca for those wishing to visit rap star Notorious B.I.G.'s old stomping ground. The cheesecake is world-famous as well, so no matter what motivates you, you'll be satisfied. If you find yourself suddenly in need of more underground mix tapes or perhaps some fresh new kicks, then it's off to the **Fulton Street Mall (Map 5)** for these and other urban necessities. The **Brooklyn Brewery (Map 2)** is also a great place to sample some of the best Brooklyn has to offer, in the form of its delicious lagers and ales.

Map 1 · Greenpoint

Newton Creek Sewage Treatment Plant	Greenpoint Ave & Provost St	Take a moment to contemplate all of the famous and beautiful peoples' shit floating around in here.

Map 2 · Williamsburg

City Reliquary	370 Metropolitan Ave	Artifacts from New York's vast and rich history.
East River State Park	90 Kent Ave · 347-297-9470	Swath of waterfront greenspace, Williamsburg style.
McCarren Pool	Lorimer St & Bayard St	Really cool abandoned pool that we hope continues to be used as a venue for concerts and film screenings.
Williamsburg Bridge	S 5th St & Driggs St	Bridge of the chosen people—Jews and well-off hipsters.

Map 3 · East Williamsburg

Pfizer Pharmaceutical	630 Flushing Ave	Look for this factory to close any day now. Bye bye jobs, hello condos..
Williamsburg Houses	176 Maujer St	A public housing project proclaimed a landmark in 2003.

Map 4 · Bushwick

St Barbara's Roman Catholic Church	138 Bleecker St	A little piece of Europe in the middle of Bushwick.

Map 5 · Brooklyn Heights / DUMBO / Downtown

Brooklyn Borough Hall	209 Joralemon St · 718-802-3700	Built in the 1840s, this Greek Revival landmark was once employed as the official City Hall of Brokly.
Brooklyn Bridge	Adams St & East River	If you haven't walked over it at least twice yet, you're not cool.
Brooklyn Heights Promenade	n/a	The best place to really see Manhattan. It's the view that's in all the movies.
Brooklyn Historical Society	128 Pierrepont St · 718-222-4111	Want to really learn about Brooklyn? Go here.
Brooklyn Ice Cream Factory	Fulton Ferry Pier · 718-246-3963	Expensive, old-fashioned ice cream beneath the bridge.
Brooklyn Navy Yard	Waterfront	Nation's first navy yard employed 70,000 people during WWII. Today, it houses a diverse range of businesses.
Brooklyn Tabernacle	17 Smith St · 718-783-0942	Home of the award-winning Brooklyn Tabernacle Choir.
Empire-Fulton Ferry State Park	n/a	Stunning views of the bridge.
Fulton Street Mall	Fulton St b/w Flatbush Ave & Borough Hall Plz	The shopping experience, Brooklyn style. Hot sneakers can be had for a song.
Jetsons Building	110 York St	View this sculptural roof from the Manhattan Bridge at night when it's lit with colored lights.
Junior's Restaurant	386 Flatbush Ave · 718-852-5257	For the only cheesecake worth its curds and whey. (Free pickles, great if you're preggers.)
Manhattan Bridge	n/a	Connecting Brooklyn to that other borough.
New York Transit Museum	Boerum Pl & Schermerhorn St · 718-694-1600	Everything one can say about the MTA.

Map 6 · Fort Greene / Clinton Hill

Broken Angel	Quincy St b/w Downing St & Classon St	Crazy architectural home soon to be condos.
Brooklyn Academy of Music	30 Lafayette Ave · 718-636-4100	Home of Dave Chappelle's *Block Party*. America's oldest continuously operating performing arts center. Never dull.
Brooklyn Masonic Temple	317 Clermont Ave · 718-638-1256	Its vestrymen have included Robert E. Lee and Thomas J. (Stonewall) Jackson.
Fort Greene Park	DeKalb Ave & Washington Park	Liquor store proximity is a plus on a warm afternoon when you visit this welcome chunk of green.
Lafayette Avenue Presbyterian Church	85 S Oxford St · 718-625-7515	Nationally known church with performing arts; former Underground Railroad stop.

General Information · **Landmarks**

Map 6 · Fort Greene / Clinton Hill—*continued*

Long Island Rail Road Station	Hanson Pl & Flatbush Ave · 718-217-5477	A low red-brick building hosting more than 20 million passengers annually. A total craphole.
Pratt Institute Power Plant	200 Willoughby Ave · 718-636-3600	This authentic steam generator gets fired up a few times a year to impress the parents. Cool.
Steiner Studios	15 Washington Ave	Film studio in the Brooklyn Navy Yard. Spike Lee's *Inside Man* was recently shot here.
Williamsburg Savings Bank Building	1 Hanson Pl	Still the tallest building in the borough and when you're lost, a sight for sore eyes.

Map 7 · Bedford-Stuyvesant

Akwaaba Mansion	347 MacDonough St · 718-455-5958	Restored 1860s villa that now operates as a beautiful B&B.
Magnolia Grandiflora	679 Lafayette Ave	One of two landmarked trees in all of NYC. Visit in spring when it blossoms.

Map 8 · BoCoCa / Red Hook

Beard Street Pier	Foot of Van Brunt St on the water	Historic 19th Century warehouses, now a cluster of shops and offices.
Brooklyn Clay Retort and Fire Brick Building	76 Van Dyke St	Red Hook's first official Landmark building dates to the mid-19th century.
Gowanus Canal	n/a	Brooklyn's answer to the Seine.
Phone Booth	Huntington St & Hamilton Ave	Where hookers, pimps, and dealers call mom for money.
Red Hook Park	Richards St & Verona St	Watch futbol and eat Central American street food every Saturday from spring through fall.
Red Hook Grain Terminal	n/a	Visit just to wonder what it's doing there.
Warren Place	Warren Pl	Public housing from the 1870s.

Map 9 · Park Slope / Prospect Heights / Windsor Terrace

Brooklyn Botanic Garden	900 Washington Ave · 718-623-7200	A beautiful and peaceful spot inside and out. Cherry blossoms in spring are awe inspiring.
Brooklyn Conservatory of Music	58 Seventh Ave · 718-622-3300	This Victorian Gothic brownstone hosts performances by its students and guest artists.
Brooklyn Public Library (Central Branch)	Grand Army Plz · 718-230-2100	The building looks like a book!
Grand Army Plaza	Flatbush Ave & Plaza St	Site of John H. Duncan's Soldiers' and Sailors' Memorial Arch.
New York Puppet Library	Grand Army Plz · 617- 623-203	The Memorial Arch at Grand Army Plaza has a funky theater at the top. A must see (summer Saturdays only).
Park Slope Food Co-op	782 Union St · 718-622-0560	These farm-fresh veggies will do for those in search of their peck of dirt. Rinse.

Map 10 · Prospect-Lefferts Gardens / Crown Heights

Brooklyn Children's Museum	145 Brooklyn Ave · 718-735-4400	Take your own kids or someone else's so you can get in on the fun without looking silly.
Brooklyn Museum	200 Eastern Pkwy · 718-638-5000	Recently completed renovations lend a futuristic air, but the collections are a Brooklyn jewel.
The Carousel	Ocean Ave & Flatbush Ave & Empire Blvd	Carved in 1912 and restored in 1990.
Prospect Park Zoo	450 Flatbush Ave · 718-399-7339	Home to approximately 400 animals.

Map 11 · Sunset Park / Green-Wood Heights

Green-Wood Cemetery	500 25th St · 718-768-7300	Lots of winding paths and greenery good for contemplation.

Map 12 · Borough Park

Shmura Matzoh Factory	36th St & 13th Ave	The real deal. Only open in the pre-passover season.

General Information · **Landmarks**

Map 13 · Kensington / Ditmas Park / Windsor Terrace

Erasmus Hall Academy	911 Flatbush Ave · 718-282-7804	Boasts famous graduates such as Alexander Hamilton, Neil Diamond, and Barbara Streisand.
Flatbush Dutch Reform Church	890 Flatbush Ave	Originally constructed in 1654 by order of Bloomberg's predecessor, Peter Stuyvesant.
Kensington Stables	51 Caton Ave · 718-972-4588	Riding horses is one of life's small pleasures. Combine that with subway proximity and you're in business.

Map 14 · Bay Ridge

69th Street Pier/9/11 Memorial	Shore Rd & Bay Ridge Ave	Once the embarkation point for the Bay Ridge-St. George ferry, it offers a panoramic harbor view.
The Barkaloo Cemetery	Narrows Ave & Mackay Pl	The smallest cemetery founded in 1725 by Dutch immigrant William Harmans Barkaloo.
Fontbonne Hall	9901 Shore Rd · 718-748-2244	Now a Catholic school, this 1890s private residence once belonged to actress Lillian Russell.
Fort Hamilton	101st St & Fourth Ave	Established in the 1820s as a garrison for protecting the harbor and city against attack.
The Gingerbread House	Narrows Ave & 83rd St	The best example of Arts and Crafts architecture in the city.
James F Farrell House	95th St & Shore Rd	This 1849 Greek Revival house evokes the neighborhood's days as a wealthy seaside retreat.
Leif Ericsson Runestone	Fourth Ave & 67th St	Commemorating the viking explorer's discovery of America…way before that other guy.
St John's Episcopal Church	9818 Ft Hamilton Pkwy · 718-745-2377	Established in 1834, the present structure dates to 1890; its vestrymen have included Robert E. Lee and Thomas J. (Stonewall) Jackson.
Verrazano-Narrows Bridge	Easternmost point of I-278 at Ft Wadsworth	The longest span in North America really puts things into perspective. Awesome views below.

Map 15 · Dyker Heights / Bensonhurst

Nellie Bly Amusement Park	1824 Shore Pkwy · 718-996-4002	Kiddie-size amusement park. Open Easter through Halloween.

Map 16 · Midwood

JC Studios	1268 E 14th St · 718-780-6400	Formerly NBC studios where *The Cosby Show* was filmed; is now the production site of *As the World Turns*.
Wyckoff House	1669 E 22nd St	What things used to look like. Not open to the public.

Coney Island / Brighton Beach

Abe Stark Ice Skating Rink	Coney Island Boardwalk & W 19th St · 718-946-6536	Like most of the 'hood, in need of a little TLC. Still, way fun and admission's cheap.
KeySpan Park	1904 Surf Ave	Baseball without steroids? Who knew?
New York Aquarium	Surf Ave & W 8th St · 718-265-3474	Sprightly seahorses and others herald the variety of the seas.
Parachute Jump	Surf Ave & W 19 St	BK's Eiffel Tower. Glows nightly thanks to a lighting installation commissioned in 2006.
Sideshows by the Seashore / Coney Island Museum	1208 Surf Ave · 718-372-5159	All manner of curiosities, both old-timey and modern. NFT pick.

Eastern Brooklyn

Lady Moody House	27 Gravesend Neck Rd	Purported home of Gravesend founder, 1643.
Old Gravesend Cemetery	Gravesend Neck Rd b/w McDonald Ave & Van Sicklen St	Dates to 1643. Burial place of Lady Moody.

Storage / Truck Rental

Storage

Storage	Address	Phone	Map
Great Storage	49 Wyckoff Ave	718-381-3871	4
Storage Deluxe	1220 Broadway	718-573-4555	4
American Self Storage	202 Tillary St	718-260-8601	5
American Self Storage	45 Clinton St	718-246-5600	5
Extra Space Storage	160 John St	718-797-4040	5
Public Storage	269 Gold St	877-788-2028	5
Shurgard Storage	30 Prince St	718-852-7100	5
Extra Space Storage	41 Flatbush Ave	718-596-4060	6
Hall Street Storage	12 Hall St	718-855-3636	6
Lockaway Self Storage	1 Carlton Ave	718-522-5050	6
Moishe's Mini Storage	22 Grand Ave	718-237-9735	6
Public Storage	72 Emerson Pl	718-638-1287	6
Storage Deluxe	945 Atlantic Ave	718-399-6037	6
Storage Deluxe	945 Atlantic Ave	718-235-2999	6
Storage Mart	50 Wallabout St	718-522-9055	6
Storage Deluxe	1220 Broadway	877-989-7867	7
Moving Officials	63 9th St	718-832-5793	8
Treasure Island Storage	183 Lorraine St	718-596-1850	8
Pack-it-Away Storage	808 Pacific St	718-622-4300	9
Premier Storage	312 3rd Ave	718-855-2100	9
Storage Mart	718 Atlantic Ave	718-399-6037	9
U-Haul	394 Fourth Ave	718-237-2893	9
Affordable Self Storage	1680 Atlantic Ave	718-363-2825	10
Public Storage	1062 St Johns Pl	718-771-0853	10
Safeguard Self Storage	115 Empire	718-282-1388	10
Harborside Self Storage	56 48th St	718-965-0474	11
Stop & Stor	534 63rd St	718-833-8600	11
Storage Mart	980 Fourth Ave	718-499-3999	11
Extra Space Storage	2207 Albemarle Rd	718-287-0496	13
Stop & Stor	40 Erasmus St	718-284-8000	13
Extra Space Storage	201 64th St	718-748-4499	14
U-Haul New Utrecht	6615 New Utrecht Ave	718-232-1400	15
Mobile Self Storage	n/a	718-439-1088	n/a
Storage Deluxe	2049 Pitkin Ave	877-989-7867	n/a
Storage Deluxe	2887 Atlantic Ave	718-235-2999	n/a
Storage Deluxe	2990 Cropsey Ave	718-373-0517	n/a
Storage Deluxe	464 Stanley Ave	877-989-7867	n/a

Truck Rental

Truck Rental		Address	Phone	Map
U-Haul	S&C Truck & Auto Center	314 McGuiness Blvd	718-349-7168	1
Penske	PSTP	470 Rodney St	718-797-4098	2
U-Haul	F&B Truck Repair	990 Metropolitan Ave	718-782-6720	3
U-Haul	Koordy Corp	1127 Flushing Ave	718-381-1763	3
U-Haul	STG DLX Van Buren St	552 Van Buren St	718-443-0857	4
Budget	JMC Automotive	376 Classon Ave	718-857-1555	6
U-Haul	Lockaway Self Storage	1 Carlton Ave	718-797-5098	6
U-Haul	Jules Management	257 Nostrand Ave	718-638-7161	6
U-Haul	STG DLX Brooklyn	945 Atlantic Ave	718-623-2450	7
U-Haul	Petroleum DeKalb	10 Malcolm X Blvd	718-573-5120	7
Budget	Park Slope Rental Corp	519 Smith St	718-596-0280	8
U-Haul	9th Street Self-Storage	88 9th St	718-788-3370	8
U-Haul	Flash Auto Sales	404 Smith St	718-694-0744	8
Budget	St Mark Park	307 St Mark's Ave	718-857-2621	9
Penske	Parkside Service Center	340 Fourth Ave	718-768-6844	9
U-Haul	U-Haul Center	394 Fourth Ave	718-237-2893	9
U-Haul	Mike's Travel & Tours	465 Fenimore St	718-756-7743	10
Budget	LAD Service	5410 Third Ave	718-836-0079	11
Budget	Perfect Car Rental	6302 17th Ave	718-837-8174	11
U-Haul	Affordable Rentals	29 Church Ave	718-972-6865	12
U-Haul	Metro Fleet Systems	705 McDonald Ave	718-431-0659	13
U-Haul	U-Haul New Utrecht	6615 New Utrecht Ave	718-232-1400	15

Gyms

	Address	Phone	Map
Exodus Fitness	510 Metropolitan Ave	718-599-1073	2
Harbor Fitness	191 15th St	718-965-6200	9

Locksmiths

	Phone
All Brooklyn Locksmiths	718-826-2800
Aladdin Locksmiths	718-693-8100
Champion Locksmiths	718-906-9665

Pharmacies

	Address	Phone	Map
Duane Reade	386 Fulton St	718-330-0363	5
Neergaard	454 Fifth Ave	718-768-0600	9
Pathmark Pharmacy	625 Atlantic Ave	718-399-6239	9
*Prescription counter closes at 9			
Pathmark	1245 61st St	718-853-8633	12
Duane Reade	436 86th St	718-833-7758	14
CVS	2925 Kings Hwy	718-677-3871	16
Walgreens	946 Kings Hwy	718-645-0417	16
*Prescription counter closes at 10 pm			
CVS	2472 Flatbush Ave	718-253-0200	p74
CVS	4901 Kings Hwy	718-252-3791	p74
Rite Aid	185 Kings Hwy	718-331-2019	p74
Rite Aid	2324 Flatbush Ave	718-951-6869	p74

Plumbers

	Phone
A-1 Water Main & Sewer Contractors	718-272-4784
Alex Figiolia	718-643-0900
Allcounty Plumbing & Heating	718-284-6200
Capital	718-492-8057
Downtown Plumbing and Sewer	718-858-7070
Fast Repair	718-645-0089
RR Plumbing Roto-Rooter	718-763-6464
Sewers	718-234-8411
Sewers	718-495-3600
Vigilante	718-522-6111

Restaurants

	Address	Phone	Map
Seventh Avenue Donuts	324 Seventh Ave	718-768-0748	9
Del'Rio Diner	166 Kings Ave	718-331-3107	p74
Kellogg's Diner	518 Metropolitan Ave	718-782-4502	2
Piaxtla es Mexico Deli	505 51st St	718-633-4816	11
God Bless Deli	818 Manhattan Ave	718-349-0605	1
Bukhara Restaurant	788 Coney Island Ave	718-462-6922	13
Farmer in the Deli	357 Myrtle Ave	718-875-9067	6
Bridgeview Diner	9011 Third Ave	718-680-9818	14
Grand Morelos	727 Grand St	718-218-9441	3
George's	753 Coney Island Ave	718-282-0152	13
El Greco Diner	1821 Emmons Ave	718-934-1288	p74

Supermarkets

	Address	Phone	Map
Peas & Pickles	55 Washington St	718-488-8336	5
Peas & Pickles	79 Henry St	718-596-8219	5
Key Food	369 Flatbush Ave	718-789-3007	9
Pathmark	137 12th St	718-788-5100	9
Pathmark	625 Atlantic Ave	718-399-6161	9
Shop Rite	1080 McDonald Ave	718-252-5770	16

Overview

Platoons of artists are moving to Brooklyn from Manhattan, so it's no surprise that many galleries have followed suit. Working-class artists are producing some great work that subverts the radar of Manhattan's upscale gallery tastemakers. Most art galleries in Brooklyn are located in Williamsburg and DUMBO, although spaces are opening up in Greenpoint, Fort Greene, Carroll Gardens, and Red Hook. The DUMBO Arts Festival and the Gowanus Open Studios Tour are solid introductions to the scene. **The Brooklyn Arts Council (Map 5)** (www.brooklynartscouncil.org) is a local organization that supports artists in addition to having its own art gallery, film festival, seminars, education programs, and other events.

DUMBO

Home to a good number of local artists, DUMBO takes center stage during the Art Under the Bridge Festival each October. Galleries and studios throw open their doors with hundreds of artists displaying their work. Permanent galleries with regular exhibitions include the **DUMBO Arts Center (Map 5)**, the group of second-floor galleries at **111 Front Street (Map 5)**, and the always-interesting **Jan Larsen Gallery (Map 5)** at 63 Pearl Street.

Williamsburg and Greenpoint

Be it an apartment, t-shirt, or gallery, all of Williamsburg is a canvas. **Jack the Pelican (Map 2)** and **McCaig-Welles Gallery (Map 2)** have consistently stellar shows. **Cave (Map 2)** features Asian artists and dance exhibitions. **Brooklyn Fire Proof (Map 2)**, in the no-man's land between Williamsburg and Greenpoint, has a large raw space featuring sculptures, installations, and paintings. The morbidly curious may enjoy a trip to the **Dabora Gallery (Map 1)** in Greenpoint for a brushstroke with the gothic.

BoCoCa/ Red Hook

Carroll Gardens and Red Hook are home to numerous studios. Many are clustered around the Gowanus Canal, Brooklyn's working-class response to Venice. This has inspired the Gowanus Open Studios Tour held every October, when local artists admit you into their spaces to view their work. There are several galleries with permanent exhibitions on Atlantic and Fulton Avenues east of Smith Street. The **Bruno Marina Gallery (Map 8)** often hosts worthwhile exhibitions that focus on serenity and naturalism.

Map 1 • Greenpoint

Dabora Gallery	1080 Manhattan Ave	718-609-9269
Galeria Janet	205 Norman Ave	718-383-9380

Map 2 • Williamsburg

AG Gallery	103 N 3rd St	718-599-3044
Art 101	101 Grand St	718-302-2242
Black & White	483 Driggs Ave	718-599-8775
Brooklyn Fire Proof	101 Richardson St	718-302-4702
Capla Kesting Fine Art	121 Roebling St	917-650-3760
Cave	58 Grand St	718-388-6780
Ch'i: An Art Space	293 Grand St	718-218-8939
Cinders	103 Havemeyer St	718-388-2311
Dollhaus	37 Broadway	917-667-2332
EX	872 Kent Ave	718-783-0060
Figureworks	168 N 6th St	718-486-7021
The Front Room Gallery	147 Roebling St	718-782-2556
Holland Tunnel	61 S 3rd St	718-384-5738
Jack the Pelican	487 Driggs Ave	718-782-0183
Like the spice, art studio	224 Roebling St	718-388-5388
McCaig-Welles Gallery	129 Roebling St	718-384-8729
Momenta Art	359 Bedford Ave	718-218-8058
Parker's Box	193 Grand St	718-388-2882
Pierogi Brooklyn	177 N 9th St	718-599-2144
Saved Tattoo	3 Hope St	718-486-0850
Williamsburg Art & Historical Society	135 Broadway	718-486-7372

Arts & Entertainment · **Art Galleries**

Map 3 · East Williamsburg

kbp	63 Stagg St	212-464-8895
NurtureArt Gallery	910 Grand St	718-782-7755
Third Ward	195 Morgan Ave	718-715-4961

Map 4 · Bushwick

A Space Gallery	1138 Broadway	917-776-0772

Map 5 · Brooklyn Heights / DUMBO / Downtown

5+5 Gallery	111 Front St	718-488-8383
BAC Gallery	111 Front St	718-625-0080
DUMBO Arts Center	30 Washington St	718-694-0831
Gloria Kennedy Gallery	111 Front St	718-858-5254
Henry Gregg Gallery	111 Front St	718-408-1090
Jan Larsen Gallery	63 Pearl St	718-797-2557
Jubilee	117 Henry St	718-596-1499
Nelson Hancock Gallery	111 Front St	718-408-1190
The Rotunda Gallery	33 Clinton St	718-875-4047
Safe-T-Gallery	111 Front St	718-782-5920
Salena Gallery – LIU	1 University Plz	718-488-1051
Sankaranka Gallery	111 Front St	718-666-3636
Spring	126 Front St	718-222-1054
Underbridge Pictures	111 Front St	718-596-0390
Wessel + O'Connor Fine Art	111 Front St	718-596-1700

Map 6 · Fort Greene / Clinton Hill

Clinton Hill Simply Art Gallery	154 Vanderbilt Ave	718-852-0227
ElevenTen Gallery	1110 Fulton St	718-857-5696
Sarafina	411 Myrtle Ave	718-522-1083
Schafler Gallery – Pratt	200 Willoughby Ave	718-636-3517

Map 7 · Bedford-Stuyvesant

Skylight Gallery Restoration Plaza	1368 Fulton St	718-636-6949

Map 8 · BoCoCa / Red Hook

Artez'N	444 Atlantic Ave	718-596-2649
Brooklyn Waterfront Artists Coalition	499 Van Brunt St	718-596-2507
Bruno Marina Gallery	372 Atlantic Ave	718-254-0808
Kentler International Drawing Space	353 Van Brunt St	718-875-2098
Metaphor Contemporary Art	382 Atlantic Ave	718-254-9126
Micro Museum	123 Smith St	718-797-3116
Object-Image Gallery	91 Fifth Ave	718-623-2434
Rocketship	208 Smith St	718-797-1348

Map 9 · Park Slope / Prospect Heights / Windsor Terrace

440 Gallery	440 Sixth Ave	718-499-3844
Brooklyn Artist Gym	168 7th St	718-858-9069
JK Flynn	471 Sixth Ave	718-369-8934

Map 11 · Sunset Park / Green-Wood Heights

Tabla Rasa Gallery	224 48th St	718-768-0305

Arts & Entertainment · **Bookstores**

Though there are still far fewer bookstores in Brooklyn than there are writers, each of the borough's major neighborhoods has a few decent options. Perhaps the top place is Williamsburg's elegant **Spoonbill & Sugartown (Map 2)**. In Cobble Hill/Carroll Gardens, check out the excellent independent **Book Court (Map 8)**, **Rocketship (Map 8)**, with its brilliant selection of graphic novels, the fire-hazard of the **Community Book Store (Map 9)**, and the funky **Freebird Books (Map 8)**, which has the perfect combo of used titles and great coffee. Park Slope is home to **Community Book Store (Map 9)**, a cozy neighborhood meeting place complete with a café and garden. Also check out the very respectable used and new selection at the small storefront **Babbo's Books (Map 9)**, late-night selections at **Unnameable Books (Map 9)**, and local author readings downstairs at the **Barnes & Noble (Map 9)**.

Despite (or maybe because of) its out-of-the-way location, **Vox Pop (Map 13)**, the left-leaning bookstore from the founder of Soft Skull Press, is one to watch. Head to Borough Park and Brighton Beach for dizzying selections of Jewish and Russian bookstores, respectively. For more specific needs, however, you'll need to head into that other borough…

Map 1 · Greenpoint

Ex Libris Polish Book Gallery	140 Nassau Ave	718-349-0468	Polish.
Polish American Bookstore	648 Manhattan Ave	718-349-3756	Polish.
Polish Bookstore & Publishing	161 Java St	718-349-2738	Polish.
Polonia Book Store	882 Manhattan Ave	718-389-1684	Polish.
Word	126 Franklin St	718-383-0096	Literary fiction, non-fiction, and kids books.

Map 2 · Williamsburg

The Read Café	158 Bedford Ave	718-599-3032	Used.
Spoonbill & Sugartown	Mini Mall, 218 Bedford Ave	718-387-7322	Art, architecture, design, philosophy, and literature. New and used.

Map 3 · East Williamsburg

Libreria Cristiana Bethel	666 Broadway	718-388-3195	Religious.

Map 5 · Brooklyn Heights / DUMBO / Downtown

A&B Books	146 Lawrence St	718-596-0872	African-American books.
A&B Books	223 Duffield St	718-783-7808	General African-American books.
Barnes & Noble	106 Court St	718-246-4996	Chain.
Heights Books	109 Montague St	718-624-4876	Rare, out of print, used.
Long Island University Book Store	1 University Plz	718-858-3888	General.
St Mark's Comics	148 Montague St	718-935-0911	Comics.
Trazar's Variety Book Store	40 Hoyt St	718-797-2478	African-American books.
Zakka	155 Plymouth St	718-801-8037	Graphic design books.

Map 6 · Fort Greene / Clinton Hill

Brownstone Books at BAM	30 Lafayette Ave	718-636-4136	General, specializing in film, music, and dance.
Dare Books	33 Lafayette Ave	718-625-4651	General.
Pratt Institute Bookstore	550 Myrtle Ave	718-789-1105	Art books.

Map 7 · Bedford-Stuyvesant

Brownstone Books	409 Lewis Ave	718-953-7328	General.

Map 8 · BoCoCa / Red Hook

Anwaar Bookstore	428 Atlantic Ave	718-875-3791	Arabic books.

Book Court	163 Court St	718-875-3677	General.
Community Book Store	212 Court St	718-834-9494	General.
Dar Us Salam	486 Atlantic Ave	718-625-5925	Islamic books.
Freebird Books	123 Columbia St	718-643-8484	Used.
Pranga Book Store	354 Court St	718-624-2927	General new and used.
Rocketship	208 Smith St	718-797-1348	Comic books and graphic novels.

Map 9 • Park Slope / Prospect Heights / Windsor Terrace

Babbo's Books	242 Prospect Park W	718-788-3475	Used & new.
Barnes & Noble	267 Seventh Ave	718-832-9066	Chain.
Community Book Store	143 Seventh Ave	718-783-3075	Used & new.
Park Slope Books	200 Seventh Ave	718-499-3064	Mostly used.
Unnameable Books	456 Bergen St	718-789-1534	General new and used.

Map 10 • Prospect-Lefferts Gardens / Crown Heights

Goodwill Gospel Store	759 Flatbush Ave	718-287-9001	Christian.
Maverick Comics	210 Parkside Ave	718-284-5185	Comics.
Yoruba Book Center	610 New York Ave	718-774-5800	Yoruba religious bookstore.

Map 11 • Sunset Park / Green-Wood Heights

Libreria Jovenes Cristianos	5703 Fifth Ave	718-439-7873	Christian.

Map 12 • Borough Park

Ateres Sofrim	5302 16th Ave	718-633-4721	Judaica.
Bulletproof Comics	4507 Ft Hamilton Pkwy	718-854-3367	Comics.
Hecht Hebrew Book & Religious	265 Coney Island Ave	718-258-9696	Judaica.
Pinters Hebrew Book Store	4408 14th Ave	718-871-2260	Hebrew Bookstore.

Map 13 • Kensington / Ditmas Park / Windsor Terrace

Brooklyn College Bookstore	2900 Bedford Ave	718-434-0333	Selection of bestsellers and children's books.
Morija Book Store	1387 Flatbush Ave	718-282-9997	Religious.
Rincher's Bookstore	2804 Church Ave	718-282-4033	General.
Shakespeare & Co	14 Hillel Pl	718-434-5326	General.
Vox Pop	1022 Cortelyou Rd	718-940-2084	Progressive coffeehouse/event space/publishing company/bookstore!

Map 14 • Bay Ridge

Bay Ridge Bookstore	8508 Fourth Ave	718-680-5137	General.
The Bookmark Shoppe	8415 Third Ave	718-833-5115	General.
Galaxy Comics	6823 Fifth Ave	718-921-1236	Comics.
Islamic Books & Tapes	6805 Fifth Ave	718-567-8540	Islamic.

Map 15 • Dyker Heights / Bensonhurst

International Bookstore	1914 86th St	718-236-1090	Russian.

Map 16 • Midwood

A Torah Treasures Books & Gifts	3005 Ave L	718-758-1221	Judaica.
Bulletproof Comics	2178 Nostrand Ave	718-434-1800	Comics.
Harnik's Happy House	1403 Ave J	718-951-9805	General.
Here's A Book Store	1964 Coney Island Ave	718-645-6675	Used & new.
Mekor Hasfarim	1973 Coney Island Ave	718-627-4385	Judaica.
Rusbook Corporation Russian	1742 E 13th St	718-336-7680	Russian.

Brooklyn used to be teeming with hundreds of grand movie theaters. Unfortunately, almost all of the neighborhood movie palaces have been lost to the bulldozer or recycled into 99-cent stores. Despite its huge population, today Brooklyn offers very few movie theaters and even fewer decent ones. Nonetheless, for those who resist the urge to hop a subway to Manhattan, there are some worthwhile options. Movie buffs who are especially interested in independent and experimental films will be happy to know that Brooklyn has the most vibrant scene in the city.

There are a number of soulless multiplexes showing typical Hollywood fare, complete with stale popcorn and annoying commercials. Check the newspaper or the Web for the latest listings in various locations around Brooklyn. A better alternative is the handful of neighborhood cinemas still in operation. What they may lack in sound quality or screen size, they make up for in grit and charm. **Cobble Hill Cinemas (Map 8)** shows first-run and independent films and offers cheap tickets on Tuesdays and Thursdays. Even though it's unrenovated, the small and intimate **Pavilion Brooklyn Heights (Map 5)** remains a favorite, due to its charming miniscule lobby and fabulous location on Henry Street. The **Kent Triplex Theater (Map 16)** in Midwood could use a major renovation, but it shows Russian films and offers reduced-rate tickets on Wednesdays. The Brooklyn Public Library has the best deal in the borough with regular free screenings.

Brooklyn's gem for the true cinemaphile is the **BAM Rose Cinemas (Map 6)**. It boasts a gorgeously appointed space with tasty popcorn, pleasant service, and an exceptional choice of art house and foreign films. The theaters are rarely overcrowded and it is always clean and inviting, which is unique to the New York movie going experience. Manhattanites have even been known to make the colossal effort to leave their sacred island every so often to attend movies there! Specifically worth checking out is BAMcinématek, which hosts retrospectives, special screenings, and appearances by the finest directors and actors.

Some of the hippest cinema in Brooklyn happens a bit under the radar. At the top of the list is **Rooftop Films** (www.rooftopfilms.com; 718-417-7362) which mixes independent cinema with fresh air on various roofs around Brooklyn during the warmer months. Café Steinhof (Map 9) shows all types of film favorites with its Austrian grub on Sundays. An annual event not to be missed is the Brooklyn International Film Festival at the Brooklyn Museum (Map 10) every June. With cutting-edge events like this taking place, Brooklyn can once again be proud of its contribution to the New York film scene.

Movie Theaters	Address	Phone		Map
BAM Rose Cinemas	BAM, 30 Lafayette Ave	718-636-4100	Great seating and mix of first runs and revivals.	6
Cobble Hill Cinemas	265 Court St	718-596-9113	Great indie destination, though theaters are small.	8
Kent Triplex	1170 Coney Island Ave	718-338-3371	Moron blockbuster destination.	16
Pavilion Brooklyn Heights	70 Henry St	718-596-7070	Intimate, classy, and just about perfect.	5
Pavilion Movie Theatres	188 Prospect Park W	718-369-0838	Nice mix of stuff right across from Propsect Park.	9
Regal/UA Court Street	108 Court St	718-246-7995	Audience-participation-friendly megaplex.	5
Rooftop Films	various locations	718-417-7362	Summer rooftop series— check website for locations!	n/a

Museums

Brooklyn is not generally known for its museums, but culture buffs still have plenty to love. The main attraction is the **Brooklyn Museum (Map 10)** which became famous (or infamous) by igniting former Mayor Giuliani's ire with its controversial *Sensation's* exhibit. In addition to viewing an extensive permanent collection, crowds can dance and socialize at their ever-popular "First Saturdays," and admire the cutting-edge architecture (a transparent, space-age exterior fronting an old-world, Romanesque facade). History aficionados will enjoy the **Brooklyn Historical Society (Map 5),** housed in a four-story Queen Anne-style building and the fascinating vintage-subway-car-depot that is the **New York Transit Museum (Map 5)**, both of which are located downtown. Williamsburg's funky and fascinating **City Reliquary Museum (Map 2)** is a must see for New Yorkophiles. And kids and adults alike shouldn't miss the touchy-feely exhibits at the **Brooklyn Children's Museum (Map 10)**, which is regarded as the best of its kind in New York.

Museums	Address	Phone	Map
Brooklyn Children's Museum	145 Brooklyn Ave	718-735-4400	10
Brooklyn Historical Society	128 Pierrepont St	718-222-4111	5
Brooklyn Museum	200 Eastern Pkwy	718-638-5000	10
City Reliquary	370 Metropolitan Ave	718-782-4842	2
Coney Island Museum	1208 Surf Ave	718-372-5159	p136
Doll & Toy Museum of NYC	280 Cadman Plz W	718-243-0820	5
Harbor Defense Museum	230 Sheridan Loop	718-630-4349	14
Jewish Childrens' Museum	792 Eastern Pkwy	718-467-0600	10
Kurdish Library and Museum	345 Park Pl	718-783-7930	9
Museum of Contemporary African Diasporan Arts	80 Hanson Pl	718-230-0492	6
New York Aquarium	502 Surf Ave	718-265-3474	p136
New York Transit Museum	Boerum Pl & Schermerhorn St	718-694-1600	5
The Old Stone House	First Ave b/w 3rd St & 4th St	718-768-3195	9
Simmons Collection African Arts Museum	1063 Fulton St	718-230-0933	6
Waterfront Museum	290 Conover St	718-624-4719	8
Wyckoff-Bennett Homestead	5816 Clarendon Rd	718-629-5400	p135

Theaters

Broadway and Lincoln Center may have the big bucks and the well-known stars, but New York's abundance of talented artists is spread throughout the five boroughs. Brooklyn is the home of many firmly rooted theater, dance, and music companies and, with the increasing number of Manhattan groups getting priced out of their venues, is welcoming many new and adventurous artists who have chosen to hop across the East River.

The Brooklyn Academy of Music (just call it BAM) serves as the centerpiece for performing arts in Kings County. Consisting of the gorgeous, if slightly in need of more restoration, Beaux-Arts **Harvey Lichtenstein Theater (Map 6)**, the **Howard Gilman Opera House (Map 6)**, Rose Cinemas, and BAMcafé, it's a popular stopping point for an assortment of international, national, and local theater, dance, and classical music companies. BAM supplies a healthy mix of the traditional, contemporary, and experimental and serves as home to the illustrious and very hip Brooklyn Philharmonic. See the full schedule at www.bam.org.

For classical recitals in a casual setting, you can't get less formal than **Bargemusic (Map 5)**, moored at the Fulton Ferry landing. Concerts (some free) are presented year round, but with a romantic view of the Manhattan skyline it's especially popular on date nights during the warmer months. www.bargemusic.org

For opera lovers on a budget who don't want to stand in the nosebleed section of the Metropolitan Opera House, where you can't tell a mezzo from a countertenor, the Regina Opera Company gives you all the classics in their cozy space **Regina Hall (Map15)**. Production values are modest, but do you really need live horses to do *La Boheme*?

The **Galapagos Arts Space (Map 2)** sneers at the thought of applying for grants while the folks at **St. Ann's Warehouse (Map 5)** happily accept private and public funding. Both spaces encourage artists to experiment into new territory that sometimes results in non-traditional theater pieces. St. Ann's has seen two of its shows move to Broadway. Galapagos regularly hosts a new breed of retro-yet-feminist-approved burlesque shows, where mixed-gender audiences cheer on female striptease dancers whose routines are so funny and bizarre you'll probably forget to become aroused. The **Brooklyn Lyceum (Map 9)** has a regular hodgepodge of vaudeville and theater shorts. **Charlie Pineapple Theater Company (Map 2)** fits no more than two dozen patrons into its intimate space, but the young company has been tempting lovers of good drama with well-received productions of edgy plays such as *True West* and *One Flew Over the Cuckoo's Nest*. www.charliepineapple.com

Is your iPod loaded up with Rodgers and Hammerstein? Can't get enough of those Neil Simon comedies and Arthur Miller dramas? **The Heights Players (Map 5)** have been entertaining Brooklynites with popular favorites and recent Broadway and Off-Broadway hits since the days when Tennessee Williams was a fresh new voice. The slightly younger **Gallery Players (Map 9)** lean more toward off-beat works by the likes of Terrence McNally and Stephen Sondheim, often mounting the first New York revivals of recently closed plays and musicals. www.heightsplayers.org, www.galleryplayers.org

Many of these companies offer subscriptions to their seasons at discount prices, but you never know when a play will pop up at some space that is suddenly being called a theater. For extensive listings of plays all over New York, visit www.broadwayworld.com and www.theatermania.com.

Theaters	Address	Phone	Map
651 Arts	651 Fulton St	718-636-4181	6
Bargemusic	Fulton Ferry Landing near Brooklyn Bridge	718-624-2083	5
The Billie Holiday Theater	1368 Fulton St	718-636-0918	7
BRIC Studio	647 Fulton St	718-855-7882	5
Brick Theatre	575 Metropolitan Ave	718-907-6189	2
Brooklyn Arts Council	55 Washington St	718-625-0080	5
Brooklyn Arts Exchange	421 Fifth Ave	718-832-0018	9
Brooklyn Conservatory of Music	58 Seventh Ave	718-622-3300	9
Brooklyn Family Theatre	1012 Eighth Ave	718-670-7205	9
Brooklyn Lyceum	227 Fourth Ave	718-857-4816	9
Charlie Pineapple Theater Company	208 N 8th St	718-907-0577	2
Gallery Players Theater	199 14th St	718-595-0547	9
Gershwin Theater	2900 Bedford Ave	718-961-5666	13
Harvey Lichtenstein Theater	651 Fulton St	718-636-4100	6
The Heights Players	26 Willow St	718-237-2752	5
Howard Gilman Opera House	30 Lafayette Ave	718-636-4100	6
Paul Robeson Theatre	54 Greene Ave	718-783-9794	6
Puppetworks	338 Sixth Ave	718-965-3391	9
Regina Hall	65th St & 12th Ave	718-232-3555	15
St Ann's Warehouse	38 Water St	718-254-8779	5
Walt Whitman Theatre, Brooklyn Center for the Performing Arts	2900 Campus Rd	718-951-4500	13

Since the 17th Century, Manhattan has reigned supreme among its sister boroughs in terms of, well, pretty much everything. When one thinks of New York City, it is never of Fresh Kills, Staten Island, or the Brooklyn Navy Yard. Tourists and outer-borough residents have long sought solace in the warmth of Manhattan's day-glo cocktails. But the supremacy of the nation's smallest county is finally being challenged. Rising rents have forced artisans to seek shelter elsewhere, and in doing so they've helped transform run-down neighborhoods into hotbeds of booze and entertainment. No other borough has benefited more from this escape from New York than Manhattan's big brother Brooklyn.

For years, Brooklyn was sort of off the radar. If you moved across the East River, you'd only communicate with Manhattanites via postcard; now they're begging for a spot on your futon. Places like Williamsburg, Park Slope, and BoCoCa are being swarmed by Manhattanites who have unwittingly joined the legions of their cursed foe: the bridge-and-tunnel crowd. Manhattan may still be number one, but Brooklyn is an ass-nipping second. In terms of nightlife, it may have left the slender isle in the dust. Live music venues (both above- and underground) are thriving; their recorded counterparts, jukeboxes, are sucking down quarters by the fistful; and every other niche from the bowling alley to the martini bar has been pushed to its epitome in Brooklyn. Below are some suggestions.

Live Music

Brooklyn is enough of a tastemaker to now demand the attention of touring acts. The largest venues, **Studio B (Map 1)**, **Warsaw (Map 1)**, **Music Hall of Williamsburg (Map 2)**, and **Southpaw (Map 9)**, book rock, hip-hop, and experimental music (respectively) for panting droves of audiophiles. For a more intimate feel, and an emphasis on folk music, check out **Pete's Candy Store (Map 2)** or **Barbes (Map 9)**. Jazz is also alive and well at places like **Zebulon (Map 2)** and **The Jazz Spot (Map 7)**.

Hipster Bars

If you're not sure whether you've stumbled into a hipster enclave, look for board games and quiz-night emcees and a swarm of oddly dressed folks trying their damnedest not to enjoy themselves. Of course, hipsters aren't all bad. At least they know how to pick bars. They've named several their own, including **Buttermilk (Map 9)** in Park Slope, **Enid's (Map 1)** in Greenpoint, and **Royal Oak (Map 2)** in Williamsburg.

Atmosphere

This is a subjective category to be sure, but there are just certain bars that you go to for more than simply the beer selection or the drink specials. You go there because the ambience is interesting and inviting. **Iona (Map 2)** in Williamsburg, with its backyard patio and fire pits, is a case in point. For a funkier vibe, try **Sputnik (Map 6)** in Clinton Hill, chock-full of "space age" furnishings from the '60s and '70s. Since 1890, **Sunny's (Map 8)** has been the bar in Red Hook. It once took in patrons on a pay-what-you-wish basis, but Red Hook's rise has given them reason to actually charge for the alcohol served in this charming hideaway. And if you just want to go somewhere to relive the glory days of your teen years (but with legal drinking), rush over to **Barcade (Map 2)**, which is filled with '80s video games including NFT fave Q*bert.

Jukebox

If the DJ won't take requests and the bartender is only interested enough to put an iPod on shuffle, then you've got to go for the jukebox. For pure eclecticism, you can't beat **Daddy's (Map 2)** in Williamsburg. Indie rock fans should visit **Commonwealth (Map 9)**. For classic rock, new wave, and everything in-between, check out **Boat (Map 8)** in Carroll Gardens.

Dive Bars

Brooklyn has a few hundred years of drinking under its belt, so many establishments' heydays happened in the last millennium. Still, these places are newly embraced for their easy-going vibe and cheep beer. The ultimate Brooklyn dive is the **Turkey's Nest (Map 2)**, because it's not a hipster joint pretending to be seedy; it is a proudly certified craphole. **Tommy's Tavern (Map 1)** in Greenpoint is also a great armpit of a bar, and on the weekends they have live music in the back room that is surprisingly good. While in Park Slope, you can always drink for cheap at **O'Connor's (Map 9)**.

Best All Around

Certain bars, for whatever reason, simply rule. It might be because they attract a certain type of patron, or play a certain type of music, or sit in a certain neighborhood. However, the real reason people revisit these places over and over is for the emotional connection. Below are examples of places that have such a pull on their customers. For Manhattan-quality cocktails at Brooklyn prices, check out **Brooklyn Social (Map 8)** in Carroll Gardens. Their old-fashioned mixology makes it worth dealing with the crowds. **Spuyten Duyvil (Map 2)** in Williamsburg is something of a hidden gem. It attracts cultish locals who go ga-ga over the 80 international beers and appreciate the warm, knowledgeable staff. Finally, **The Gutter (Map 2)**, Brooklyn's first bowling alley to open in the borough in 50 years, draws those looking to knock 'em down while enjoying a great selection of craft brews.

Map 1 • Greenpoint

Black Rabbit	91 Greenpoint Ave	718-349-1595	Fantastic fireplace, delicious mini-burgers. Trivia night is packed.
Coco 66	66 Greenpoint Ave	718-389-7392	Like an LA bar. Dark, druggy and full of people talking about themselves.
The Diamond	43 Franklin St	718-383-5030	Wine, massive beer selection, and shuffleboard.
Enid's	560 Manhattan Ave	718-349-3859	Greenpoint's finest hipster stand-by.
Europa	98 Meserole Ave	718-383-5723	Strobe light extravaganza.
Jack O'Neil's	130 Franklin St	718-389-3888	Irish pub in a sea of Polish.
Lost and Found	113 Franklin St	718-383-6000	Skee-ball, Big Buck Hunter, free hot dogs, and occasional live bands.
The Mark Bar	1025 Manhattan Ave	718-349-2340	Wide selection of beer.
Matchless	557 Manhattan Ave	718-383-5333	Rock 'n' roll trivia nights are a must.
Pencil Factory	142 Franklin St	718-609-5858	Great beer; great vibe.
Red Star	37 Greenpoint Ave	718-349-0149	A real sports bar. 2 floors and terrific wings.
Studio B	259 Banker St	718-389-1880	Fluorescent lights, eclectic bands, and DJs.
Tommy's Tavern	1041 Manhattan Ave	718-383-9699	Super-dive with live music on weekends.
Warsaw	261 Driggs Ave	718-387-0505	Brooklyn's best concert venue.

Map 2 • Williamsburg

The Abbey	536 Driggs Ave	718-599-4400	Great jukebox and staff.
Alligator Lounge	600 Metropolitan Ave	718-599-4440	Ignore the décor, and enjoy the free brick oven pizza with your beer.
Barcade	388 Union Ave	718-302-6464	Paradise for '80s console champions and craft-beer guzzlers.
Bembe	81 S 6th St	718-387-5389	Hookahville.
Black Betty	366 Metropolitan Ave	718-599-0243	Dark, exotic, and inviting.
Brooklyn Brewery	79 N 11th St	718-486-7422	Open Friday nights only. Tours on Saturdays.
Charleston	174 Bedford Ave	n/a	Still going.
Clem's	264 Grand St	718-387-9617	Classic narrow bar space and good drink specials make this a neighborhood staple.

Daddy's	437 Graham Ave	718-609-6388	Friendly hipster hideaway.
East River Bar	97 S 6th St	718-302-0511	Fun interior, patio, and live music.
Greenpoint Tavern	188 Bedford Ave	718-384-9539	Cheap beer in Styrofoam cups.
The Gutter	200 N 14th	718-387-3585	Vintage style bowling alley with great brews on tap—what could be better?
Iona	180 Grand St	718-384-5008	Plenty of choices on tap.
Larry Lawrence	295 Grand St	718-218-7866	Laid-back bar with a lovely loft for smokers.
The Levee	212 Berry St	718-218-8787	Pinball, Connect Four, and Frito pies in a laid-back setting. Formerly Cokies, now a laid back vibe with free cheese balls.
Mugs Ale House	125 Bedford Ave	718-486-8232	Surprisingly good food, great beer selection, cheap.
Music Hall of Williamsburg	66 N 6th St	212-260-4700	Formerly Northsix, now Brooklyn's Bowery Ballroom.
Pete's Candy Store	709 Lorimer St	718-302-3770	Live music, trivia nights, awesome back room, and Scrabble.
Radegast Hall & Biergarten	113 N 3rd St	718-963-3973	German beer hall with retractable roof. Only in Williamsburg
Royal Oak	594 Union Ave	718-388-3884	It seems like everybody ends up here.
Savalas	285 Bedford Ave	718-599-5565	A narrow lounge, but people find space to dance.
Spuyten Duyvil	359 Metropolitan Ave	718-963-4140	Join the Belgian beer cult.
Trash	256 Grand St	718-599-1000	Punk rock, PBR, and free tater tots.
Turkey's Nest	94 Bedford Ave	718-384-9774	Best dive in Williamsburg.
Union Pool	484 Union Ave	718-609-0484	Good starting point—D or finishing point.
Zebulon	258 Wythe Ave	718-218-6934	World-fusion and jazz music with Mediterranean bar food.

Map 3 · East Williamsburg

Asterisk Art Space	258 Johnson Ave	n/a	Outsider bands for insiders.
Bushwick Country Club	618 Grand St	718-388-2114	"Muffy, I've got a feeling we're not in Greenwich anymore."
Don Pedro	90 Manhattan Ave	718-218-6914	Lively local watering hole that frequently hosts local bands.
duckduck	153 Montrose Ave		Badly needed neighborhood bar.
Harefield Road	769 Metropolitan Ave	718-388-6870	Spacious, unpretentious spot for microbrews and hot toddies.
Office Ops	57 Thames St	718-418-2509	The Rock and Rollerskate party should not be missed.
Sweet Ups	277 Graham Ave	718-384-3886	Great neighborhood bar with karaoke on Tuesdays.
Third Ward	195 Morgan Ave	718-715-4961	Art shows and parties in East-burg's industrial wilderness.
Wreck Room	940 Flushing Ave	718-418-6347	Get completely "over-served" at this live music spot.

Map 5 · Brooklyn Heights / DUMBO / Downtown

68 Jay Street Bar	68 Jay St	718-260-8207	Arty local bar.
Henry St Ale House	62 Henry St	718-522-4801	Cozy, dark space with good selections on tap.
Jack the Horse Tavern	66 Hicks St	718-852-5084	Oustanding upscale pub/New American cuisine, great feel.
Low Bar	81 Washington St	718-222-1569	Asian-themed basement bar.

Arts & Entertainment · **Nightlife**

Map 5 · Brooklyn Heights / DUMBO / Downtown—*continued*

Okeefe's	62 Court St	718-855-8751	Sports bar (large Met's following), surprisingly decent food.
St Ann's Warehouse	38 Water St	718-254-8779	Live music, theater. Challenging entertainment.
Water Street Bar	66 Water St	718-625-9352	Roomy Irish pub.

Map 6 · Fort Greene / Clinton Hill

The Alibi	242 DeKalb Ave	718-783-8519	Real deal neighborhood bar.
BAMcafé	30 Lafayette Ave	718-636-4100	Fine food, cocktails, and live music in a classy, cavernous space.
Frank's Lounge	660 Fulton St	718-625-9339	When you need to get funky.
Grand Dakar	285 Grand Ave	718-398-8900	Occasional live music; skip the jazz but check out the African sets.
Moe's	80 Lafayette Ave	718-797-9536	Laid-back, friendly, fun.
Reign Bar & Lounge	46 Washington Ave	718-643-7344	Posh, pricey club.
Sputnik	262 Taaffe Pl	718-398-6666	Fabulously furnished Pratt hangout.
Stonehome Wine Bar	87 Lafayette Ave	718-624-9443	Dark cave for serious oenophiles.
Thomas Beisl	25 Lafayette Ave	718-222-5800	Straight outta Vienna.

Map 7 · Bedford-Stuyvesant

Goodbye Blue Monday	1087 Broadway	718-453-6343	An antique shop and café with live music nightly.
The Jazz Spot	375 Kosciusko St	718-453-7825	Hot food and tasty jazz in a café atmosphere.
Sista's Place	456 Nostrand Ave	718-398-1766	Jazz, poetry, and open mic nights.
Solomon's Porch	307 Stuyvesant Ave	718-919-8001	Café with live jazz and spoken word.

Map 8 · BoCoCa / Red Hook

Abilene	442 Cort St	718-522-6900	Cozy and unpretentious. Drink specials galore.
Black Mountain Wine House	415 Union St	718-395-2614	Try the Lebanese wine!
Boat	175 Smith St	718-254-0607	Dank, dark, and friendly. Nice tunes to boot.
Brazen Head	228 Atlantic Ave	718-488-0430	Cask ale, mixed crowd.
Brooklyn Inn	148 Hoyt St	718-625-9741	When you're feeling nostalgic.
Brooklyn Social	335 Smith St	718-858-7758	Old boy's lounge revamped. Cocktails still the same. NFT Pick.
Cody's Bar & Grill	154 Court St	718-852-6115	Great sports bar. Seriously.
Downtown Bar & Grill	160 Court St	718-625-2835	Gets the package games. More beers than God intended for man.
Floyd	131 Atlantic Ave	718-858-5810	Indoor bocce ball court!
Gowanus Yacht Club	323 Smith St	718-246-1321	Dogs, burgers, and beer. Love it.
Issue Project Room	232 3rd St	718-330-0313	Art and performance space next to Gowanus Canal.
Kili	81 Hoyt St	718-855-5574	Nice space and chilled vibe.
Last Exit	136 Atlantic Ave	718-222-9198	Still trying to win trivia night. $10 pails of PBR.
Montero Bar and Grill	73 Atlantic Ave	718-624-9799	A taste of what things used to be like.
Moonshine	317 Columbia St	718-422-0563	You supply the meat; they supply the grill.
PJ Hanley's	449 Court St	718-797-4057	Booze since 1874.
Red Hook Bait & Tackle	320 Van Brunt St	718-797-4892	Kitschy, comfy pub with cheap drinks and good beers on tap.
Sugar Lounge	147A Columbia St	718-643-2880	Hammocks, hummus, and happy people.

Sunny's	253 Conover St	718-625-8211	No longer pay-what-you-wish, but still cheap and good.
Tini Wine Bar & Café	414 Van Brunt St	718-855-4206	Wine-soaked snacking on the Red Hook waterfront.
Waterfront Ale House	155 Atlantic Ave	718-522-3794	Renowned burgers and sizable beer list.

Map 9 · Park Slope / Prospect Heights / Windsor Terrace

Bar Toto	411 11th St	718-768-4698	Great bar food.
Barbes	376 9th St	718-965-9177	Smart-looking space with eclectic entertainment. Recommended.
Beast	638 Bergen St	718-399-6855	Great, great local vibe.
Buttermilk	577 Fifth Ave	718-788-6297	Hippest on the block.
Canal Bar	270 Third Ave	718-246-0011	Dive near the Gowanus, but not into it.
The Cherry Tree	65 Fourth Ave	718-399-1353	Rowdy Irish pub with a stately back yard.
Commonwealth	497 Fifth Ave	718-768-2040	So many beers, so little time.
Flatbush Farm	76 St Marks Ave	718-622-3276	Great bar, great food, great everything, really.
Fourth Avenue Pub	76 Fourth Ave	718-643-2273	1. Toss darts. 2. Drink fine draft beer. 3. Repeat.
Freddy's Bar and Backroom	485 Dean St	718-622-7035	Music and readings for finger-snapping hepcats.
The Gate	321 Fifth Ave	718-768-4329	Large outdoor area, twenty beers on tap.
Ginger's	363 Fifth Ave	718-788-0924	Nice and casual for center Slope.
Good Coffeehouse Music Parlor	53 Prospect Park West	718-768-2972	Brooklyn's home for acoustic roots music.
Great Lakes	284 Fifth Ave	718-499-3710	Laid-back hipster dive. Great jukebox, cheap beer.
Hank's Saloon	46 Third Ave	718-625-8003	Sweaty, hillbillyesque.
Lighthouse Tavern	243 Fifth Ave	718-788-8070	Don't miss Local Yokel night every Monday.
Loki Lounge	304 Fifth Ave	718-965-9600	Darts and billiards tone down the classic wood bar. Good music.
O'Connor's	39 Fifth Ave	718-783-9721	Friendly dive in need of a designer.
Pacific Standard	82 Fourth Ave	718-858-1951	Drinking and board games most certainly mix.
Park Slope Ale House	356 Sixth Ave	718-788-1756	Good pub grub and beer selection.
Patio Lounge	179 Fifth Ave	718-857-3477	Verdant boozing.
Puppet's Jazz Bar	294 Fifth Ave	718-499-2627	Jazz and wine preside in this wee club.
Soda	629 Vanderbilt Ave	718-230-8393	Nice summer drinkin' spot. NFT pick.
Southpaw	125 Fifth Ave	718-230-0236	Best live music in the Slope.
Timboo's	477 Fifth Ave	718-788-9782	Nothin' fancy—just booze, TVs and talk of gentrification.
Union Hall	702 Union St	718-638-4400	Quirky spot for indie shows and stuffed birds.

Map 10 · Prospect Lefferts-Gardens / Crown Heights

Empire Roller Skating Center	687 Sixth Ave	718-462-1400	Gospel night and adult night rollerskating.
Maximillian Bells	1146 Nostrand Ave		Reliable and lovable dive bar.
Wingate Field	Brooklyn Ave & Winthrop St	718-469-1912	Live music every now and then.

Map 11 · Sunset Park / Green-Wood Heights

Kitchenbar	687 Sixth Ave	718-499-5623	Comfortable and stylish lounge in South Slope.
Melody Lanes	461 37th St	718-832-2695	Way better than Bowlmor.

Map 13 · Kensington / Ditmas Park / Windsor Terrace

Michelle's Cocktail Lounge	2294 Bedford Ave	718-284-1185	Rustic pub.
Shenanigans Pub	802 Caton Ave	718-633-3689	Tavern-like with a dark, tropical feel.

Map 14 · Bay Ridge

Bean Post	7525 Fifth Ave	718-745-9413	Popular pub/sports bar.
Delia's Lounge	9224 Third Ave	718-745-7999	When you need to get in the mood.
Hall of Fame Billiards	505 Ovington Ave	718-921-2694	Large poolhall with celeb cache.
JJ Bubbles	7912 Third Ave	718-745-8790	Comfortable dive bar.
Kelly's Tavern	9259 Fourth Ave	718-745-9546	Classic NY Irish bar.
Kitty Kiernan's	9715 Third Ave	718-921-0217	Another Irish pub.
Peggy O'Neill's	8123 Fifth Ave	718-748-1400	Standard Irish.
Salty Dog	7509 Third Ave	718-238-0030	Good food and boisterous dancing. (Don't tell Bloomberg.)
Speakeasy	9427 Fifth Ave	718-833-3941	Cozy bar with live music nights.
Wicked Monk	8415 Fifth Ave	718-921-0601	Intimate Gothic pub.

Map 16 · Midwood

Blue Velvet Lounge	341 Ave U	718-266-5196	Cocktail central.

Eastern Brooklyn

The Wrong Number	168 Ave T	718-373-6865	Friendly neighborhood bar.

To eat in Brooklyn—the stuff that dreams are made of…

Welcome to Italy

You got ya two kinds of Italian places in Brooklyn—the old ones and the new ones. And, with a few notable exceptions, the new ones are waaay better than the old ones. A few exceptions—**Ferdinando's (Map 8)** for killer Sicilian (no pun intended), **Queen (Map 5)** for classic white-linen Italian, and **Joe's of Avenue U (Eastern Brooklyn)** for buffet-style. But for daily life in the 21st Century, almost every nabe in BK has got it goin' on—so check out **Acqua Santa (Map 2)** in Williamsburg, **Locanda (Map 6)** in Clinton Hill, **Noodle Pudding (Map 5)** in Brooklyn Heights, **Al Di La (Map 9)** in Park Slope, **Fragole (Map 8)** and **Panino'teca 275 (Map 8)** in Carroll Gardens, **The Good Fork (Map 8)** in Red Hook, **Bocca Lupo (Map 8)** in Cobble Hill, **Scopello (Map 6)** in Ft. Greene, and **The Tuscany Grill (Map 14)** in Bay Ridge. Trust us—any one of these "new" joints will make you feel quite close to the old country.

Liberté, égalité, fraternité!

In case you thought that the other great cuisine of the world was underrepresented, think again. There is pretty much at least one, if not more than one, French response to the Italian options above—so be sure and check out **Belleville (Map 9)** in Park Slope, **Quercy (Map 8)** and **Bar Tabac (Map 8)** in Cobble Hill, **Chez Oskar (Map 6)** and **Chez Lola (Map 6)** in Fort Greene, and **Fada (Map 2)** and **Juliette (Map 2)** in Williamsburg. A moment of silence for the fabulous but closed 360 in Red Hook.

The Rest of the World

The entire world's ethnic make-up is represented in Brooklyn, somewhere or other. Fortunately this translates into an abundance of food choices—from the great Mexican at **Alma (Map 8)** in Carroll Gardens West to the extremely simple and unpretentious Middle Eastern **Zaytoons (Map 8)** on Smith Street. And then, everything else…**Madiba (South African Map 6)**; **Lomzynianka** (Polish **Map 1**); **Convivium Osteria** (Portuguese **Map 9**); **Thomas Beisl** (Austrian **Map 6**); **Joya** (Thai **Map 8**); **Nyonya** (Malaysian **Map 11**); **Kush** (African **Map 6**); **Grand Dakar** (Senegalese **Map 6**); **Sheep Station** (Australian **Map 8**); etc…

The Pizza War

You just can't beat Brooklyn for pizza, although trying to come to some sort of consensus as to which is the "best" is beyond impossible. The classics in each neighborhood include **Grimaldi's (Map 5)** in Brooklyn Heights (always top-rated by Zagat), the utterly fresh+brilliant **Franny's (Map 9)** in Park Slope/Prospect Heights, **Totonnos (p. 136)** in Coney Island (the thinnest thin-crust of them all), **DiFaras (Map 16)** in Midwood (see Dominic DeMarco take the pizzas out of the oven with his bare hands), **Lucali (Map 8)** in Carroll Gardens, and the furthest out there of them all, **L&B Spumoni Gardens (Eastern Brooklyn)** in Bensonhurst (get the Sicilian).

Where Everyone Knows Your Name

This is by no means an exhaustive list, but there just happen to be a few places in each nabe that are simply cool, friendly places to go to. **The Hope & Anchor (Map 8)** is close to the top of this list (that's three Red Hook mentions so far for those of you counting at home), followed closely by **Tom's (Map 9)** in Prospect Heights, **DuMont (Map 2)** in Williamsburg, **Maggie Brown (Map 6)** in Fort Greene, and **Sherwood Café (Map 8)** in Carroll Gardens. Insert your own here:_____.

Our Favorite Restaurants

Again, just a few picks to stir things up: **Applewood (Map 9)**—slow food comes to Brooklyn; **Blue Ribbon (Map 9)**—surely you didn't think we'd forget; **Stone Park Café (Map 9)**—any place with marrow is a friend of ours; **Relish (Map 2)**—cool in every possible aspect of the word; **Bar Tabac (Map 8)**—anything open past 10 pm in Brooklyn is a godsend; **Convivium Osteria (Map 9)**—one of the best interiors (especially the basement) this side of the Atlantic; **Henry's End (Map 5)**—elk chops + Samuel Smith's Nut Brown Ale = Bliss; and, of course, **Peter Luger (Map 2)**—the best steak this world has ever seen. And the best spinach. And the best potatoes. And…you get the point.

Arts & Entertainment · **Restaurants**

Key: $: Under $10 / $$: $10–$20 / $$$: $20–$30 / $$$$: $30–$40 / $$$$$: $40+;
     * : Does not accept credit cards / † : Accepts only American Express / †† : Accepts only Visa and MasterCard

Map 1 · Greenpoint

Closing time on weekend nights

Name	Address	Phone	Price	Close	Notes
Acapulco Deli & Restaurant	1116 Manhattan Ave	718-349-8429	$	10 pm	Authentic Mexican food with some American standards.
Amarin Café	617 Manhattan Ave	718-349-2788	$*	11 pm	Good, cheap Thai food.
Baldo's Pizza	175 Nassau Ave	718-349-7770	$$*	10 pm	Pizza; best when delivered.
Brooklyn Label	180 Franklin St	718-389-2806	$	9 pm	Scrumptious sandwiches in the stately Astral building.
Casanova	338 McGuinness Blvd	718-389-0990	$$	11 pm	Italian fare.
Christina's	853 Manhattan Ave	718-383-4382	$*	10 pm	Traditional Polish food, cheap breakfasts!
Dami's	931 Manhattan Ave	718-349-7501	$$	10 pm	Brand new Polish-American joint.
Divine Follie Café	929 Manhattan Ave	718-389-6770	$$	10 pm	Large selection of meats, pastas, and pizza.
Enid's	560 Manhattan Ave	718-349-3859	$$	10 pm	Popular brunch on weekends; also dinner weeknights.
Erb	681 Manhattan Ave	718-349-8215	$$††	11:30 pm	Try the curry noodles.
Fresca Tortilla	620 Manhattan Ave	718-389-8818	$$	11 pm	Cheap Mexican takeout.
God Bless Deli	818 Manhattan Ave	718-349-0605	$*	24-hrs	The only 24-hour joint in the 'hood. Cheap sandwiches and burgers.
Johnny's Café	632 Manhattan Ave	718-383-9644	$$	1 am	Home-cooked Polish standards.
Lamb & Jaffey	1073 Manhattan Ave	718-389-3638	$$$	1 am	Classy date spot.
Lomzynianka	646 Manhattan Ave	718-389-9439	$*	9 pm	Get your kitschy Polish fix dirt cheap.
Manhattan 3 Decker	695 Manhattan Ave	718-389-6664	$$	9:30 pm	Greek and American fare.
Monsignor's	905 Lorimer St	718-963-3399	$$	11 pm	Cheap Italian.
Old Poland Restaurant	190 Nassau Ave	718-349-7775	$*	9 pm	Polish/American.
OTT	970 Manhattan Ave	718-609-2416	$$	10:30 pm	Another excellent Thai choice on Manhattan Ave.
Queen's Hideaway	222 Franklin St	718-383-2355	$$$††	10:30 pm	Home cookin' with something new every day.
Relax	68 Newell St	718-389-1665	$*	9:30 pm	Polish diner w/ good prices and excellent soups—a neighborhood favorite.
San Diego	999 Manhattan Ave	718-389-7747	$$	12 am	Mexican kitchen.
Sapporo Haru	622 Manhattan Ave	718-389-9697	$$††	12:30 am	Fresh sushi, friendly service.
Thai Café	925 Manhattan Ave	718-383-3562	$*	11 pm	Vast menu, veg options, eat in or take out.
Valdiano	659 Manhattan Ave	718-383-1707	$$*	8:45 pm	Southern Italian.

Map 2 · Williamsburg

Name	Address	Phone	Price	Close	Notes
Acqua Santa	556 Driggs Ave	718-384-9695	$$	12 am	Bistro Italian—amazing patio.
Anna Maria Pizza	179 Bedford Ave	718-599-4550	$	4 am	A must before late-night drinking.
Bacci & Abracci	204 Grand St	718-599-6599	$$	12 am	Old-world Italian in a modern setting.
Blackbird Parlour	197 Bedford Ave	718-599-2707	$		Cozy European style café with tasty sandwiches.
Bonita	338 Bedford Ave	718-384-9500	$	12 am	Americanized Mexican in a nice atmosphere.
Bozu	296 Grand St	718-384-7770	$$††	1 am	Amazing Japanese tapas and sushi bombs.
Diner	85 Broadway	718-486-3077	$$	1 am	Amazing, simple food like you've never tasted—never disappoints.
Dokebi	199 Grand St	718-782-1424	$$$	12 am	Cook your own Korean BBQ with tabletop hibachi.
Dressler	149 Broadway	718-384-6343	$$$$	12 am	So darn classy, you'll feel like you're in Park Slope.
DuMont	432 Union Ave	718-486-7717	$$	12 am	Continually changing market-fresh menu and yummy desserts.
DuMont Burger	314 Bedford Ave	718-384-6127	$$	2 am	The mini burger is even better proportioned than the original.
Fada	530 Driggs Ave	718-388-6607	$$$	1 am	Cuisine Marseillaise.
Fette Sau	345 Metropolitan Ave	718-963-3404	$$	11 pm	Enjoy pounds of meat and casks of beer in a former auto-body repair shop.

Arts & Entertainment · **Restaurants**

Key: $: Under $10 / $$: $10–$20 / $$$: $20–$30 / $$$$: $30–$40 / $$$$$: $40+;
* : Does not accept credit cards / † : Accepts only American Express / †† : Accepts only Visa and MasterCard

Map 2 · Williamsburg —continued

Juliette	135 N 5th St	718-388-9222	$$	1 am	Northside bistro with rooftop deck.
Kate's Brooklyn Joint	295 Berry St	718-218-7167	$$	10 pm	Fake-meat comfort food.
Lola's	454 Graham Ave	718-389-7497	$$	11 pm	Mexican brunch.
Marlow & Sons	81 Broadway	718-384-1441	$$$	1 am	Oysters and beer, old timey-like—go for Happy Hour
Moto	394 Broadway	718-599-6895	$$*	12 am	Triangular nook with horseshoe bar and comfort food.
Oasis	161 N 7th St	718-218-7607	$	3 am	Cheap Middle Eastern delights right by the L, and open late.
Peter Luger Steak House	178 Broadway	718-387-7400	$$$$$*	10:45 pm	Best steak, potatoes, and spinach in this solar system.
PT	331 Bedford Ave	718-388-7438	$$$	12 am	D.O.C.'s sophisticated older brother.
Radegast Hall & Biergarten	113 N 3rd St	718-963-3973	$$	11:30 pm	German fare (schnitzel and strudel) in old-timey bier hall atmosphere.
Raymund's Place	124 Bedford Ave	718-388-4200	$$*	11 pm	The Polish "Hooters."
Relish	225 Wythe St	718-963-4546	$$	1 am	Comfort food gone eclectic with a touch of class.
Roebling Tea Room	143 Roebling St	718-963-0760	$$$	3 am	Fancy tea eatery.
Sparky's/Egg	135A N 5th St	718-302-5151	$$	12 am	Organic breakfast and free range burgers.
Taco Chulo	318 Grand St	718-302-2485	$$	11 pm	Handmade, decadently pimped out tacos. Gotta love that!
Teddy's Bar and Grill	96 Berry St	718-384-9787	$††	1 am	Best bar food ever. Hipster and Polish locals unite.
Yola's Café	542 Metropolitan Ave	718-486-0757	$*	1 am	Terrific, authentic Mexican in a claustrophobic atmosphere.

Map 3 · East Williamsburg

Bahia	690 Grand St	718-218-9592	$$	11 pm	Try the mouth-watering pupusas.
Barzola	197 Meserole St	718-381-4343	$$	11 pm	Ecuadorean fare in mirrored splendor.
Café Nijasol	173 Montrose Ave	718-599-1612		6 pm	A friendly neighborhood café serving coffee, breakfast, and sandwiches to the Montrose L crowds.
Carmine's	358 Graham Ave	718-782-9659	$	11 pm	Amazing slices.
Cono and Sons O'Pescatore	301 Graham Ave	718-388-0168	$$	11 pm	Old World elegance, Neapolitan style.
Danny's Pizzeria	241 Bushwick Ave	718-381-1669	$	12 am	Not the best, but the only pizza in town.
El Brillante Restaurant	159 Graham Ave	718-782-3323	$*	11 pm	Friendly Spanish-American luncheonette.
El Nuevo Yauca	465 Bushwick Ave	718-386-5913	$$*	11 pm	South of the border delicacies.
Garden Grill	318 Graham Ave	718-384-8668	$$	10 pm	Classic diner grub with good donuts.
Grand Morelos	727 Grand St	718-218-9441	$$††	24-Hrs	24-hour Mexican diner/bakery.
Latin Cuisine	804 Grand St	718-302-6146	$$	11 pm	Good Columbian fare.
Life Café NINE83	983 Flushing Ave	718-386-1133	$$	1 am	Same as Life on Ave B with excellent happy hour.
Lily Thai	615 Grand St	718-218-7522	$	10:30 pm	Extensive menu with good lunch specials.
Loco Burrito	243 Bushwick Ave	718-456-9114	$$	11 pm	A place for the new, unadventurous hipsters.
Los Primos	704 Grand St	718-486-8449	$$	3 am	Authentic Latin spot with tasty seafood.
Manna's Restaurant	829 Broadway	718-218-8575	$*	9 pm	Pay-by-the-pound soul food buffet.
Mojito Loco	102 Meserole St	718-963-2960	$$††	11 pm	Yummy Latin fusion. Love the corn.
Najeeb's	374 Graham Ave	718-387-8333	$$*	10 pm	Tasty Middle Eastern fare.
Ricos Tacos y Antojitos Mexicanos	107 Graham Ave	718-384-9076	$*	8 pm	Best Mexican food in the 'hood.
Tony's Pizzeria	355 Graham Ave	718-384-8669	$$	12 am	Pizza, pasta, espresso.
Wombat	613 Grand St	718-218-7077	$$*	11 pm	Aussie cuisine lands in Billyburg.

Key: $: Under $10 / $$: $10–$20 / $$$: $20–$30 / $$$$: $30–$40 / $$$$$: $40+;
        * : Does not accept credit cards / † : Accepts only American Express / †† : Accepts only Visa and MasterCard

Map 4 • Bushwick

Bojangles'	1291 Broadway	718-443-7913	$	3 am	Unbelievable biscuits and fries.
Northeast Kingdom	18 Wyckoff Ave	718-386-3864	$$	11 pm	Cozy, hip ski lodge–style eatery in gritty nabe.

Map 5 • Brooklyn Heights / DUMBO / Downtown

Bubby's	1 Main St	718-222-0666	$$	11 pm	It's all about the pie.
Curry Leaf	151 Remsen St	718-222-3900	$$	10:30 pm	Terrific Indian food.
DUMBO General Store	111 Front St	718-855-5288	$$	8 pm	Food and drink for artists.
Fascati Pizzeria	80 Henry St	718-237-1278	$*	11 pm	Excellent slice pizza.
Five Front	5 Front St	718-625-5559	$$	12 am	Tasty newcomer with a beautiful garden.
Five Guys	138 Montague St	718-797-9380	$	10 pm	Burger joint with tasty fries and free peanuts while you wait.
Grimaldi's	19 Old Fulton St	718-858-4300	$*	11:45 pm	Excellent, though not the best, NY pizza.
Hale & Hearty Soup	32 Court St	718-596-5600	$$	7 pm	Super soups.
Heights Café	84 Montague St	718-625-5555	$$$	12 am	Decent dining near the Promenade.
Henry's End	44 Henry St	718-834-1776	$$$	11 pm	Inventive, game-oriented menu.
Jack the Horse Tavern	66 Hicks St	718-852-5084	$$$$	11 pm	Oustanding upscale pub/New American cuisine, great feel.
Junior's Restaurant	386 Flatbush Ave	718-852-5257	$	2 am	American with huge portions.
Miso	40 Main St	718-858-8388	$$$	11 pm	Japanese fusion cuisine.
Noodle Pudding	38 Henry St	718-625-3737	$$*	11 pm	Excellent Northern Italian fare.
Pete's Downtown	2 Water St	718-858-3510	$$	11 pm	Italian food and a view.
The Plant	25 Jay St	718-722-7541	$$	11 pm	Raw and organic foods.
Queen Ristorante	84 Court St	718-596-5954	$$$$	10:30 pm	Good, white-tablecloth, bow-tied-waiter, Italian joint
Rice	81 Washington St	718-222-9880	$$*	11 pm	Tasty Asian for less.
River Café	1 Water St	718-522-5200	$$$$$	11 pm	Great view, but overrated.
Siggy's Good Food	76 Henry St	718-237-3199	$$††	10 pm	Vegan pal café.
Superfine	126 Front St	718-243-9005	$$	11 pm	Mediterranean-inspired menu, bi-level bar, local art and music. NFT pick.
Sushi California	71 Clark St	718-222-0308	$$	11 pm	Sushi Express, reasonable prices.
Thai 101	101 Montague St	718-237-2594	$$	10:30 pm	Die for this Thai.
Theresa's	80 Montague St	718-797-3996		11 pm	Polish-American comfort food. Come hungry.
Toro Restaurant	1 Front St	718-625-0300	$$	12 am	Spanish-Asian fusion.

Map 6 • Fort Greene / Clinton Hill

1 Greene Sushi and Sashimi	1 Greene Ave	718-422-1000	$$	11 pm	Fresh sushi, familiar standardized setting.
67 Burger	67 Lafayette Ave	718-797-7150	$$	10 pm	Super-cool stop for a quick bite before your movie at BAM.
BAMcafé	30 Lafayette Ave	718-636-4100	$$	12 am	Café with live music weekend evenings.
Black Iris	228 DeKalb Ave	718-852-9800	$$*	11:30 pm	Middle Eastern.
Buff Patty	376 Myrtle Ave	718-855-3266	$	10 pm	Excellent and super-cheap Mex; nice and spicy.
Café Lafayette	99 S Portland Ave	718-858-6821	$$$	12 am	French goodness near BAM; small, intimate.
Castro's Restaurant	511 Myrtle Ave	718-398-1459	$$	12 am	Burritos delivered con cervesas, if you like.
Chez Lola	387 Myrtle Ave	718-858-1484	$$$	11 pm	French, inventive specials; a Fort Greene favorite.
Chez Oskar	211 DeKalb Ave	718-852-6250	$$$	1 am	French cuisine in a good neighborhood bistro.
Choice Market	318 Lafayette Ave	718-230-5234	$*	9 pm	Excellent sandwiches, baked goods, burgers, etc. served w/ maddening slowness. Outside.

Arts & Entertainment · **Restaurants**

Key: $: Under $10 / $$: $10–$20 / $$$: $20–$30 / $$$$: $30–$40 / $$$$$: $40+;
* : Does not accept credit cards / † : Accepts only American Express / †† : Accepts only Visa and MasterCard

Map 6 · Fort Greene / Clinton Hill—*continued*

Grand Dakar	285 Grand Ave	718-398-8900	$$$	1 am	Friendly, insanely laid-back Senegalese.
Habana Outpost	757 Fulton St	718-858-9500	$*	12 am	Grilled corn and free movies in a solar-powered restaurant.
Ici	246 DeKalb Ave	718-789-2778	$$$	11 pm	Beautiful new addition to FG restaurant scene, and worth the splurge.
Kush	17 Putnam Ave	718-230-3471	$$	12 am	West African café and restaurant; killer short ribs.
Locanda Vini & Olii	129 Gates Ave	718-622-9202	$$	11:30 pm	Rustic but pricey neighborhood Italian. Marvelous décor.
LouLou	222 DeKalb Ave	718-246-0633	$$$	12 am	Rustic Breton/French gem where seafood rules.
Luz	177 Vanderbilt Ave	718-246-4000	$$$	12 am	Yuppie interior with requisite brunch.
Madiba	195 DeKalb Ave	718-855-9190	$$$	12 am	South African-Bunny Chow, need we say more? Shebeen with live music.
Maggie Brown	455 Myrtle Ave	718-643-7001	$$*	12 am	Food by the fireplace; great burgers.
Mojito Restaurant	82 Washington Ave	718-797-3100	$$	10:30 pm	Classy Cuban cuisine.
Night of the Cookers	767 Fulton St	718-797-1197	$$$	12:30 am	Hip bistro with southern accents.
Olea	171 Lafayette Ave	718-643-7003	$$	12 am	Retooled Mediterenean.
Pequena	86 S Portland Ave	718-643-0000	$$*	12 am	Killer quesadillas.
Red Bamboo	271 Adelphi St	718-643-4352	$$$	3 am	Leafy patio, friendly service, veggie treats. Edamame that will make you believe.
Rice	166 DeKalb Ave	718-858-2700	$$*	11 pm	Tasty Asian for less.
Ruthie's Restaurant	96 DeKalb Ave	718-246-5189	$$*	11 pm	Soul food in mega portions.
Scopello	63 Lafayette Ave	718-852-1100	$$	11 pm	Sicilian chic in stylish surroundings.
The Smoke Joint	87 S Elliiot Pl	718-797-1011	$$	11 pm	BBQ with the right sauce. Holla!
Soule	920 Fulton St	718-399-7200	$$	12 am	Everything from king crab to roti to curry goat to blackened salmon. Tons of sides.
Thai 101	455 Myrtle Ave	718-855-4615	$$	11 pm	Die for this Thai.
Thomas Beisl	25 Lafayette Ave	718-222-5800	$$$	12 am	Pricey pre-BAM Austrian. Definitely go once.
Zaytoons	472 Myrtle Ave	718-623-5522	$$	12 am	Above-average Middle Eastern's second outpost.

Map 7 · Bedford-Stuyvesant

A&A Bakes & Doubles	481 Nostrand Ave	718-230-0753	$*	3 pm	A neighborhood favorite—no one leaves without their doubles.
Ali's Roti Shop	1267 Fulton St	718-783-0316	$*	9 pm	West Indian roti.
Dabakh Malick Resaurant	1191 Fulton St	718-399-1588	$$*	2 am	Senegalese steam table for the adventurous hungry.
Ricardo Pizza	528 Nostrand Ave	718-638-6924	$*	9 pm	Best pizza in the Stuy, period. Pops is no joke with a pie.
SugarHill Supper Club	609 DeKalb Ave	718-797-1727	$$††	24-Hrs	Downtown soul(food).

Map 8 · BoCoCa / Red Hook

Alma	187 Columbia St	718-643-5400	$$$	11 pm	Top NYC Mexican with great views of Lower Manhattan.
Atlantic Chip Shop	129 Atlantic Ave	718-855-7775	$$	12 am	Heart attack on a plate.
Bar Tabac	128 Smith St	718-923-0918	$$	3 am	Open late; fabulous frites, burgers, et al.
Bocca Lupo	391 Henry St	718-243-2522	$$$	12 am	Postmodern panini by day and (late) night. We love NYC.
Caserta Vecchia	221 Smith St	718-624-7549	$$	11 pm	Excellent, fresh brick-oven and friendly smiles; garden.
Chance	223 Smith St	718-242-1515	$$$$	12 am	Upscale Asian fusion—recommended.
Chestnut	271 Smith St	718-243-0049	$$$	11 pm	Seasonal fare. Severely underrated.

209

Arts & Entertainment • **Restaurants**

Key: $: Under $10 / $$: $10–$20 / $$$: $20–$30 / $$$$: $30–$40 / $$$$$: $40+;
* : Does not accept credit cards / † : Accepts only American Express / †† : Accepts only Visa and MasterCard

Map 8 • BoCoCa / Red Hook —continued

Chicory	243 DeGraw St	718-797-2121	$	10 pm	Gavin McAleer kicks major ass. Everything's great.
Cubana Café	272 Smith St	718-858-3980	$$*	11:30 pm	Colorful, authentic Cuban Ñlively staff.
El Nuevo Portal	217 Smith St	718-246-1416	$*	11 pm	Killer breaded steak.
Ferdinando's Focacceria Restaurant	151 Union St	718-855-1545	$*	10 pm	Sicilian specialties you won't find anywhere else! Get the panelle special.
Fragole	394 Court St	718-522-7133	$$	11:30 pm	Fresh and cozy Italian. An absolute gem.
Frankie's 457	457 Court St	718-403-0033	$$*	12 am	Fantastic meatballs. Cool space.
The Good Fork	391 Van Brunt St	718-643-6636	$$$	10:30 pm	Yep. It's good.
The Grocery	288 Smith St	718-596-3335	$$$$$††	11 pm	Magnificent. Reservations recommended.
Hadramout	172 Atlantic Ave	718-852-3577	$*	12 am	Great Yemeni diner–order the salta and don't fear the fenugreek foam!
Hanco's	85 Bergen St	718-858-6818	$*	9 pm	Banh Mi for people who won't trek to Sunset Park.
Hope & Anchor	347 Van Brunt St	718-237-0276	$$	1 am	Great upscale diner.
Joya	215 Court St	718-222-3484	$$*	12 am	Excellent, inexpensive, but super-noisy Thai.
Ki Sushi	122 Smith St	718-935-0575	$$	12 am	Affordable sushi in sleek surroundings.
Le Petite Café	502 Court St	718-596-7060	$$	10:30 pm	Great bistro food–check out the garden.
Lucali	575 Henry St	718-858-4086	$$	6 pm	One man makes every perfect pizza by hand.
Panino'teca 275	275 Smith St	718-237-2728	$$	12 am	Great paninis and fab cheese lasagna.
Patois	255 Smith St	718-855-1535	$$$$	11:30 pm	French bistro. Killer brunch.
Quercy	242 Court St	718-243-2151	$$$$	11 pm	Sister restaurant to La Luncheonette in Manhattan, and equally sublime.
Sam's Restaurant	238 Court St	718-596-3458		1 am	An Italian institution. Go for the pizza.
Saul	140 Smith St	718-935-9844	$$$	11 pm	Romantical.
Sherwood Café/ Robin des Bois	195 Smith St	718-596-1609	$$*	1 am	Mellow French vibe—best croque monsieur in town.
Soul Spot	302 Atlantic Ave	718-596-9933	$$††	11 pm	American and Afro-Caribbean soul food.
Yemen Café	176 Atlantic Ave	718-834-9533	$	11 pm	More good Yemeni food, because you can never have too much lamb.
Zaytoons	283 Smith St	718-875-1880	$$	12 am	Excellent Middle Eastern pizzas and kebabs.

Map 9 • Park Slope / Prospect Heights / Windsor Terrace

12th Street Bar and Grill	1123 Eighth Ave	718-965-9526	$$$	11 pm	Outstanding gourmet comfort fare.
2nd Street Café	189 Seventh Ave	718-369-6928	$$	12 am	Clamoring brunch crowd.
Al Di La Trattoria	248 Fifth Ave	718-783-4565	$$$	11 pm	Chandelier & brick-walled Italian. Super.
Amorina	624 Vanderbilt Ave	718-230-3030	$$$	11 pm	Watch your perfect pizza get made with sea salt and love.
Anthony's	426 Seventh Ave	718-369-8315	$$	12 am	New neighborhood fave for brick-oven 'za.
Applewood	501 11th St	718-768-2044	$$$	11 pm	Elegant, cheerful slow food.
Beast	638 Bergen St	718-399-6855	$$$	11:30 pm	American tapas.
Belleville	332 Fifth Ave	718-832-9777	$$$$$	12 am	Fab bistro French; they've perfected entrecote.
Blue Ribbon Brooklyn	280 Fifth Ave	718-840-0404	$$$$	4 am	The one and only!
Bogota Latin Bistro	141 Fifth Ave	718-230-3805	$$$	1 am	Stylish South- and Central-American restaurant.
Bonnie's Grill	278 Fifth Ave	718-369-9527	$$	12 am	Habit-forming contemporary diner.
Brooklyn Fish Camp	162 Fifth Ave	718-783-3264	$$$	11 pm	Mary's Fish Camp redux.
ChipShop	383 Fifth Ave	718-832-7701	$*	11 pm	Brits dish fish, chips, and the Beatles.
Convivium Osteria	68 Fifth Ave	718-857-1833	$$$$	11:30 pm	Delicious Italian with a Portugese influence. Rustic, warm setting.
Flatbush Farm	76 St Mark's Ave	718-622-3276	$$	11 pm	Local, seasonal, and delish.
Franny's	295 Flatbush Ave	718-230-0221	$$††	11:30 pm	Brilliant pizza, drop-dead fresh. NFT fave.

Key: $: Under $10 / $$: $10–$20 / $$$: $20–$30 / $$$$: $30–$40 / $$$$$: $40+;
 * : Does not accept credit cards / † : Accepts only American Express / †† : Accepts only Visa and MasterCard

Map 9 • Park Slope / Prospect Heights / Windsor Terrace—continued

Jpan Sushi	267 Fifth Ave	718-788-2880	$$$	11:30 pm	Excellent, inventive special rolls; weird space.
Kinara	473 Fifth Ave	718-499-3777	$$	10 pm	Large selection of vegetarian and non-vegetarian Indian dishes.
La Taqueria	72 Seventh Ave	718-398-4300	$	10 pm	Easy y barato, meaning cheap. Autentico.
The Minnow	442 9th St	718-832-5500	$$$	11 pm	Excellent surf, not so good on the turf.
Mitchell's Soul Food	617 Vanderbilt Ave	718-789-3212	$*	10:30 pm	Seedy, cheap soul food.
Moim	206 Garfield Pl	718-499-8092	$$$		Innovative Korean in a swanky setting.
Nana	155 Fifth Ave	718-230-3749	$$*	12 am	Absolutely delicious Pan-Asian.
Noo Na	565 Vanderbilt Ave	718-398-6662	$$*	2 am	Authentic Korean, finally!
Olive Vine Café	54 Seventh Ave	718-636-4333	$*	10:30 pm	Crispy Mediterranean pizzas.
Red Hot	349 Seventh Ave	718-369-0700	$$	11 pm	Fake meat for vegetarians who like to pretend they're not.
Rose Water	787 Union St	718-783-3800	$$$	11 pm	Intimate, airy Mediterranean.
Sheep Station	149 Fourth Ave	718-857-4337	$$*	12 am	Australian craft beers and Aussie-themed food. Mate.
Stone Park Café	324 Fifth Ave	718-369-0082	$$$$	11 pm	Already a contender for best Park Slope dining. NFT pick.
Sushi Tatsu	347 Flatbush Ave	718-638-7900	$$	11:30 pm	A breath of Japan on busy Flatbush.
Tom's	782 Washington Ave	718-636-9738	$$*	4 pm	Old-school mom-and-pop diner since 1936. A cholesterol love affair.
Watana	420 Seventh Ave	718-832-1611	$$	11 pm	Best Thai food on the slope. BYOB.

Map 10 • Prospect-Lefferts Gardens / Crown Heights

Ali Roti Shop	589 Flatbush Ave	718-462-1730	$$*	10:30 pm	Caribbean with style.
Bombay Masala	678 Franklin Ave	718-230-7640	$$	11 pm	Surprisingly good Indian.
Brooklyn Exposure	1401 Bedford Ave	718-783-8220	$$	4 am	The classiest date place in the neighborhood.
Culpepper's	1082 Nostrand Ave	718-940-4122	$	11 pm	Deliciousness from Barbados. Get the fish over cous cous and a side of coconut bread
Enduro	51 Lincoln Rd	718-282-7097	$$$*		Go with a margarita, fish tacos, and guac.
Golden Krust	1014A Nostrand Ave	718-604-2211	$*	9 pm	West Indian chain with a bent toward home cooking.
Golden Krust	568 Flatbush Ave	718-282-1437	$	9:30 pm	West Indian chain with a bent toward home cooking.
Irie Vegetarian	804 Nostrand Ave	718-493-2451	$$*	11 pm	Caribbean for herbivores.
The Islands	803 Washington Ave	718-398-3575	$$*	10:30 pm	Moan-worthy mac and cheese.
Lily's	707 Nostrand Ave	718-363-9515	$*	8 pm	Solid Jamaican grub, spicy ginger beer, and friendly staff.
Mike's International Restaurant	552 Flatbush Ave	718-856-7034	$$††	12 am	International/Jamaican.
Paradise Foods	843 Franklin Ave	718-953-2270	$$*	9 pm	Tasty, inexpensive West Indian.
Peppa's Jerk Chicken	738 Flatbush Ave	718-856-0950	$		Scrumptious and spicy.
Sabah Falafel	1166 Nostrand Ave	718-484-1933	$*		Tasty Middle Eastern.
Saje	710 Franklin Ave	646-393-5897	$$	11 pm	Innovative Asian & Caribbean cuisine. Great brunch spot.
Sushi Tatsu II	609 Franklin Ave	718-398-8828	$$	11:30 pm	Japanese.
Tavern on Nostrand	813 Nostrand Ave	718-778-8703	$$	10:30 pm	Tasty new American food with live jazz.

Map 11 • Sunset Park / Green-Wood Heights

Bar BQ	689 Sixth Ave	718-499-4872	$	11 pm	B is for brews, blues, and barbeque. And Brooklyn!
Brothers Pizza and Restaurant	647 Fourth Ave	718-768-1700	$$	12 am	Pizza, pasta, and sandwiches.

(211)

Key: $: Under $10 / $$: $10–$20 / $$$: $20–$30 / $$$$: $30–$40 / $$$$$: $40+;
 * : Does not accept credit cards / † : Accepts only American Express / †† : Accepts only Visa and MasterCard

Map 11 · Sunset Park/Green-Wood Heights—continued

Castillo Ecuatoriano	4020 Fifth Ave	718-437-7676	$$*	10:30 pm	Wide range of Ecuadorian platters.
Double Dragon	4318 Fourth Ave	718-369-1535	$$*	11:30 pm	Cheap and great Chinese food.
Eclipse	4314 Fourth Ave	718-965-1602	$$	10 pm	Mexican and American diner.
El Tesoro Ecuatoriano Restaurant	40-15 Fifth Ave	718-972-3756	$$	2 am	Ecuadoran grub, great seafood.
Elite Turkish Restaurant	805 60th St	718-633-3535		10 pm	Great food. Must wear tuxedo for dinner.
Full Doe	5905 Fourth Ave	718-439-8880	$*	8 pm	Inexpensive Chinese goodies.
Gina's	3905 Fifth Ave	718-438-9870	$$*	10 pm	Pizzeria and sandwiches.
International Restaurant	4408 Fifth Ave	718-438-2009	$$	12 am	Awesome Dominican-style breakfast.
Jade Plaza	6022 Eighth Ave	718-492-6888	$$	11 pm	Surprisingly good Chinese.
Kakala Café	5302 Eighth Ave	718-437-9688	$*	11 pm	Sweet, milky teas and oodles of noodles for the "new generation."
Mas Que Pan	5401 Fifth Ave	718-492-0479	$	6 pm	Latino bakery with killer Cuban sandwiches.
Nick's Restaurant	876 Fourth Ave	718-832-3181	$$*	6 pm	Fine diner.
Nyonya	5323 Eighth Ave	718-633-0808	$$*	11:30 pm	Hokey interior; excellent Malaysian.
Pacificana	813 55th St	718-871-2880		11 pm	Filling that dim sum-sized hole in your heart. Yum.
Piaxtla es Mexico Deli	505 51st St	718-633-4816	$*	10 pm	Cheap and delicious tacos and tortas.
Rosticeria Mexicana Los Pollitos	5911 Fourth Ave	718-439-9382	$*	11 pm	Chicken that dreams are made of.
Shi Wei Xian	5701 Seventh Ave	718-567-7628	$*	2 am	Quality Chinese.
Sunset Park Empanada Cart	Fifth Ave & 48th St		$*		Munch and stroll.
Super Pollo Latino	4102 Fifth Ave	718-871-5700	$$*	9:30 pm	Peruvian food famous for their chicken.
Tacos Matamoros	4503 Fifth Ave	718-871-7627	$*	1 am	You can't get more Mexican than this!
Ti An	5604 Eighth Ave	718-492-1592	$$*	10:30 pm	One of many good Vietnamese options in these parts

Map 12 · Borough Park

Agnati Meze	4720 16th Ave	718-833-7033		11 pm	Local outpost of the Astoria favorite. Try rooster!
AJ's Restaurant & Pizzeria	4412 Ft Hamilton Pkwy	718-871-5745	$*	10 pm	Extra-crunchy, extra-cheesy pie.
Cheskel's Shwarma King	3715 13th Ave	718-435-7100	$	3 am	Shwarma, salad bar, baba ghanoush.
China Glatt	4413 13th Ave	718-438-2576	$$	11 pm	Kosher Chinese. Only in New York.
Cracovia Deli	5503 13th Ave	718-851-7357	$$	9 pm	Best Polish Deli in Borough Park? Why not? No one's reading this anyway.
Crown Deli	4909 13th Ave	718-853-9000	$$*	10 pm	Authentic Jewish deli.
Donut Man	4708 13th Ave	718-436-7318	$$	6:30 am	Authentically retro luncheonette.
El Morro	4018 14th Ave	718-851-8976	$$	1 am	South and Central American.
Glatt a la Carte	5123 18th Ave	718-438-6675		10 pm	Fancy pants kosher steakhouse.
Kosher Delight Family Restaurant	4600 13th Ave	718-435-8500	$$	11:30 pm	Kosher fast food.
La Asuncion	3914 Ft Hamilton Pkwy	718-437-0864	$*	11 pm	Authentic Mexican.
Mendel's Pizza`	4923 18th Ave	718-438-8493		9 pm	Kosher pizza plus blintzes, falafel, and such.
Vesuvio	4720 16th Ave	718-745-0222	$$	12 am	Red sauce. Meh.
World Tong Seafood	6202 18th Ave	718-236-8118	$$*	11:30 pm	Good dim sum, rest assured, despite chef Joe Ng's departure

Map 13 · Kensington / Ditmas Park / Windsor Terrace

Bahar	984 Coney Island Ave	718-434-8088	$$	11:30 pm	Authentic Afghan cuisine (like we'd know).
Cinco De Mayo Restaurant	1202 Cortelyou Rd	718-693-1022	$*	10 pm	Great taste, large portions.

Key: $: Under $10 / $$: $10–$20 / $$$: $20–$30 / $$$$: $30–$40 / $$$$$: $40+;
* : Does not accept credit cards / † : Accepts only American Express / †† : Accepts only Visa and MasterCard

Map 13 · Kensington / Ditmas Park / Windsor Terrace—*continued*

Douglas BBQ & Grill	4310 18th Ave	718-686-8080	$$	11 pm	Kosher barbeque.
Farm on Adderley	1108 Cortelyou Rd		$$$	11:30 pm	An unlikely gem in a reviving 'nabe. Killer desserts and a heated garden.
Friendly's	125 Church Ave	718-854-8500	$*	11:30 pm	Good ol' American.
George's	753 Coney Island Ave	718-282-0152		24-Hrs	Multi-cuisine—American, Greek, and Italian smorgasbord.
Jhinuk	478 McDonald Ave	718-871-5355	$	11 pm	Homestyle Bangladeshi food. Utensils optional.
Joe & Joe Pizzeria & Restaurant	121 Church Ave	718-854-3340	$$	10 pm	A slice of Sicily.
Korner Pizzeria	226 Church Ave	718-633-9828	$*	10:30 pm	Pizzeria/Italian.
Little Bangladesh	483 McDonald Ave	718-871-7080	$$	11:30 pm	Bangladeshi delight.
Los Mariachis	805 Coney Island Ave	718-826-3388	$$$	12:30 am	Muy authentic, especially on weekends with live mariachi music.
Mirage Restaurant	2143 Cortelyou Rd	718-941-4452	$*	9:30 pm	Tasty traditional Nigerian.
Picket Fence	1310 Cortelyou Rd	718-282-6661	$$††	10 pm	Wonderful comfort food.
San Remo Pizza	1408 Cortelyou Rd	718-282-4915	$$††	11 pm	Try the fresh mozzarella pie.
Strictly Vegetarian Restaurant	2268 Church Ave	718-284-2543	$*	11:30 pm	Vegetarian Caribbean with an every changing menu.
Sybil's	2210 Church Ave	718-469-9049	$$	10 pm	Delicious Caribbean bakery.
Yen Yen	404 Church Ave	718-633-8711	$$	11:30 pm	Above-average Szechuan/Hunan cuisine.
Yummy Taco	129 Church Ave	718-431-8062	$	11 pm	Enough grease to cut the booze.

Map 14 · Bay Ridge

Anopoli	6920 Third Ave	718-748-3863	$$*	10 pm	Classic coffee shop with backyard seating.
Areo	8624 Third Ave	718-238-0079	$$$$	12:30 am	Big Italian.
Arirang Hibachi Steakhouse	8814 Fourth Ave	718-238-9880	$$$$	11 pm	Japanese hibachi with a free show.
Bally Bunion	9510 Third Ave	718-833-2801	$$$	12 am	Country Irish pub.
Banana Leaf	6814 Fourth Ave	718-238-5531	$$	10:30 pm	Malaysian, Indian, and Thai fusion.
Bridgeview Diner	9011 Third Ave	718-680-9818		24-Hrs	Bay Ridge's best diner.
Canteena	8001 Fifth Ave	718-745-5427		4 am	Mexican from the 'Circles' chain.
Casa Pepe	114 Bay Ridge Ave	718-833-8865		12 am	Festive Spanish-Mexican joint with decent chow and a cute patio.
Chianti	8530 Third Ave	718-921-6300	$$$	9:30 pm	High-quality rustic Italian; nearly everything made in-house.
Chopstix	8205 Fourth Ave	718-238-1300	$	11 pm	Asian trifecta: Chinese, Japanese, and Thai.
Damascus Gate	7224 Fifth Ave	718-680-8844	$$	10:30 pm	Authentic Syrian fare.
Embers	9519 Third Ave	718-745-3700	$$$	11 pm	Massive steaks—try the potato potpie.
Gino's	7414 Fifth Ave	718-748-1698	$$	11 pm	Classic Brooklyn Italian.
Grandma's Original Pizza	6918 Third Ave	718-833-4646	$	10:30 pm	Great pizza.
Greenhouse Café	7717 Third Ave	718-833-8200	$$$$	10:30 pm	An elegant favorite for that special night.
Henry Grattan's	8814 Third Ave	718-833-6466	$$	10 pm	Cozy bar and restaurant.
Hinsch's Confectionary	8518 Fifth Ave	718-748-2854	$$*	7:30 pm	Timeless ice cream parlor.
Karam	8519 Fourth Ave	718-745-5227	$	1 am	Best of the growing Mid-Eastern.
La Maison Du Couscous	484 77th St	718-921-2400	$$	12 am	Delightful Moroccan food
Lighthouse Café	7506 Third Ave	718-238-7102		10 pm	Classic diner grub, with a side of Brooklyn attitude.
Mambo Italiano	8803 Third Ave	718-833-4432	$$$	11 pm	Family-style—great for parties.
Mazza Plaza	8002 Fifth Ave	718-238-9576		11 pm	Cheap and tasty Middle Eastern. Get the vegetarian platter!
Mezcals	7508 Third Ave	718-748-7007	$$	11 pm	Fine Mexican fare, but we came for the tequila.

Key: $: Under $10 / $$: $10–$20 / $$$: $20–$30 / $$$$: $30–$40 / $$$$$: $40+;
      * : Does not accept credit cards / † : Accepts only American Express / †† : Accepts only Visa and MasterCard

Map 14 · Bay Ridge—continued

Mr Tang	7523 Third Ave	718-748-0400	$$$	12:30 am	Upscale Chinese Institution.
MyThai Café	7803 Third Ave	718-833-1700	$$††	3 am	Slammin' Pan-Asian eats.
Nouvelle	8716 Third Ave	718-238-8250	$$$$	1 am	Brooklyn's answer to Nobu; creative sushi/Asian fusion.
The Pearl Room	8201 Third Ave	718-833-6666	$$$$	11 pm	Hip and modern seafood.
Sancho's	7410 Third Ave	718-748-0770	$$	12 am	Spanish fare.
Skinflints	7902 Fifth Ave	718-745-1116	$$	11:30 pm	Get the burger with bleu cheese.
Taj Mahal	7315 3rd Ave	718-836-1512	$$	12 am	The best Indian food in Brooklyn. Period.
Tanoreen	7704 Third Ave	718-748-5600	$$	10:30 pm	Small Middle Eastern with big flavors.
Tuscany Grill	8620 Third Ave	718-921-5633	$$$$	11 pm	Worth going to/staying in Bay Ridge; NFT pick.
Yiannis Café	6901 Fourth Ave	718-238-7510	$$	11 pm	Greek bistro.

Map 15 · Dyker Heights / Bensonhurst

Casa Calamari	1801 Bath Ave	718-234-7060	$$	11 pm	Italian seafood…just ask the locals.
Columbus Restaurant & Deli	6610 18th Ave	718-236-8623	$*	6:30 pm	Club sandwiches to die for.
Gino's Focacceria	7118 18th Ave	718-232-9073	$*	9 pm	Great Sicilian sandwiches and snacks. Try any of the Gino's Specialities.
Il Colosseo	7704 18th Ave	718-234-3663	$$††	11 pm	Hands down the best pizza in the 'hood.
Outback Steakhouse	1475 86th St	718-837-7200	$$$	11:30 pm	A little taste of suburbia.
Shiki	1863 86th St	718-837-1586	$$	11:30 pm	Hibachi-style Japanese.
Tenzan	7116 18th Ave	718-621-3238	$$	11:30 pm	Japanese on pretty pillows.
Tommaso's	1464 86th St	718-236-9883	$$$	10:30 pm	Good enough for the Godfather.
Vermicelli House	7524 18th Ave	718-331-9259	$	11 pm	Fab Vietnamese selection.

Map 16 · Midwood

Adelman's Kosher Deli	1906 Kings Hwy	718-336-4915	$	10 pm	Pastrami piled high.
Anna's Luncheonette	2925 Ave I	718-951-7617	$*	8 pm	Counter service.
Burgers Bar	813 55th St	718-998-3200		3 am	Local fave imported from Israel. No cheeseburgers allowed.
DiFara	1424 Ave J	718-258-1367	$*	10 pm	Top NYC pizza; well worth the wait. Say hi to Dom.
Essex on Coney	1359 Coney Island Ave	718-253-1002	$	2:30 pm	Glatt kosher deli.
Jerusalem Steak House	533 Kings Hwy	718-336-5115	$$	11 pm	Kosher steakhouse. Yummy kebobs.
Kosher Bagel Hole	1431 Coney Island Ave	718-377-9700	$		They know bagels.
La Villita	1249 Ave U	718-998-0222	$	11 pm	Authentic, hearty Mexican.
Lucky's Diner	557 Kings Hwy	718-645-6551	$	1 am	'50s-style kosher diner.
Mabat	1809 E 7th St	718-339-3300	$$	12 am	Hole-in-the-wall with tasty Moroccan dishes.
Napoli Pizza	2270 Nostrand Ave	718-338-0328	$$	11 pm	If you can't get over to DiFara's.
Olympic Pita	1419 Coney Island Ave	718-258-6222	$	12 am	Heaven in a pita. Fantastic sauces—try the zhoug.
Pizza Time	1324 Ave J	718-252-8801	$*	2:30 pm	Kosher Italian.
Schnitzi	1299 Coney Island Ave	718-338-4015	$	1 am	Lots and lots of schnizel.
Sunflower Café	1223 Quentin Rd	718-336-1340	$	2 am	Surprising selection of foo-foo Kosher, including pizza.
Taci's Beyti	1955 Coney Island Ave	718-627-5750	$$	11 pm	Really fresh, really tasty Turkish cuisine.
Tblisi	811 Kings Hwy	718-382-6485	$$††		Good Georgian food—we're not talking pecan pie, we're talking former Soviet chicken hearts.
Tea for Two	547 Kings Hwy	718-998-0020	$$	11 pm	Kosher. Slammin' seafood.

Key: $: Under $10 / $$: $10–$20 / $$$: $20–$30 / $$$$: $30–$40 / $$$$$: $40+;
     * : Does not accept credit cards / † : Accepts only American Express / †† : Accepts only Visa and MasterCard

Coney Island / Brighton Beach

Name	Address	Phone	Price	Hours	Notes
Café Glechik	3159 Coney Island Ave	718-616-0766	$$*	10 pm	A cozy space decorated with authentic Russian folk art. Go for the Siberian pelmeni.
Creperie Blinnaya	109 Oriental Blvd	718-332-2736	$$	9 pm	Outdoor seating, but make no mistake—you're sitting in a driveway. Decent grub.
Footprints	1521 Surf Ave	718-265-2530	$$	3 am	Real deal Caribbean (um, curried goat, anyone?) and occasional live entertainment.
Gargiulo's	2911 W 15th St	718-266-4891	$$	11:30 pm	One of the remaining vestiges of turn-of-the-century Coney Island. Heavenly pasta.
Gina's Cappuccino	409 Brighton Beach Ave	718-646-6297	$$	11:30 pm	If you can forgive the menu's broken English, some excellent Ukrainian dishes await.
Nathan's Famous Hotdogs	1310 Surf Ave	718-946-2202	$*	10 pm	Famous for deliciousness and quick despite the line.
National	273 Brighton Beach Ave	718-646-1225	$$	12 am	Two floors of Russian food and fun.
Tatiana Restaurant	3152 Brighton 6th St	718-891-5151	$$	2 am	Moscow meets Vegas.
Totonno Pizzeria	1524 Neptune Ave	718-372-8606	$*	7:30 pm	Thin as paper, go early—they run out. Awesome.

Eastern Brooklyn

Name	Address	Phone	Price	Hours	Notes
Del'Rio Diner	166 Kings Hwy	718-331-3107	$	24-hrs	Cozy, long-time favorite on Sundays and after parties
El Greco Diner	1821 Emmons Ave	718-934-1288	$	24-hrs	Usually packed, even at 3am. Stick with reliable diner food. Getting fancy's a mistake.
Frank's Pizza	2134 Flatbush Ave, Flatlands	718-377-8100	$	12 am	Quality Italian.
Joe's of Avenue U	287 Ave U	718-449-9285	$*	8:30 pm	Rustic, real Sicilian food.
John's Deli	2438 Stillwell Ave	718-714-4377	$*	6 pm	Monster sandwiches. Most famous: Roast beef.
Jordan's Lobster Dock	2771 Knapp St, Sheepshead Bay	718-934-6300	$††	10:30 pm	Dockside dining at reasonable prices.
King's Buffet	2637 86th St	718-265-9362	$	11 pm	Decent all-you-can-eat Asian joint.
L&B Spumoni Gardens	2725 86th St	718-449-6921	$$	11 pm	Astounding Sicilian slice factory. Long live L&B!
La Palina	159 Ave O	718-236-9764	$$$	12 am	Family Italian.
Liman	2710 Emmons Ave	718-769-3322	$$$††	11:30 pm	Fish nets and sand dollars set the ambiance.
Mill Basin Kosher Delicatessen	5823 Ave T, Mill Basin	718-241-4910	$$	10 pm	When you want a LOT of pastrami.
Peter Pizza	2637 86th St	718-266-0033	$	10 pm	Great pizza and specialties.
Randazzo's	2017 Emmons Ave, Sheepshead Bay	718-615-0010	$$$	12:30 am	Historic cafeteria-style clam bar. Just try to score cheaper or tastier steamed lobster.
Roll-n-Roaster	2901 Emmons Ave, Sheepshead Bay	718-769-6000	$	3 am	Greasy goodness.
Sahara	2337 Coney Island Ave	718-376-8594	$$	2:30 am	Awesome Turkish food with ambience.
U Shweika	2027 Emmons Ave, Sheepshead Bay	718-332-0330	$$$	11 pm	Bloated bellies, pints of German beer, and wiener schnitzel. It's a party.
XO Creperie	2027 Emmons Ave	718-368-4477	$$$$$	12 am	Crepes are a mere garnish for posh, Russian-interpreted French fare. Delish!

Arts & Entertainment • Shopping

Brooklyn has been called the world's largest small town, and we feel this most strongly when strolling down charming streets lined with fruit stands, cheese shops, charcuteries, bargain basements, bookstores, clothing boutiques, and other essentials. You can pretty much find everything you need without ever leaving the better borough. Most of the good stuff is concentrated in Williamsburg, BoCoCa, and Park Slope, but every neighborhood has something to offer.

Food

Be sure to check out one of the many bakeries in BoCoCa (**Map 8**). (**Caputo's**, **Marquet**, and **Mazzola** are all great.) For anything and everything Italian, get thee to Bensonhurst. **Villabate Pasticceria & Bakery (Map 15)** will make you quiver with delight—or wait, that might just be all the sugar. For all your cheese needs, the recently relocated and expanded **Bedford Cheese Shop (Map 2)** in Williamsburg is your best bet, though **Stinky (Map 8)** in BoCoCa is the new pretender. Check out the specialty dry goods at **Sahadi Importing Company (Map 8)** in Cobble Hill. In BoCoCa, **D'Amico Foods (Map 8)** is definitely a top NYC destination for fresh-ground coffee, and butcher **Staubitz (Map 8)** delivers up one of the city's best meat selection. With all of the above, who needs restaurants?

Clothing

For unique boutiques, take a stroll along Smith and Court Streets in Carroll Gardens or Fifth Avenue in Park Slope. **Beacon's Closet (Map 2)** is a great vintage shop in Williamsburg. We also love **Pop's Popular Clothing (Map 1)** in Greenpoint. For all your underwear needs, check out the bargains at **Underworld Plaza (Map 12)** in Borough Park. For those with suburban nostalgia, the soul-sucking **Atlantic Terminal Mall (Map 6)** provides a home to Victoria's Secret, Old Navy, Daffy's, and other chains we secretly love. And, of course, we can't forget the **Century 21 (Map 14)** in Bay Ridge—not as good as its Manhattan counterpart, but still a madhouse any day of the week.

Home

Brooklyn has an array of big-time chains such as **Target (Map 6)**, and **Costco (Map 11)** that have a little bit of everything. Some good spots for home furnishings include **Design Within Reach (Map 5)**, and **West Elm (Map 5)**. For something posher and hipper, check out Smith Street's **Environment 337 (Map 8)**. For jewelry, **Swallow (Map 8)** and **Clay Pot (Map 9)** are two excellent gift-giving destinations—they both also carry a lot of fun, random eclectic items. Williamsburg's **Golden Calf (Map 2)** sells a unique selection of Chinese antiques and furniture crafted by local artists. For vintage, mid-century, and modern pieces, try Williamsburg's **Two Jakes (Map 2)**, DUMBO's **City Barn Antiques (Map 5)**, or Park Slope's **Trailer Park (Map 7)**. We've all heard the rumors about an Ikea in Red Hook—we hope it's true for the sake of convenience, but hope that it falls through for fear of the traffic!

Miscellaneous

Check out **Earwax Records (Map 2)** and the **Academy Records (Map 2)** in Williamsburg or the well-curated **Somethin' Else (Map 9)** in Park Slope for great tunage, **American Beer Distributors (Map 8)** on Court Street for hundreds of imported brews, and the McSweeney's shop/tutoring center, **Brooklyn Superhero Supply (Map 9)**, on Fifth Avenue in the Slope. Bookworms can happily while away the hours amidst the stacks at Cobble Hill's **Book Court (Map 8)**. **Bierkraft (Map 9)** covers at least three obsessions—cheese, chocolate, and beer—while **Blue Marble (Map 8)** has a great slant: Organic ice cream. Come summertime, handmade jewelry, clothes and bags, used books, and irresistibly hip baby clothes are sold for a song at the many crafts fairs that land in artsy Williamsburg—the Renegade Arts Fair (www.renegadecraft.com) in McCarren Park is always a good bet. And on warm weekends, we love trolling neighborhoods like Park Slope and Williamsburg for stoop sales—you'll find incredible bargains, unique finds, and you may just make a new friend.

Map 1 • Greenpoint

Brooklynski	145 Driggs Ave	718-389-0901	Quirky little gifts for cool Brooklynites.
Chopin Chemists	911 Manhattan Ave	718-383-7822	Polish-speaking; useful location.
Dee & Dee	777 Manhattan Ave	718-389-0181	Mega dollar store; cheap stuff.
Film Noir	10 Bedford Ave	718-389-5773	One of Greenpoint's top video rental destination.
The Garden	921 Manhattan Ave	718-389-6448	Organic groceries *and* Polish goth chicks!
Mini Me	123 Nassau Ave	718-389-0333	Babies' and kids' clothing.
Petland Discounts	846 Manhattan Ave	718-349-8370	Shit you need for your stupid pet.
Photoplay	928 Manhattan Ave	718-383-7782	Ben's favorite Greenpoint video store.
Polam	952 Manhattan Ave	718-383-2763	Quality Polish meat market with cheap bulk pickles.
Pop's Popular Clothing	7 Franklin St	718-349-7677	Great second-hand clothing, especially jeans.
Sikorski Meat	603 Manhattan Ave	718-389-6181	Tender, salty, smoky, Polish…meat.
Steve's Meat Market	104 Nassau Ave	718-383-1780	Sausages double smoked for her pleasure.
Syrena Bakery	207 Norman Ave	718-349-0560	Very nice Polish bakery with an espresso bar and bagels.
The Thing	1001 Manhattan Ave	718-349-8234	Unusual second-hand store offers thousands of used LPs.
Uncle Louie G's	172 Greenpoint Ave	718-349-1199	So many flavors, so little time.
Wedel	772 Manhattan Ave	718-383-3933	Old-school chocolate shop, straight out of Poland.
Wizard Electroland	863 Manhattan Ave	718-349-6889	Electronics store.

Map 2 · Williamsburg

Academy Records	96 N 6th St	718-218-8200	Bins and bins of new and used LPs.
Amarcord Vintage Fashion	223 Bedford Ave	718-963-4001	Well-edited vintage goodies, many pieces direct from Europe.
Artist & Craftsman	761 Metropolitan Ave	718-782-7765	Art supplies.
Beacon's Closet	88 N 11th St	718-486-0816	Rad resale with lots of gems.
Bedford Cheese Shop	229 Bedford Ave	718-599-7588	Best cheese selection in the borough.
The Brooklyn Kitchen	616 Lorimer St	718-389-2982	A primer on housewares for the Converse set.
Built By Wendy	46 N 6th St	718-384-2882	Brooklyn outpost of NYC-based independent label.
Earwax Records	Mini Mall, 218 Bedford Ave	718-486-3771	Record store with all the indie classics.
Emily's Pork Store	426 Graham Ave	718-383-7216	Broccoli rabe sausage is their specialty.
Future Perfect	115 N 6th St	718-599-6278	The coolest assemblage of cutting-edge housewares and cute furnishings.
Houndstooth	485 Driggs Ave	718-384-8705	Vintage clothing for male hipsters seeking the authorial look.
Jumelle	148 Bedford Ave	718-388-9525	Motivation to get a real job or a rich husband.
KCDC Skateshop	90 N 11th St	718-387-9006	Shop and gallery featuring locally designed gear.
The Mini-Market	Mini Mall, 218 Bedford Ave	718-302-9337	Hodge-podge of tchotchkes and fun clothes.
Model T Meats	404 Graham Ave	718-389-1553	Meat, meat, and more meat. Also, cheese.
Moon River Chattel	62 Grand St	718-388-1121	Cute store offering antiques and architectural salvage.
Otte	132 N 5th St	718-302-3007	A small well-edited roster of established and emerging designers.
Passout Record Shop	131 Grand St	718-384-7273	Subversive media and in-store shows.
Pegasus	355 Bedford Ave	718-782-2842	Vintage finds at near-thrift store prices.
Roulette	188 Havemeyer St	718-218-7104	Choice vintage housewares at affordable prices.
Scandinavian Grace	167 N 9th St	718-384-7886	All things Scandinavian design.
Sodafine	119 Grand St	718-230-3060	Hot little numbers with big price tags.
Soundfix	110 Bedford Ave	718-388-8090	Independent record store with a café/performance space in back.
Spoonbill & Sugartown	Mini Mall, 218 Bedford Ave	718-387-7322	Excellent indie bookstore.
Sprout	44 Grand St	718-388-4440	Contemporary home and garden store.
Spuyten Devil Grocery	132 N 5th St	718-384-1520	Belgium beer lovers' bar sells the goods in Williamsburg's mini mall.
Treehouse	430 Graham Ave	718-482-TREE	Quirky, one-of-a-kind clothing and jewelry. Plus, crafting classes!
Two Jakes	320 Wythe Ave	718-782-7780	Furniture: Mod, metal, misc.
Ugly Luggage	214 Bedford Ave	718-384-0724	Small storefront packed with antiques.
Videology	308 Bedford Ave	718-782-3468	Videos. Rental.
Yoko Devereaux	338 Broadway	718-302-1450	Hip menswear line's first retail shop.

Map 3 · East Williamsburg

The Archive	49 Bogart St	718-381-1944	Top video store in East Williamsburg.
Brooklyn Natural	49 Bogart St	718-381-0650	Upscale deli—check out the new late-night delivery menu.
Fortunato Brothers	289 Manhattan Ave	718-387-2281	Old-school pastry and espresso shop.
GreenDepot	20 Rewe St	718-782-2991	Al Gore would shop here if he lived in Brooklyn.
Moore Street Market	108 Moore St	718-384-1371	Latino fresh food for 50+ years (multi-vendor).
The Vortex	222 Montrose Ave	718-609-6066	Hidden treasures waiting to be found.
Zukkie's	279 Bushwick Ave	718-456-0048	Some good finds amongst the junk.

Map 4 · Bushwick

Green Village	276 Starr St	718-599-4017	Piles of resale items for you to spend the day rummaging through.
Kenco Retail Shops	1451 Myrtle Ave	718-456-8705	Absolutely everything.

Map 5 · Brooklyn Heights / DUMBO / Downtown

Almondine Bakery	85 Water St	718-797-5026	Pastry smells waft to the street.
Design Within Reach	76 Montague St	718-643-1015	Not really, but the stuff IS cool.
Halcyon	57 Pearl St	718-260-9299	Vinyl for DJ fanatics.
Half Pint	55 Washington St	718-875-4007	Ditch Gap Kids!
Heights Prime Meats	59 Clark St	718-237-0133	Butcher.

Map 5 · Brooklyn Heights / DUMBO / Downtown—*continued*

Jacques Torres Chocolate	66 Water St	718-875-9772	The Platonic ideal of chocolate.
Lassen & Hennigs	114 Montague St	718-875-6272	Specialty foods and deli.
Montague Street Video	143 Montague St	718-875-1715	Good selection serving the Heights.
New Balance Store	125 Court St	718-858-8550	Running sneaks and the like.
Pomme	81 Washington St	718-855-0623	Pricey imports for baby hipsters. Haircuts, too.
Recycle-A-Bicycle	35 Pearl St	718-858-2972	Bikes to the ceiling.
Stewart/Stand	165 Front St	718-407-4197	Another very cool design shop for DUMBO.
West Elm	75 Front St	718-875-7757	Cool home décor at reasonable prices.
Wonk	68 Jay St	718-596-8026	Furnish your penthouse.

Map 6 · Fort Greene / Clinton Hill

Atlantic Terminal Mall	Atlantic Ave & Flatbush Ave		Blah.
Blue Bass Vintage	431 DeKalb Ave	347-750-8935	Thrift store with wide selection and rummage-sale-feel.
Carol's Daughter	1 S Elliot Pl	718-596-1862	Skincare with a cult following.
Dope Jams	580 Myrtle Ave	718-622-7977	Soul, funk, hip-hop, but no dope.
Frosted Moon	154 Vanderbilt Ave	718-858-3161	Full of pretty things.
The Greene Grape	765 Fulton St	718-797-9463	Nice new wine shop.
Gureje	886 Pacific St	718-857-2522	West African–flavored clothing, with a music club in the back!
Kiki's Pet Spa	239 DeKalb Ave	718-857-7272	For pet-worshippers.
Malchijah Hats	225 DeKalb Ave	718-643-3269	Beautiful and unique hats.
The Midtown Greenhouse Garden Center	115 Flatbush Ave	718-636-0020	Fully stocked with plants and gardening supplies.
My Little India	96 S Elliot Pl	718-855-5220	Furniture, candles, textiles.
Owa African Market	434 Myrtle Ave	718-643-8487	Beads galore.
Pratt Institute Bookstore	550 Myrtle Ave	718-789-1105	Art supplies, bookstore, cool stuff for students.
Target	Atlantic Terminal, 139 Flatbush Ave	718-290-1109	Bull's eye!
White Elephant Gallery	572 Myrtle Ave	718-789-9423	Mindset is key. It could be treasure.
Yu Interiors	15 Greene Ave	718-237-5878	Modern furniture, bags, and candles.

Map 7 · Bedford-Stuyvesant

Andrew Fish Market	1228 B Fulton St	718-623-6774	You pick it, they cook it. Fried to perfection on the spot.
Birdell's Records	535 Nostrand Ave	718-638-4504	If it's been recorded, they have it.
Foot Locker	1258 Fulton St	718-399-6979	For all your footwear needs.
Happiness Fruit Farm	1307 Fulton St	718-638-1773	Freshest produce.
Original Barber Shop	409 Nostrand Ave	718-638-3470	Old techniques are still in use at this tidy little shop.
Tony's Country Life	1316 Fulton St	718-789-2040	Best health emporium in the 'hood with a friendly and helpful staff.

Map 8 · BoCoCa / Red Hook

A Cook's Companion	197 Atlantic Ave	718-852-6901	A fantastic shop with everything for your kitchen (except the food).
Adam's Fresh Bakery by Design	144 Smith St	888-363-7374	Heaven in a cupcake.
American Beer Distributors	256 Court St	718-875-0226	International beer merchant. NFT pick.
Blue Marble	420 Atalntic Ave	718-858-1100	Organic ice cream and other treats; great space too.
Book Court	163 Court St	718-875-3677	The neighborhood spot for books.
Butter	389 Atlantic Ave	718-260-9033	Very cool and very expensive boutique.
Caputo's Fine Foods	460 Court St	718-855-8852	Italian gourmet specialties.
D'Amico Foods	309 Court St	718-875-5403	The best coffee in the 'hood, if not the city.
Environment337	337 Smith St	718-522-1767	Another Smith Street hit.
Exit 9	127 Smith St	718-422-7720	Quirky gifts.
Fish Tales	296 Smith St	718-246-1346	The place for fish.
Flight 001	132 Smith St	718-243-0001	Luggages etc, for the pampered traveler.
Marquet Patisserie	221 Court St	718-855-1289	Mouth-watering croissants and quiches.
Mazzola Bakery	192 Union St	718-643-1719	Top bakery in CG.
Refinery	254 Smith St	718-643-7861	Great bags and accessories.
Rocketship	208 Smith St	718-797-1348	Nice selection of comic books and graphic novels.

Sahadi Importing Company	187 Atlantic Ave	718-624-4550	Middle Eastern specialty and fine foods since 1948.
Staubitz Meat Market	222 Court St	718-624-0014	Top NYC butcher.
Stinky	261 Smith St	718-522-7425	I get it! It's a cheese store!
Swallow	361 Smith St	718-222-8201	An exquisite selection of glass, jewelry, and books.

Map 9 · Park Slope / Prospect Heights / Windsor Terrace

3R Living	276 Fifth Ave	718-832-0951	Eco-friendly and organic products and gifts.
Artesana Home	170 Seventh Ave	718-369-9881	Housewares better traveled than you.
Beacon's Closet	220 Fifth Ave	718-230-1630	Rad resale with lots of gems.
Bierkraft	191 Fifth Ave	718-230-7600	Cheese, chocolate, and nearly 1000 varieties of beer.
Bird	430 Seventh Ave	718-768-4940	Unique women's clothes and accessories.
Brooklyn Superhero Supply	372 Fifth Ave	718-499-9884	Capes, treasure maps, and bottled special powers. Also, McSweeney's publications.
Buttercup's PAW-tisserie	63 Fifth Ave	718-399-2228	
Clay Pot	162 Seventh Ave	718-788-6564	Hand-crafted gifts, jewelry.
Fabrica	619 Vanderbilt Ave	718-398-3831	Elegantly designed home furnishings.
JackRabbit Sports	151 Seventh Ave	718-636-9000	Mecca for runners, swimmers, and cyclists.
Leaf and Bean	83 Seventh Ave	718-638-5791	Coffees and teas.
Loom	115 Seventh Ave	718-789-0061	Irresistible gifts and housewares.
Mostly Modern	383 Seventh Ave	718-499-9867	Winsome wares for space-age bachelor pads.
Movable Feast	284 Prospect Park W	718-965-2900	Catering to your every need.
Nancy Nancy	244 Fifth Ave	718-789-5262	Cards, gifts, novelties.
Rare Device	453 Seventh Ave	718-301-6375	Cool design shop.
Root Stock & Quade	297 Seventh Ave	718-832-1888	The yummiest place for flowers, plants, and bouquets.
Somethin' Else	294 Fifth Ave	718-768-5131	Meticulously cool music and clothes.
Stitch Therapy	176 Lincoln Pl	718-398-2020	Luxurious yarns. Plus knitting classes.
Traditions	465 Fifth Ave	718-768-1430	Organic food heaven for those who are choosy about protein powder.
Trailer Park	77 Sterling Pl	718-623-2170	Unique and handcrafted furnishings.
Uncle Louie G's	741 Union St	718-623-6668	So many flavors, so little time.
United Meat Market	219 Prospect Park West	718-768-7227	All-American fare with a veggie bent.

Map 10 · Prospect-Lefferts Gardens / Crown Heights

Allan's Quality Bakery	1109 Nostrand Ave	718-774-7892	Lines into the night.
Barbara's Flower Shop	615 Nostrand Ave	718-773-6644	Smells as good as the Botanic Garden.
Phat Albert's	495 Flatbush Ave	718-469-2116	Cheap is good.
Scoops	624 Flatbush Ave	718-282-5904	Tasty ice cream.

Map 11 · Sunset Park / Green-Wood Heights

Costco	976 Third Ave	718-965-7603	Get loaded.
East Coast Beer Co	969 Third Ave	718-788-8000	For all your beer needs—kegs included.
Hong Kong Supermarket	6023 Eighth Ave	718-438-2288	Massive Asian grocery.
Petland Discounts	5015 Fifth Ave	718-871-7699	Crap for your stupid pet.
Ten Ren Tea & Ginseng	5817 Eighth Ave	718-853-0660	Lovely selection of teas.

Map 12 · Borough Park

Antiques & Decorations	4319 14th Ave	718-633-6393	Bubbe's living room, for sale!
Benetton	4610 13th Ave	718-853-3420	Orthodox-approved selection of modest clothes.
Bulletproof Games II	4507 Ft Hamilton Pkwy	718-854-3367	Down with Yu-Gi-Oh! tournaments?
Circus Fruits	5915 Ft Hamilton Pkwy	718-436-2100	Fantastic selection and prices; some exotic stuff.
Coluccio & Sons	1214 60th St	718-436-6700	Imported Italian specialties.
Jacadi	5005 16th Ave	718-871-9402	European-style children's boutique.
Kaff's Bakery	4518 Ft Hamilton Pkwy	718-633-2600	Kosher bread-a-plenty.
Kosher Candy Man	4702 13th Ave	718-438-5419	Yummy holiday and gift arrangements.
Scribbles	3720 14th Ave	718-435-8711	Classroom supplies and crafts.
Strauss Bakery	5115 13th Ave	718-851-7728	Amazingly fancy cakes.
Trainworld	751 McDonald Ave	718-436-7072	Wholesale prices on hundreds of model trains. A choo choo paradise.
Underworld Plaza	1421 62nd St	718-232-6804	Underwear city.
Weiss Bakery	5011 13th Ave	718-438-0407	Wedding cakes to party-size challahs.

Map 13 · Kensington / Ditmas Park / Windsor Terrace

Belle & Maxie	1209 Cortelyou Rd	718-484-3302	The neighborhood tot shop.
Cortelyou Vintage	1118 Cortelyou Rd	718-287-6300	Gorgeous, affordable deco antiques.
Flatbush Food Co-op	1318 Cortelyou Rd	718-284-9717	The place for all your organic goods.
Natural Frontier Market	1104 Cortelyou Rd	718-284-3593	Specializing in natural and organic products.
Newkirk Plaza	Above Newkirk Ave Subway		Rumor has it that this was America's first mall.
Old Navy Outlet	1009 Flatbush Ave	718-693-7507	Cheaper-than-cheap wardrobe basics.
Trailer Park	1211 Cortelyou Rd	718-282-2800	Unique and handcrafted furnishings.
Uncle Louie G's	1306 Flatbush Ave	718-434-2600	So many flavors, so little time.

Map 14 · Bay Ridge

Arayssi Bakery	7216 Fifth Ave	718-745-2115	Popular Lebanese bakery.
The Bookmark Shoppe	8415 Third Ave	718-833-5115	Your friendly neighborhood book store.
Century 21	472 86th St	718-748-3266	Discounted apparel, housewares, and linen—everything!
Havin' a Party	8414 Fifth Ave	718 836-3701	Party supplies and novelties.
Leske's Bakery	7612 Fifth Ave	718-680-2323	There's only one Babka left...watch out for elbows!
Little Cupcake Bakeshop	9102 Third Ave	718-680-4465	Now, who doesn't just love a good cupcake?
Modell's	531 86th St	718-745-7900	Sports. Sports. Sports. Get your Cyclones stuff here!
Nordic Delicacies	6909 Third Ave	718-748-1874	Norwegian carryout and grocery store.
Panda Sport	9213 Fifth Ave	718-238-4919	Full line of ski equipment. Ask about ski trips!
Pretty Girl	8501 Fifth Ave	718-492-0216	Inexpensive women's clothing.
Village Irish Imports	8508 Third Ave	718-238-2582	Cead Mille Failte! Bits and pieces direct from the Emerald Isle.

Map 15 · Dyker Heights / Bensonhurst

3 Guys from Brooklyn	6502 Ft Hamilton Pkwy	718-748-8340	Fresh produce from nice guys.
Arcobaleno Italiano	7306 18th Ave	718-259-7951	For all your Fellini needs.
Lioni Latticini	7819 15th Ave	718-232-7852	Lots and lots of mighty fine mozzarella.
Pastosa Ravioli	7425 New Utrecht Ave	718-236-9615	Pasta heaven.
Queen Ann Ravioli	7205 18th Ave	718-256-1061	18 varieties of ravioli—totally awesome.
SAS Italian Records	7113 18th Ave	718-331-0539	Italian music, games, beauty products, and soccer paraphernalia.
Sea Breeze	8500 18th Ave	718-259-9693	Fresh fish at great prices.
Villabate Pasticceria & Bakery	7117 18th Ave	718-331-8430	This place is da bomb!!! Don't go on an empty stomach.

Map 16 · Midwood

Canal Jean Company	2236 Nostrand Ave	718-421-7590	Not as good as Manhattan locales, but still has nice deals.
Chiffon Bakery	1373 Coney Island Ave	718-258-8822	Holla at the challah, kid.
Chuckies	1304 Kings Hwy	718-376-1003	Possibly the best shoe store in Brooklyn. We're talking Manolos and Jimmy Choos.
Downtown	2502 Ave U	718-934-8280	Trendy in a junior high sorta way. But (hollah!) they do midnight madness sales.
Eichler's	1401 Coney Island Ave	718-258-7643	Everything Judaica—literally!
Fish Expo	2370 Nostrand Ave	718-253-6400	Tropicals for your viewing pleasure.
Image	1310 Kings Hwy	718-336-7058	Cool youthful labels like Juicy Couture and D&G, often at a discount.
Jinil Au Chocolat	1371 Coney Island Ave	718-758-0199	Pricey custom-made chocolate.
Mansoura	515 Kings Hwy	718-645-7977	Amazing bakery with Jewish specialties. Best baklava on the planet.
Sea Bay	1237 Ave U	718-382-8889	Any Asian ingredient you could want.
Wig Showcase	820 Kings Hwy	718-339-8300	Lots of oddly coiffed mannequin heads.
Zelda's Art World	2291 Nostrand Ave	718-377-7779	Art Supplies.

Coney Island / Brighton Beach

M&I International	249 Brighton Beach Ave	718-615-1011	A European foods behemoth. Enjoy tea and sweets on a newly added rooftop terrace.
Prime Meat Market	1516 Mermaid Ave	718-372-8091	Tiny butcher shop that's been around since the old days. Great skirt steak and kind service.

Eastern Brooklyn

AKO	2184 McDonald Ave	718-265-3111	One of four locations. Good-looking furniture, a step above IKEA in price and quality.
Dairy Maid Ravioli	216 Ave U	718-449-2620	House-made pastas. Been there, like, forever.
Enterprize	1601 Sheepshead Bay Rd	718-769-5800	Sleek Italian wares from Alessi and the like. There's a gift registry, too.
Le Monti	2070 McDonald Ave	718-375-4634	Furs that recall an Ivana Trump aesthetic. Not that there's anything wrong with that…
Leohmann's	2807 E 21st St	718-638-1256	A generations-old yenta stomping ground. This one's back room is just so-so.
Meat Supreme	181 Ave U	718-372-4555	Meat, seafood, Italian groceries.
Mini Centro	1659 Sheepshead Bay Rd	718-651-1481	No shelves, just stacks of Italian shoes. C'mon, don't be scared.
Nuts & Candy	2079 86th St	718-266-8234	What it sounds like, but the gourmet stuff.
Omni Health	265 Ave U	718-714-6664	Vitamins, herbs, organic food.
Pisa Pork Store	306 Kings Hwy	718-336-1828	Mini Little Italy.
Sheepshead Bay Gourmet	1518 Ave Z	718-891-2300	Quaintly decorated market. European specialties, from stuffed cabbage to Napoleon.

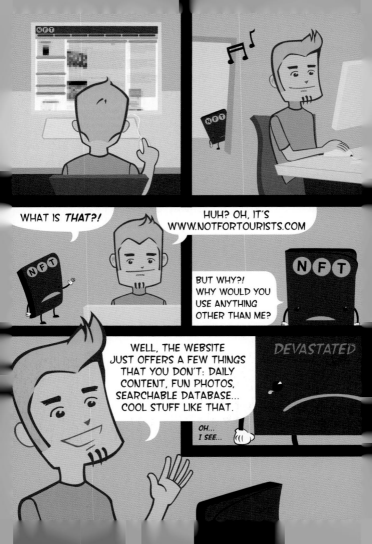

NEW YORK PRESS

WHAT'S GOING ON

Sign up for the New York Press
weekly e-newsletter for the latest in
food, *culture* and *nightlife*.

www.nypress.com

LIFE,
LIBERTY
AND THE
PURSUIT OF
HAPPY HOUR
>JOIN THE PARTY
SVEDKA
Imported Swedish
VODKA
Product of Sweden

Understanding Your World, So You Don't Have To

Lead anchor Brandon Armstrong and the rest of the Onion team bring you, the ignorant masses, hard-hitting news, videos, and opinions you can't find anywhere else.

FREE IN PRINT WEEKLY AND ONLINE DAILY AT ONION.COM

America's Finest News Source

CELEBRATE BROOKLYN!
MUSIC DANCE WORD FILM
PROSPECT PARK BANDSHELL
JUNE
THROUGH
AUGUST
BRICONLINE.ORG/CB

DO MORE.

SPEND LESS.

Discover 52 restaurants. Save $10 every time.
Also available: The Bar & Lounge Deck. Do more. Spend less.

www.cityshuffle.com

Where do you go when your desire to help is larger than your zip code?

You go to Morocco, Mongolia, or 71 other countries. And when you return, your own community will benefit in ways you can't imagine.

PEACE CORPS

800.424.8580
www.peacecorps.gov

Life is calling.
How far will you go?

Medusa
Salon, Inc
177 Seventh Avenue,
Brooklyn *(718) 965- 3999*

_____
_____
_____
_____
_____
_____
_____
_____
_____
_____
_____

Street Index

Street / Range		
36th St		
(200-699)	11	A1/A2
(1100-1598)	12	A1/A2
E 36th St		
(1000-1749)	*	F4
(1750-2199)	*	G5
W 36th St	*	H2
37th St		
(201-899)	11	A1/A2
(960-1599)	12	A1/A2
E 37th St		
(69-200)	10	B2
(241-999)	*	E4
(1013-1799)	*	F4
(1800-2199)	*	G5
W 37th St	*	H2
38th St		
(300-449)	11	A1
(1000-1599)	12	A1/A2
E 38th St		
(69-204)	10	B2
(205-894)	*	E4
(895-1649)	*	F4
(1650-1849)	*	F5
(1850-2299)	*	G5
39th St		
(1-899)	11	A1/A2
(930-1698)	12	A1/A2
E 39th St		
(1-116)	10	B2
(113-957)	*	E4
(1029-1312)	*	F4
40th St		
(100-948)	11	A1/A2
(959-1699)	12	A1/A2
E 40th St		
(1-929)	*	E4
(930-1299)	*	E4
(1301-1449)	*	F5
41st St		
(100-949)	11	A1/B1/B2
(950-1699)	12	B1/B2
E 41st St	*	F5
42nd St		
(1-899)	11	B1/B2
(970-1798)	12	B1/B2
E 42nd St		
(25-969)	*	E4
(950-1198)	*	F5
43rd St		
(1-899)	11	B1/B2
(1000-1799)	12	B1/B2
E 43rd St		
(1-72)	*	D4
(73-592)	*	E4
(593-834)	*	E5
(867-1699)	*	F5
44th St		
(40-949)	11	B1/B2
(950-1799)	12	B1/B2
45th St		
(200-899)	11	B1/B2
(1000-1799)	12	B1/B2
E 45th St		
(73-171)	*	D4
(227-315)	*	D5
(331-1162)	*	E5
(1159-1749)	*	F5
46th St		
(200-899)	11	B1/B2
(1000-1799)	12	B1/B2
E 46th St		
(67-310)	*	D5
(340-1098)	*	E5
(1162-1799)	*	F5
47th St		
(100-949)	11	B1/B2
(950-1941)	12	B1/B2
E 47th St	*	E5
48th St		
(52-899)	11	B1/B2
(1000-1899)	12	B1/B2
E 48th St		
(24-304)	*	D5
(339-1034)	*	E5
(1166-1899)	*	F5
49th St		
(100-899)	11	B1/B2
(1000-1899)	12	B1/B2
E 49th St		
(73-305)	*	D5
(336-1010)	*	E5
(1161-1899)	*	F5
50th St		
(100-949)	11	B1/B2
(950-1998)	12	B1/B2
51st St		
(1-899)	11	B1/B2
(950-2099)	12	B1/B2
E 51st St		
(2-294)	*	D5
(321-966)	*	E5
(1151-1872)	*	F5
(1927-2049)	*	G5
52nd St		
(1-899)	11	B1/B2
(1000-1999)	12	B1/B2
E 52nd St		
(2-228)	*	D5
(253-1016)	*	E5
(1100-1899)	*	F5
(1951-2099)	*	G5
E 53rd Pl	*	G5
53rd St		
(1-956)	11	B1/B2
(1001-1999)	12	B1/B2
E 53rd St		
(2-215)	*	D5
(216-244)	11	B1
(245-1023)	*	E5
(1071-1859)	*	F5
(2000-2099)	*	G5
54th St		
(100-899)	11	B1/B2
(971-1999)	12	B1/B2
E 54th St		
(1-154)	*	D5
(166-999)	*	E5
(1025-1815)	*	F5
(2000-2099)	*	G5
55th St		
(100-899)	11	B1/B2
(900-2099)	12	B1/B2
E 55th St		
(1-104)	*	D5
(140-1000)	*	E5
(1001-1950)	*	F5
56th Dr	*	G5
56th St		
(80-899)	11	B1/B2
(900-2099)	12	B1/B2
E 56th St		
(2-79)	*	D5
(109-850)	*	E5
(851-1999)	*	F5
E 57th Pl	*	G5
57th St		
(1-899)	11	B1/B2
(1000-1799)	12	B1/B2
(2000-2198)	*	F3
E 57th St		
(1-53)	*	D5
(54-699)	*	E5
(800-1999)	*	F5
(2000-2099)	*	F3
58th St		
(100-899)	11	B1/B2
(1000-1899)	12	B1/B2
(2050-2167)	*	F3
E 58th St		
(1-884)	*	E5
(801-2099)	*	F5
E 59th Pl	*	G5
59th St		
(200-899)	11	B1/B2
(950-1999)	12	B1/B2
(2050-2299)	*	F3
E 59th St		
(1-699)	*	E5
(800-1999)	*	F5
E 60th Pl	*	G5
60th St		
(200-938)	11	B1/B2
(2050-2363)	*	F3
(939-2384)	12	B1/B2
E 60th St	*	F5
61st St		
(200-935)	11	B1/B2
(936-1999)	12	B1/B2
(2050-2399)	*	F3
E 61st St	*	F5
62nd St		
(200-933)	11	B1/B2
(934-2049)	12	B1/B2
(2050-2349)	*	F3
(2350-2414)	*	G3
63rd St		
(200-929)	11	B1/B2
(930-1999)	12	B1/B2
(2050-2299)	*	F3
(2250-2499)	*	G3
E 63rd St		
(1400-2199)	*	F5
(2300-2799)	*	G5
64th St		
(200-499)	11	B1
(600-849)	14	A2
(850-2014)	15	A1/A2
(2023-2199)	*	F5
(2200-2299)	*	F5
(2250-2499)	*	G3
E 64th St		
(1295-2249)	*	F5
(2400-2549)	*	G6
(2550-2799)	*	G5
65th St		
(200-849)	14	A1/A2
(850-2049)	15	A1/A2
(2101-2199)	*	F3
(2200-2550)	*	G3

Street Index

Street Index

Street Index

Street Index

NOT FOR TOURISTS™ Custom Mapping

We'll map your world.

Need a custom map?

NFT will work with you to design a custom map that promotes your company or event. NFT's team will come up with something new or put a fresh face on something you already have. We provide custom map-making and information design services to fit your needs—whether simply showing where your organization is located on one of our existing maps, or creating a completely new visual context for the information you wish to convey. NFT will help you—and your audience—make the most of the place you're in, while you're in it.

For more information, call us at 212-965-8650 or visit
www.notfortourists.com/custommapping.aspx

Not For Tourists™
www.notfortourists.com
Atlanta · Boston · Chicago · London · Los Angeles · New York City · Philadelphia · San Francisco · Seattle · Washington DC